I AM A REFUGEE

Camillo Adler

ISBN: 1477664084

ISBN 13: 9781477664087

Printed by CreateSpace, North Charleston, SC

7/21/14

To Chris & Jessica
I hope this raises the
consciousness of that time
best wishes

Michel

Translated from the German

by Michel F. Adler

CONTENTS

Part III
Observations and Reflections

Translator's Note

Not granted a work permit as a refugee in Switzerland, my father spent much of his time writing. He authored three manuscripts, which came to light only in my brother, Paul's, artifacts after he passed away in March 2004. The first manuscript, *Der Kaefig* (*The Cage*), is an autobiographical portrayal, fictionalized but accurate, of my father's family in the anti-Semitic environment of Vienna in 1930; it culminates with his departure to France, a common outcome for many Jews seeking employment and trying to escape the poisonous, discriminatory atmosphere. This story contains much Viennese dialect, and I have therefore not attempted to translate it. The second manuscript, *Mensch ohne Heimat* (*Man without a Country*), tells the story of my father's path from the internment camps into the French Foreign Legion, from basic training in Algeria and Morocco through the return home after France's swift surrender to Germany in the summer of 1940. Also autobiographical fiction, an edited version was serialized in the Swiss newspaper *Die Volkstimme* in 1945. The last manuscript, *Ich bin ein Fluechtling* (*I Am a Refugee*), a nonfiction account of the conditions in Lyon under the second German occupation, relates our family's escape from France into Switzerland, life in the refugee camps, and eventual settlement in the "house on the mountain."

In *Man without a Country*, I have changed aliases of immediate family names back to the actual names thus providing continuity with *I Am a Refugee*. Having no way of knowing the real names of all the other characters, they remain as per the original. I have added clarifying footnotes to both works.

I hope through the publication of my father's writings to add to the written history of those dreadful times and contribute in a small way to remembering the actualities of the Holocaust. Myriad recollections have already been written; on one level the theme of survival is a common element, yet each unique story needs to be preserved. The surviving heroes who fought to save the world from totalitarianism are today in their late eighties and nineties; similarly most Holocaust survivors of today were then mere children. In a few years, all those lives will be snuffed out as well, leaving only the historical record.

MICHEL ADLER

PART I

MAN WITHOUT A COUNTRY

Original Manuscript dated April 1945

1

Drawn into War

On August 13, 1939, my wife, Martha; my three-and-a-half-year-old boy, Paul; and I began our vacation in the Ardèche. A worrisome year lay behind us. Though Austrians, we had lived in France for many years, and the Anschluss affected us deeply. We were Jews, and we clung to our country of origin as any human clings to his homeland. Our parents and relatives lived in Vienna. We never missed an opportunity to spend our vacation with them in that trusted land.

We loved Austria. All people love their country, the place in which they grew up and spent their youth, those years most filled with life's richest experiences. What humans—if they deserve to be called that—remain cold remembering the mountains and valleys they traversed as youths? Who isn't struck with an odd feeling when images of small lanes and places where one once lingered materialize? But now we no longer had any part of it. The teachings of a gruesome political party thrust us out of our original community and banished us. That is painful.

At the same time, our circle of people was severed. All around, spring moved into the land, extolling the grace of the Creator with flowers and chirping birds; at the same time, his pursued and harassed creations stowed themselves away over border crossings and begged for

3

admittance and rescue. But the world hardened their hearts, courting the favor of the persecutors and ridiculing sacrifice. Still, perhaps that too had to be, in order to cap it all and not undeservedly have the criminal courts trump humankind. Our loved ones had fled, their fate filled with worry and sorrow, robbed of everything: their possessions and their human dignity.

* * *

Bold headlines again filled the newspapers. Should Danzig become part of Germany? We had become more than accustomed to the dramatic performance again unfolding before the eyes of a blunted humankind: challenges and threats from one side; initially powerful and sharp retorts from the other; escalating rhetoric, until the world finally swallowed the reality as a "given"—until it finally, full of self-deceit, hoping to be spared and perhaps achieve real peace, relinquished a scrap to the unappeasable.

We had no illusions. After the Munich compromise, Europe appeared to us as Hitler's hunting preserve. The rape of the Czech people testified to the fact that an aggressor without conscience possessed limitless power when the defenders of the law were too weak to stand up to the sacrifice. How could someone, through Hitler's emasculation of Bohemia, peacefully approve the surrender of one's natural flow! Against all promises, Czechoslovakia was sold out to the brazen plunderers. Mutual assistance, as established by treaty, dictated by sensibility—and even more so by self-preservation—no longer applied. The given word was no longer a word, and fear was simply fear. Hitler could only see the circumstances of Munich, underlined by the total absorption of Czechoslovakia on March 15, as a license for future conquests. His opponents' speeches appeared to him targeted only for internal political consumption. He no longer needed to take seriously threats that would never be executed.

We, just as the French among whom we lived, had little faith the sword would be drawn; why "die for Danzig" when one had refused to die for Prague or even Vienna? Should the politics of retreat from the criminals have reason and purpose? Let Russia confront Germany regarding the Polish cadaver. "Oh, holy St. Florian," we read from the wounded declarations of the statesmen, "spare our houses and kindle the others." Wasn't it clearly evident from the relationship with Russia that it recognized these intentions as those of the Western powers? Russia was not at Munich because it recognized the Western powers' yearning for peace transcended any instinct for self-preservation; it made a pact with Germany so as to legally benefit from the development of an apparently unavoidable situation, and arm—as long as there was time.

Though Hitler prepared for war according to a deliberate plan, he counted on achieving some bloodless results. And let's be honest: Didn't he develop a propaganda abroad whose reverberation seemed to declare him and all pessimists on our continent in agreement? Why a war with France? Hitler looked on while undermining this country from within. Didn't he always win more admirers to his teachings in those French population tiers who, with the power of their money, were the most influential and surely remained the most goal-conscious even after the Popular Front elections?

* * *

I had been a resident of France since 1930. Shortly after my immigration, I joined a silk-weaving firm and had not changed my position since. My fellow employees were all French, with one exception; he was multilingual and, as I, engaged with foreign sales. The patrician establishments of Lyon did not employ foreigners unless they had need for their language skills to carry on trade outside of France.

Until this time, I lived there in peace. Austrians were gladly seen everywhere. Vienna reminded one of joyous things, of Mozart and Strauss. Until 1933 no one worried about the Jewish question. I had then made the friendship of a student, and at the beginning of our acquaintance, bearing in mind my experiences in my homeland, I made him aware that I was a Jew. The young man shrugged his shoulders indifferently. What concern was it of his? Who was asking?

5

And so it was in the office. Religion was a private matter.

At the beginning of the thirties, Germany obtained much valuable product from the French silk industry. One of the biggest German textile companies, Karstadt AG, employed many young Germans in its purchasing office in Lyon. I had made friends with several of them. We spoke German, as we were not yet sufficiently fluent in French. We ate together in a family guesthouse. Of the twelve table companions, three were Jewish. As the Jewish Day of Atonement neared, one of the Jews told the guesthouse head he would not be coming for meals the next day. The brave woman then inquired after the religious beliefs of the others. "Are you also a Jew?" she asked a young Berliner sitting next to me, the epitome of a Germanic, blond, blue-eyed youth. By God, how he turned red. No one had ever held him for a Jew. The dignified Madam Perrin laughed about his embarrassment. "There, there, now, your religion is not written on your face. Do you take it as a shame to be a Jew?"

I could cite other examples of French indifference to race. Enough. In broader circles, this question was simply not discussed.

But after 1933, the picture changed. It became obvious, more and more publications, which later received plenty of German intellectual and in some cases financial support, carried the race and Jewish question with an openness that was not at all necessary.

Through misuse of freedom of the press, publications such as *Je suis partout* and *Gringoire* spread unpunished the most obscene lies about Jews and Jewish influence and, under the protection of democracy, sang the praises of total tyranny. Eventually, Hitler's propaganda was so successful and his fifth column so strong that one had to be prepared for the deciding point in time when France could not muster sufficient will to defend itself against Germany. Even if it didn't join Germany, it would not stop Hitler.

* * *

The Anschluss made my wife and me legally homeless. The Germans seized the Austrian interests abroad without encountering any resistance. England even handed over a gold treasury. Austrians living abroad, who did not want to bend to its power, joined the army of the disenfranchised. No one protected us, exactly as no one concerned themselves with the expelled Spaniards, Italians, and Germans. Silence was the big password. A refugee conference convened in Evian testified to their lack of power. At the renewal of our papers, the French official wrote into the identification card: "Ex-Austrian." And that was that.

As Jews, could we count on living in our country of choice unmolested for the long term? The further the situation developed, the bleaker the future became. After the Munich Agreement, our part of the world was forever handed over to the powers of the irrational. When I read one of the above-mentioned newspapers—they were available everywhere—I became sick. Hadn't it started that way in Germany also? Every day I saw the poison of hate engulfing us. So we resolved to emigrate[1] overseas and thought we still had time to leisurely make our preparations. We expected further concessions to Germany, maybe even a war between Germany and Russia, but in any case a longer breathing pause.

Humans tend to simplify the questions of the day. Who is at fault? "The Jew and the bicycle rider," replies the joker. Here it's the Communists; there again, the capitalists; elsewhere the Jesuits, the Pope, the foreigners, and so on and so forth. It isn't just the blacks of the bush that believe in demons and fetishes; we ourselves, the proud white race, are controlled by dark powers: we believe in the evil eye, the boogey man, and the unlucky number thirteen. On one side, God; the other, the devil. We ourselves are goodness. Who doubts that? So there must be evil powers at fault for everything—groups about whom we know very little, but whisper about even more so. One of these evil powers—who are at fault for every misfortune, who possess all the money in the world, force themselves into everything, strive for world domination—for thousands of years have been the Jews. Sixty generations ago, it is said, they crossed someone in their midst. For that they are cursed, and even today are attributed with everything evil. For isn't it true, other people have never slain a single good person in their midst. So then?

All kinds of discussions with colleagues from work and acquaintances poisoned our existence. All at once we appeared to people as something

---

1 However, with the outbreak of war, the United States cancelled all visa applications.

peculiar and puzzling. Some believed with all seriousness in an unfathomable international Jewish organization that strived to attain world domination. In view of this stupidity and ignorance, we almost lost the will to live. One day I heard a Frenchman from so-called better circles, and certainly not an anti-Semite, concoct the following nonsense: "A misfortune for the Jew that America devalued the dollar just at the time of Hitler's rise to power. Had the Jewish financial businesses not had such a stake in the dollar transactions, it would have known how to prevent the rise of Hitler." Of course this assertion is pure rubbish. Where are the Jewish international financial interests hidden? Since when does big Jewish business feel solidarity with the little Jew of his own country, let alone a foreign one? Did his conscience stop Mr. Manfred Weiss of the Czepel munitions factory from delivering arms to the Axis powers and with access any time to Admiral Nicholas Horthy? Didn't Fritz Mandl, munitions manufacturer, though forced by his Jewish heritage to leave Austria, forcefully support fascism from South America? The Jewish financial magnate generously contributed a few dollars to his needy co-religionists. In short, he behaved exactly the same as any munitions manufacturer, establishing an endowment for widows and waifs from their blood money. He was first a capitalist, then British, French, or American, and totally last a little bit Jewish.

* * *

Under these circumstances we particularly looked forward to our vacation. We decided on a nice country inn at a quiet little spot in the Ardèche away from the modern hustle and bustle, where many families with children sought recuperation in nature.

In this blessed area, the newspapers came a little late. What difference does it make! Here, we wanted to know nothing about politics.

The Ardèche is a charming, picturesque low mountain range. The soft rounded peaks are covered with pine forests, and in the valley magnificent cows graze in juicy meadows. Peace permeates the countryside. We enjoyed the fresh air of the forest, the smell of the fields, and the innocent chatter of our firstborn; and the sky was as blue as on a postcard.

Those sunny vacation days today appear to me like a fairytale dream, those last cheerful days before the storm of war, whose awful scale we fortunately could not fathom. But one day, posters appeared—attached to trees on all crossroads, like an evil rash disfiguring the face of the forest—and spoke of the threat of war and conscription. Like a cascade, they followed one another, calling each age group to service until over-taken at the end of August by the general mobilization.

Our inn became the stage for touching scenes. The men took leave of their families. But they hoped unceasingly, that this time, just like the time in April or in September of 1938, with the march to the borders, nothing would come of it. Why fear the worst over a city like Danzig?

My situation was simple enough. Several months ago I voluntarily made myself available to my guest country. In my pocket I carried the invitation for the medical examination for military service for September 21, 1939.

We thought the war might yet surprise us in Europe. As a precaution, my wife and I agreed that it would be my duty to serve in the war. Should Germany emerge victorious, a Jew would find no country left on earth in which to live unchallenged. If anyone, we Jews had to be among the first warriors to oppose Hitler's Germany. Could we be bystanders when others carried on the struggle that for us meant victory or total annihilation? We loved peace. But hadn't the Nazis long ago declared a gruesome war against us? So much as my wife cared for me, and as close as she was to her brother who also found refuge in France, there was no choice but to follow our conscience: we must serve.

So at the end of August, I traveled back to Lyon. For the time being, Martha and little Paul stayed in the Ardèche, as the civilian population feared the bombing of the major cities that must follow the start of the war.

* * *

The business where I was employed suffered from a total depletion of its core personnel. Several young co-workers had already left, and the others would return in a few days to their hometowns. Our staff consisted of seventeen men. Remaining were several older men beyond the qualifying service age, an office assistant whose World War I injuries made him unfit for service, the bookkeeper, whose arm was partially paralyzed following an accident, and the foreigner. This citizen of a neutral state, like the others released from war service, was looked upon disparagingly.

No one was enamored with the possibility of war. The sudden quiet in business left us with ample time to express many observations, among which lay the hope of a last-minute "understanding." I will always remember, in the course of the debates, the wicked words of a fellow worker: "All the Jews should be sent directly to the front lines." Our response, "You'd like that; then you might be able to just stay at home," shut him up. This Jew-hater and coward later emerged logically enough as an ardent collaborator and advocate of a united Europe under German rule.

On my return to Lyon, my first act was to visit the recruitment office to see if I could enlist right away. I bought a newspaper in a kiosk near the headquarters on Place du Président Carnot. The sales woman told me, "The government is mobilizing the nation to prevent a revolution." I was astonished that twenty-four hours after the expiration of the ultimatum someone dared to view matters from this point. But while the attitudes of many totally justified such an interpretation, the mood of the people was sooner directed toward war. Regarding my report for service, I had time. I need not worry about my examination for military service until the twenty-first.

In general, in case of war the French hoped to be able to peacefully wait out the collapse of Germany through hunger and inner unrest, behind the protection of the Maginot Line. Daily the newspapers hammered us with how France possessed the strongest fortification lines and the most powerful army. And the Germans waited only for the opportunity to rise up against Hitler. The German tanks were just dummies. The Germans were merely playing military, as suited their nature, yet incapable of disputing France's well-grounded superiority. The government and the press deceived us shamelessly.

But following England's actions, everyone realized that France most reluctantly slipped into the war. Could it actually tolerate the bloodletting of another world war?

The thinking was: Of the forty-two million inhabitants of European France, three million were foreigners, or approximately 7 percent. The constituency of foreigners in the working age group was markedly higher. The children of immigrants were, for the most part, born in France, and were French. That's how it was with our Paul. There were many families in which only the husband was a foreigner and the wife and children were French. Considering that the parents of many immigrants stayed in the country of origin, one was forced to estimate to a far greater extent the significance of the foreigners to the population. You couldn't go wrong, if you assumed that the foreigners constituted a fifth of the working inhabitants of France. And of the French numbers, it had also to be considered that a great many were naturalized.

There was nothing to be done. The people remembered all too well the great slaughters from 1914 to 1918. Every French family mourned their dead. The question of the Marne: was it something other than the heroic self-sacrifice of the best sons of the people, whose government failed miserably to organize an effective defense? One only had to skim through the weighty reports of the first months of the First World War. The lack of foresight, failing weapons—all led to the defeat of France in June of 1940 and had also played a disastrous role in the year 1914. And if the French succeeded in the last instant, despite the lack of technical means, to build a rampart with their own bodies against the aggressor, it was only because the methods of war at that time didn't possess the penetration power of 1940 technology. France paid the price of victory in the First World War with one and a half million lives, the majority of which fell at the beginning of the war. The laying down of French blood marked a further decline in the already suffering French family. No woman whose brother, father, or spouse fell in war likes bringing children into the world to have them one day handed over and led to the slaughter.

Many causes contributed to the demise of the French family: the weightiest being the war of 1914. Another such bloodletting and the depopulation of France would force her to invite more foreigners into the country and make areas of the country heavily foreign. Every French government knew that. You couldn't go into war with a declining population.

* * *

Even among the many acquaintances within my immigrant circles, the war elicited very mixed feelings. They were, however, unanimous in the view that the war could only end with the defeat of Germany. No one wanted to believe in the crowning of a victory over the civilized world, bringing with it so much injustice, and so many violent deeds.

Many refugees had served in the First World War and experienced firsthand the German fighting power and organizational capability. They warned of extreme expectations. Germany would resist to the end. I saw my need to enlist as self-evident, yet I was so painfully taken aback when our family physician once declared, "All Jews must register for war service." With what right could he make rules for others? He went into the service as a physician and didn't have to participate in any battle attacks. For him, it was a foregone conclusion that France would open a wide-ranging offensive.

Now, concerning my small person, I must confess that I still very much valued my life. Dimly, I hoped that a merciful Providence, dear God would protectively reign over me if I did the duty of an honorable man. Far distant was an arrogant hero consciousness: I am led by a sense of duty and rest my hope on God.

For the time being, we had not yet come that far. Barely had the ultimatum expired and conditions of war been instituted, when green posters appeared on the advertising pillars. "Listen," a Frenchman told me, "The Boches are being imprisoned." Satisfied, he rubbed his hands. "This time they won't catch us the way they did in 1914." Prior to the First World War, many Germans were resident in France. Most of them had been notified by the German consulate and cleared out in time and fought against their guest country. The French never forgot.

You could search with spotlights for Reich Germans in French firms, but you couldn't find too many of them. Of course there were men that originated from enemy territory, but were they Germans according to their country's national law? Some were "fellows without a native country," meaning Communists and Socialists. Also a few devout Catholics and Protestants emigrated, but Hitler had pushed these out of the German community quite a while ago. To say nothing of Jews, who purely "blood-wise," had nothing in common with the noble race. Well, the French officials didn't follow Hitler's racial and popular teachings. In truth, the posters appeared to be printed for us refugees. We were the men from the enemy territory, who were to assemble at certain gathering places with all our papers and food provisions for forty-eight hours for the purposes of internment.

It took several days for that to sink in. This reality by itself would never have entered our thick skulls, for who would lock their friends behind bars? But the police cooperated; they gradually arrested and delivered refugees from Germany, Austria, and Czechoslovakia. I directed myself to the commissioner for foreigners in my neighborhood, who had known me for many years and knew where I belonged. But rules are rules. "I understand your feelings," the good man consoled me, and raised his hands toward the heavens. "But you must understand that we must inspect the papers of suspicious foreigners. It's a precautionary measure. Go there without worrying. In a few days, they will release you."

What could I say? We had no choice. In the end, I thought, I'll be enlisted on September 21, and then, in any event, this farce will be over.

So I tied my bundle. I didn't confide in my office companions. Truly, I was ashamed—as if I had something to be ashamed about. I only explained to my director what it was about. He too thought I would be back home in two or three days.

In the evening, I went to the Gerland Sports Stadium, designated as the Lyon assembly point for men from the enemy territory. Seven o'clock had long passed. Fortunately the guards were not too exacting in their duty. They asked me to come back tomorrow; there was no hurry.

No, there was no hurry, certainly none as far as I was concerned. But the fool that I am, I was ashamed to go down the stairs, fearing the malicious looks of the building residents and having to reply to the nasty question of the waiting concierge—that I was going to an assembly place for Germans.

But nothing helped. On September 16, two weeks after the declaration of war, I had to report to Gerland, and was interned. That's how the war started for me and other stateless people—not the war against Hitler's Germany in which we had planned to participate, but the battle against human stupidity and capriciousness. And even today this battle has not blown away.

2

INTERNMENT BEGINS

W e had explained our position to the guards—wasn't a French victory of even greater importance for us than for France?— nonetheless, the soldiers didn't trust us. We had been delivered as Boches; therefore, we were Boches.

They took everything from us: cigarettes, matches, lighters, writing paper, pencils, and most of all, fountain pens, as well as pocketknives and house keys. Strangely enough, they let us keep our money. They said everything would be returned to us in the internment camp just as soon as they examined our files and knew everyone's individual situation.

I spent two days in Gerland. In our broken state, we suffered terribly from the no smoking rule. Finally, the sergeant on duty explained that for a good tip he would return the cigarettes. We could smoke them in the privy. Our group consisted of twenty men, who certainly were not Nazis. We were so stunned. How could they do that to us? We had lived in France for years, and our papers had been repeatedly examined; they knew what each one of us did. For every resident, the French police carefully established a file on their political convictions based on information from neighbors or informants. Most every concierge belonged to the trusted circle of the police. Actual spies would obviously not be brought here, as their clients provided them with identification papers from a neutral country. What did they want from us? Why couldn't we see anyone? Why couldn't we smoke? Would France be defeated if we smoked? Longingly we looked at the high, wrought iron fence, where on the other side people moved freely about. A few pedestrians nosily looked at the hated Bosches. Now and then a crying woman came to the fence wanting to speak with her husband, but was denied. No angel with sword drawn—only a soldier with bayonet and rifle—guarded the portal: the entrance to the paradise of free men beckoned. When questioned, their retort to me was that, unfortunately, also refugees and even Jews were in the service of the Gestapo, and that unpleasant events forced the French government for the time being to take all Germans and Austrians into custody, contrary to its original intentions. Correct: even among the refugees and Jews there were a few scoundrels. They could cite as an excuse that their next of kin in Germany were at the mercy of attacks by the Gestapo, and everyone knew what such a threat signified. But why apologize? Hitler found willing coworkers in all people who sold out their homeland not under pressure, but for cash. After all, are refugees better humans? The fifth column was no greater under those without means, those under the threat of extortion and harassment, than under the free citizens of a free France. For that reason, did they put all the French behind barbed wire?

The long bayonets of the guards appeared to us as slaughter knives. The soldiers were under orders to use their weapons against us at the least sign of resistance. The world had gone mad. We slept on straw, and our care was far below civilian standards; but these concerns seemed secondary, as we were so dazed about what happened to us. We suffered only from spiritual anguish. A fellow sufferer rejected every bite of food. He wanted to rattle the world with his hunger strike, to protest against his treatment, to show that France was not worthy. But his strike served no purpose. No one gave a damn whether he ate or not.

After two days, a transport was arranged for suspects. We were transferred to the Chambaran internment camp in the Isère. During the trip, the noncommissioned officer that accompanied us entrusted me with the package of confiscated fountain pens. Today, I can't understand how I could have been so dumb. It never occurred to me to take back my beautiful gold fountain pen. We never saw those pens again. There were some very valuable pieces in the lot. Refugees were not permitted to take gold out of Germany. So among other things, they acquired expensive fountain pens. In this war we forfeited so much—much more than a gold pen. It seems childish to mourn after such a petty object. But it was the first time that in a moral country something like that happened to us.

In Chambaran, the guards welcomed us with fixed bayonets. It rained buckets. As some of us tried to find cover in a barrack, the guards pointed their bayonets toward us.

How low did we sink in just a few days! They finally shoved us into a barrack in which the length of each side was spread with straw. A big drum, in which to relieve ourselves, stood in the middle. It stank unbearably from excrement and urine. The barrack was locked behind us. We feared the drum would leak. We were overcome with tiredness; we threw ourselves onto the straw and fell asleep. Yet, this gruesome night went by. A peaceful morning broke. The door was opened. We stepped out and looked around the camp.

These disgusting barracks, now home, were encircled by barbed wire and guarded in front by soldiers with fixed bayonets. I dared not think that we had been convicted to stay here for a very long time. How often had I been quartered behind barbered wire? In how many camps had soldiers guarded me, in France and elsewhere? How often had I guarded other people, with cartridge belt and weapon? Because the bayonet, in truth, was symbolic of our bloody time, its drawn blade an expression of the misdeeds of our bottomless evil. Then, I had not yet comprehended that humanity is split into two parts: those without rights who are guarded, and the others, who are guarded by those without rights.

Here I learned for the first time to swallow my tears, to be calm and present myself in a moral and friendly way even though one wanted to become a murderer in this irrational world. We were approximately eight hundred people in the camp: for the greater part, Jewish refugees from Germany and Austria; to a lesser extent, German "Aryans" who had lived in France for years and married French woman; as well as German Democrats and Catholics, who did not want to subjugate themselves to Hitler's yoke. Finally there were a large number of Germans from Alsace, born in Alsace, who had the choice at the age of twenty-one to declare themselves for France. But France had mandatory military service of eighteen months or a year and Germany, at the time, had no military service mandate. It's not every person's thing to join the military. Now those that had shunned military service in France were considered Germans and deported here as enemy aliens. Some of the interned were rumored to be Nazis.

I need not emphasize the shock we suffered from our internment, and the spiritual suffering we endured anew every day. We walked around aimlessly, silent and grim, like animals in a cage, to and fro, fro and to. We were determined to never come to terms with our fate—no, no, never.

One day we read in the local paper that eighty German prisoners were conveyed to Chambaran. "German" prisoners? I was a German prisoner—stripped of citizenship by Hitler and designated German by the French. Some days I hated this country. Had reason been totally extinguished? What to do, dear God, what to do?

* * *

Every second day we went to work at one of the nearby airfields. I still laugh today when I think about it. They loaded us into trucks. In the front and in the rear guards traveled on motorcycles mounted with machine guns to counter any possible escape. To where shall we escape? To Germany? The machine guns were pointed in our direction even during work. We had to pick out the stones from the grassy field. With wooden sticks we poked the ground everywhere, doing more harm than good, for we were not in a state to do useful work. The stones were thrown into the trucks and dumped into a mound. For weeks we worked on the airfield. Finally it occurred to them that we only scarred the grass with our digging and turned the beautiful green pitch into a desert. One day, without reason, the work was terminated. The food at the airfield was cold and awful, and in the end we had had enough. We threw the pieces of shoe leather that masqueraded as meat at the feet of the cooks. That protest drew a hefty and loud tongue-lashing from the camp director, but after that the food improved.

They had not yet introduced food stamps. For us the camp leadership installed a special canteen in which we could buy bread, butter, sugar, and so forth. The prices in the canteen for the internees were considerably higher than in stores or even in the French soldier's canteen. We had no idea where the profits went; certainly we received no benefit. And also, we were strictly prohibited from purchasing goods elsewhere.

On another work assignment, we gathered wood from the little nearby forest. It was not possible to guard us on the narrow paths, and so the gathering of wood provided a welcome opportunity to take a stroll. It was considered a thing of honor to carry back the thinnest possible "walking sticks."

We were further used constructing shelters in which the townspeople could find protection in the event of an aerial attack. These shelters were naturally located outside the confines of the camp. Though it was forbidden to enter into any business or talk to the peasants, in exchange for an aperitif, the guard was happy to make all kinds of concessions. To venture beyond the confines of the barbed wire fence, to move about in the open air, to talk with people who wore no uniforms! This work gang suffered no shortage of workers.

Well, the circumstances…When it rained, the water didn't run off but instead puddled up on the floor. The weak camouflage of leaves and branches could not tolerate any strong movement. Only with effort could you squeeze into the shelter. No one with all his or her senses would seek shelter here in an emergency. Of course we could care less. Our supervisors were responsible for the quality of our work. And they were happy with our effort, as it depended only on the certification.

* * *

I almost forgot about it. At the end of September, the camp leadership called together all those who had volunteered for war service and had received an invitation to appear for the military service medical examination. We went to the recruiting office in Lyon. Although under guard, the escort team knew we were volunteers and was friendly toward us. We were brought to Gerland and marched from there, in formation, to Place Président Carnot, where the examination took place.

19

A huge throng of foreigners waited in the forecourt, many Spaniards. The military authorities did not particularly welcome the latter, in view of their political leanings, and many were declared unfit for service.

Finally we were called in. Most of us were fit. I was in line and convinced I would not be rejected. Though I wasn't a giant, the French in general aren't difficult and my papers were in perfect order. Everything had proceeded according to my wishes, and I thought the doctor was already prepared to advance me to the French soldiers, when at the eye exam, my eyes failed me. One eye gave out. It was as if I fell on my head; in civilian life, this one-sided weakness never bothered me; I never ever wore glasses. The doctor declared me "unfit for the infantry."

"But there are other weapons," I interjected. "No," said the doctor. "Fundamentally, foreigners may be assigned only to the infantry. If you absolutely want to be a soldier, get yourself some glasses and come again."

I bade him to declare me fit on the spot and swore I would get glasses. But the doctor had already written down his findings and called the next person. I was dismissed.

Done! I was unsuited! I could not collect myself I was so boiling over with anger. Naturally, foreigners could only be used in the infantry, the lowest sort of cannon fodder. Why offer the suspicious foreigners a better chance? You want to serve, then be good and put yourself into the front line. There we feel secure about you, and should you fall, you will be buried as a hero. In discussion with a companion, the doctor criticized the great number of businesspeople among the refugees. Didn't he know that refugees were barred from accepting other employment? That they were merely tolerated shopkeepers? Yes, we stood outside the civilian society. The stateless are people of second order. But we too are God's creation.

I hardly dared to look my fellow sufferers in the eyes. My God, I was so childish. I should have been happy. The findings were irrelevant, for also the fit were not conscripted. Fundamentally, they didn't want any Germans serving in the French military and had no regard in any way for our convictions. But we didn't know that then; for us the examination was just an examination, and not a farce.

Back to Gerland...The grounds commander permitted the guard to let us bring wine at our expense. We should drink to the medical examination in the usual way. We were so tired; we asked the commander's permission to spend the night at home. At home…We could not despite all the volunteering. Again the partitioning gate shut behind us. We wished good luck to our companions who on our march through the city had secretly sent postcards to notify our families. The next morning, all the women were at the train station. Unfortunately, my Martha was still in the Ardèche. A heartfelt exchange of kisses took place. A Viennese, a girl of short stature, jumped up to embrace her tall husband around the neck, in sheer jubilation of joy. "Just show those Nazis," she chattered between two kisses, and clenched her small fist. Her cluelessness hurt; how did the poor thing perceive the war? Next to her a woman consoled her unsuitable-for-service beloved, "You are fit for me." Gently she caressed his cheeks. "If you could just stay with me." Yes, if…That was not possible. Within a few minutes, the train began to roll. We returned to the camp as if nothing had happened, and the officials never mentioned another word about the medical examination for military service.

3

CHAMBARAN

For most, internment duration had already stretched to a couple of weeks. Nothing budged. Our worries escalated. Would we spend the entire war here? Only one way led out of the camp: the Foreign Legion, for which they eagerly recruited among us. In every way they sought to make us understand that we had no other way out. Should we sign up? For five years?

We shuddered at the thought, the more so because in Chambaran we had the opportunity to observe a variety of former Legionnaires. The wounded from the Rif War in Morocco, state pensioners, and those with distinguished service awards for their bravery—they had no doubts about their country's thanks in the form of their internment. They all sat with us in the camp. In one respect they naturally had an advantage: they could play head of the barracks. "Join the Foreign Legion," we teased each other, "then in the next war you too can be head of the barracks in the internment camp." "So why don't you join the Foreign Legion again?" we asked them. "You are after all experts in your field." "No," they refused with wrath. "Exactly because we know the Legion, we prefer Chambaran. Once and never again."

Now, they offered some choices to the Legionnaires residing in France. Many married, carried on a respectable skilled craft, and for better or for worse slogged through. With horror they thought back to the foolishness of their youth. They were offered the possibility to enlist for the duration of the war, whereas they demanded of us a five-year obligation. Five years with these troops. Of eight hundred men, only two were talked into it. Had we known that the war would last longer than five years, we still wouldn't have signed on—for no one would have enlisted voluntarily. But if humankind were so disposed with sufficient fantasy to fully picture what were to be in store for them, would war even be possible?

This Foreign Legion! No, it was not an effective recruitment method. It was so ugly how they attempted to drive us into the Legion, despite convincing us of untold thorough disrespect. Just maybe for that reason. During the day, the Legionnaires lay listlessly on the straw; and in the evening, if they had a little money, they boozed to capacity. The camp commander entrusted them to supervise us, from which they assumed the right to dodge work. Their bodies were for the most part covered with gruesome tattoos. Some were also at loggerheads with their hygiene. When I happened to stand next to a Legionnaire at the washing trough, a louse from his filthy laundry swam toward me.

These beings, for their service standing up for France, had endured the internment worse than we. Occasionally sharp confrontations erupted between them and the guard. One day, a young lad with well-deserved medals for bravery fell into a major crisis. "I have fought and suffered more for France than you," he yelled embittered to the guard. "Why do you lock me up here?" The eyes of the poor lad stood out and became violent. The captain had him taken away. In jail, in a rabid rage, he tore the clothing from his body into rags. Then he sat naked on them and calmed down.

Despite the prescribed recruitment, the Foreign Legion didn't attract anyone. We wanted to serve with Frenchmen in orderly units and not with the homeless in the Foreign Legion. Only later did our eyes open fully, and we recognized that we were the disenfranchised, that for us there was only one place of refuge, the home of the homeless, the Foreign Legion. *Legio patria nostra*, the Legion is our fatherland—this adage, which I would later see so often on the walls of the mess halls, was not known to me then. Only with time did we recognize its bitter truth.

* * *

In this camp of the disenfranchised, I soon found some like-minded souls. Would camp life have been bearable without comrades to bring solace and comfort and talk things out with? One of my unforgettable friends of that time, a former member of the Republican Defense Confederation, came from Württenberg, where he was born into a family with deeply rooted, basic democratic convictions. Hunted by the Gestapo at the start of the Reign of Terror, he had lived in France since 1933. He married a sweet French girl, who bore him two loving daughters. Gustav, a competent housefather and an upstanding man, never compromised his convictions, even to his own detriment. Our treatment did not surprise him. He used to say, "We can't expect anything else from this society. Have military reactionaries ever looked upon socialists and Jews as fellow nationals?"

I developed an especially close relationship with another fellow, Sertorius, a former lieutenant from Prussia. The cadet academy drills remained in his blood and were revealed in all his gestures. Prussian militarism rested on the conviction that the whole world is united— old Prussia was not only ruled by a single class but also a caste state. Hitler's prerogative, then, raised despotism to a legal norm, and this extremism provoked some people of the old army to reflection—not many, but still a few, including Sertorius for whom National Socialism and independent thinking were incompatible.

An unusual journey led Sertorius to democracy. One day, forced to quit his service and suffer through many obstacles, the most incriminating rumors spread about this man. They described him as affiliated with the fifth column. No one knew the real circumstances. I would have given a lot to find out, but as it was, I became very fond of him. He impressed me as sincere. Now, he was a broken man, distracted and restless. He loved his country, though he knew and acknowledged its deviant course. He suffered mental and physical anguish. And for years he never found appropriate work. With meager subsidies, he dragged with him the little remaining spark of life.

In his hopelessness he clung to God, searched for him with all his heart, searched for him with a Jew, for the God after whom we thirsted, to whom we fervently sent prayers—not the God of one religion, but God and Father of all humankind. Could my companion find solace by a priest in the camp? A clergyman once declared during a service that he did not pray for captured German civilians. To which particular national God had this strange priest prayed? I am not exaggerating. This one time sufficiently impressed upon us, innocent prisoners, in the worst way and once and for all to keep our Christian companions suffering from mental anguish away from priests.

Behind our barbed wire on a tiny fleck of grass, reserved for us, we went to and fro and back again and guided by our fate, attempting to find God's strength. We uselessly asked ourselves why the Almighty permitted all this injustice, and what purpose our wretched lives held. We had to wonder if it weren't just all happenstance, and God was just the fruit of human arrogance, giving meaning to meaningless events. Yet our need for God was stronger than our doubt; with all our strength, we had to cling to a power over us. We had to pray in our deep, innocent deprivation; we had to hope for a divine reconciliation of justice. As slaves once hoped for life in the hereafter, so we hoped for the triumph of justice, for reparations, for a new and better and more beautiful world. For my friend Gustav, socialism was his religion, from which he created hope for the future. We had to believe in something, to lean on something; else we would never have survived that gruesome time.

The world didn't make our belief for the future easy.

* * *

We, the interned, were of the same opinion: the measurements, which the government instituted against us, were aimed less at "suspicious" foreigners as against foreigners in general. Without a doubt, we belonged to the most unwelcome type of aliens, from the territory of the archenemy. Whether we Jews or democrats were anti-Hitler was, for the French, immaterial—we were all Boches. The Jews perceived that they were a more unpopular variety of Boches. The Christians on the other hand had the impression that the French military authority showed no understanding for their democratic, antifascist stance and treated them with particular contempt in some measure as turncoats. In an effort to solve the sensitive foreigner question once and for all, with the war as a pretext and lever, the government started with us, by imprisoning us. We were sure they would also screen the other foreigners. We were easy to screen. According to official figures, approximately forty-five thousand persons of German and Austrian origin enjoyed asylum rights in France, and of these, thirty thousand were women, children and the aged, and fifteen thousand civilian prisoners.

Over five years of the most horrible war have since passed through the land. When the war started, it was a most peculiar war, a *drôle de guerre*. Throughout the difficult test of waiting, the French people retrenched themselves and leaned on the foreigners who served reluctantly; we couldn't be totally ignored because the French needed us much more than they wanted to admit.

Our files were to be examined. We anticipated that, as we proved to be harmless, we would be set free and summoned to service without weapons. After all, we formed an unnecessary burden for the government. But was anyone honestly concerned with screening our situation? We had the firm impression that our entrusted guard officers and civilian corps worked against resolving the internment camps. In fact, our camp's continued existence guaranteed the continued existence of their nice, comfortable jobs. The internment camps were actually eliminated only when the legislature withheld further funding for their maintenance. Internees were then methodically promoted to *prestateurs* overnight. We didn't gain much. Most of the prestateurs remained in the same camps, without being somehow deployed. Nonetheless, we received uniforms.

It was understood that at the beginning of the internments our employers could request us. I wrote my firm but received no reply. The government ignored all petitions, giving them no serious consideration, even when the employer interceded.

* * *

I would have been thankless toward God had I not thought of the gracious chances of fate, which eased some of my sad days. I was personally acquainted with the chief inspector of the civilian prison camp in our zone. After the Anschluss, he even extended me the courtesy of visiting my parents in Vienna and brought me their treasured greetings. Troiville… Troiville—often I came across this name in the camp, without suspecting that behind this smart-looking officer with the gold-trimmed beret, hid my acquaintance, the easygoing silk businessman. And even had I known, in this awful situation, in my wretched civilian prisoner's getup, I could never have brought myself to approach him. By coincidence, some errand once took me to his office, without knowing he was there. I greeted him, feeling awkward and confused. Indeed, we were not in the busy office of a silk factory, and the two of us were strangely transformed. He didn't deny my presence, but greeted me kindly. His human response did me good. Faced with the insult and feeling of inferiority, which the misdeeds of the French world engendered in us, his friendly salutation filled the breach. Yes, there were good people too, and the fewer there were, the more cherished they would become in our memory. Troiville made the effort to ebb our deprivation. He managed to release several sick people from the camp. Per guidelines, he unfortunately could do nothing for me. On the contrary he cautioned me to be ready for a lengthy internment. At that time in the camps, a movement eagerly—though ultimately for naught—recruited for an Austrian Legion. Troiville strongly suggested I sign on, saying that in this way I could escape the camp and join with my fellow countrymen. Lacking sufficient drawing power, the Austrian Legion never came into existence. Outcast Austrian Jews would not give up the façade so that Prince Starhemberg, the once half-fascist leader of home defense, could parade around in his proud uniform. What cause should we support? The fascism of Dollfuss? The brouhaha was unbecoming.

* * *

One day a notice hung on the bulletin board in front of the commander's office. I can't recall if it rained or if the sun was shining. For me it was a memorable day, and for me the sun was shining. For there it was written that all internees with French wives or children, all those whose father, brother, or son had served in the French army could in principle be freed provided that a screening commission considered them reliable. These regulations applied to a majority of us, and we rejoiced as we already saw us in freedom.

Earlier we had anticipated from rumors that releases would be based upon these criteria. Another rumor maintained that American newspapers had reported on the abusive treatment of refugees in France. And even if behind the well-guarded fence of the camp every waiting day seemed like an eternity, one day an opportune hour would toll for us. We needed to be prepared for just such a moment. A long time before, I had my wife obtain a legally authenticated proof of my little son's French citizenship. In addition, through my voluntary enlistment, I could flawlessly demonstrate my convictions. I felt I could count on a much faster handling of my case as Mr. Troiville knew me personally and was ready to vouch for me. Now I owed my little boy my soon anticipated freedom. The little one had no idea how we cherished him. Right after his birth, as a French citizen he had helped me to secure without hassle the extension of my identity papers. Before, I had had to deal with the employment office and security police every year; then suddenly I received my work permit for a full three years. Who says children are a burden? What would have happened without our children? The first one helped regain my freedom from the internment camp; the second, due to the bare reality of his helpless age, protected us from deportation and obtained our entrance into rescuing Switzerland. Could we have known that when we bade God for a child?

"You have it made," said Sertorius, in a depressed state as we sat together in the barrack in the evening. "We couldn't have children in the woefulness of the emigration. Are we therefore Nazis?"

"Had you lived according to the Bible, you would have a whole bunch now," teased Gustav. "Just wait; after the war we family fathers will really increase in value." And burrowing in his thick hair, he added thoughtfully, "I'm afraid that of the three of us only Camillo will be released; the military authorities don't put any stock in population expansion through communism."

The poor man proved right. His convictions kept him banished into the camp. Even if he had been French, he would hardly have enjoyed

29

his freedom. If you openly express your views, you must bear the consequences. Not only did Gustav make the mistake of being a convinced socialist, but he also adopted the foolish practice of fathering girls instead of boys. Girls are not future soldiers—at most able to dress wounds, not inflict them. And there are enough of them, particularly after a world war. For whom does one have children if not for the state?

The examination of each case took a very, very long time. Time and time again, hope vanished. The screening committee met two to three days per week and worked on three to four files. It took a long time to be released.

Martha had returned to our apartment in the skyscraper quarter of Villeurbanne, a suburb of Lyon. Up to then, no air attacks had occurred, and the cost of staying in the countryside ultimately exceeded our modest means. My office didn't pay me any salary, and things didn't work out with the refugee committee.

Most of the refugee committee members sat with the common heap in the camp, and only our valuable head, Herr Professor Gumbel from Heidelberg, by decree of the French government was made a French citizen and had no further business with his captured lambs. It is always advantageous to be able to approach others, and in general to be in a higher position. It provides all kinds of connections that permit taking timely precautions and also to steam across the rescuing ocean to courageously continue the fight against National Socialism from a secure bastion. Not that I could blame anyone for caring for themselves, particularly when the enemy is the Gestapo. Too many leaders escape unharmed the catastrophe that they unload with full force upon those they lead.

The military authority didn't even authorize enlistment into the Foreign Legion for several courageous fellows because of the perceived danger of spreading intellectual infection. These young men spent the entire war festering in the camps, where the Gestapo promptly found them and took them into custody.

Fifteen thousand refugees from Germany and Austria were interned at the outbreak of the war. Releases were rarely approved and only a few could take advantage of the right to emigrate. Some of the emigrants who, guarded by police (not of the Vichy regime, but of the Third Republic), boarded an America-bound ship, stepped on French soil again in 1944 in American uniforms as liberators.

Among the internees were many elderly and sickly people. The awareness of one's refugee status and the consequences of physical and mental suffering compromise one's health. And what kind of treatment did the refugees experience in France prior to the war? They were pursued from one place to another, expelled from individual departments—yes, from the entire country; these were the orders of the day. One must not forget that prior to the establishment of the Popular Front government, Laval was France's premier, and the guidelines that went from Paris to the prefects were not conceived in the spirit of benevolent tolerance. It should be noted that the Popular Front took over the entire civil service and the alien's branch of the police; hostility to refugees continued to function anew and as cheerfully as before.

Among the internees—subject to all the torments of an evil administration—half decided in favor of the difficult service in the Legion. In exchange for asylum, they offered their highest sacrifice: their lives.

* * *

Finally Martha wrote to me that the police had made inquiries in our building, questioning the concierge, the Cerberus of life, regarding the goings-on and convictions of the inhabitants. We thought I would be home soon, and in this expectation didn't even permit ourselves the pleasure of a visit, which naturally depended upon all kinds of difficulty and expense.

Visits depended on our value in the camp leader's estimation. The small and unwelcoming courtyard in the town's inn served as the reception lounge twice per week. Joy and sorrow were neighbors and pressed for space and time.

A lot happened in those two hours they gave us with our loved ones, under the nosy eyes of a bored soldier. Some wives had sunk so low that they nearly offered themselves to the soldiers in exchange for a favor. The procuring host understood his business. Courting couples rented his guestroom for half an hour at a time! Can people be so subservient to their drives? Yes, even that existed—the total completion of our disgrace.

Acquaintances also called me twice into the visiting courtyard. To see me, these dear people claimed to be relatives. One of them surreptitiously pressed a doctor's certificate into my hand from our family physician, who several months before had treated me for ulcers. The certificate confirmed that I absolutely needed home care. It did me good to see that this nice man hadn't forgotten me; I would otherwise have never thought of this possibility for release from the camp. After this kind bestowal, just prior to the outbreak of war, I felt fit as a fiddle. The light physical labor in the fresh country air strengthened the body; we received more than enough bread—that tasty, aromatic French white bread. Butter and sugar were available in the canteen.

I did not want to be released on the basis of an illness certification. I wanted to obtain my freedom because my convictions were pure, because I didn't belong to the enemies of France, because I—I had to smile, but it was so—because I was raising a boy for this country. I was entitled to freedom and did not want to obtain it through tainted means. So I thanked the doctor for his kindness and left the certificate in my briefcase. As if in life only honesty wends its way.

* * *

When overcome by worries, we sought to sing them away from our spirits and wash them away with wine. An elder worker from Vienna also lived in my barrack; years ago he was a coachman. After the First World War, he hung up his unemployable trade and moved to France, where he had resided for eighteen years. His children were French, his wife Italian, and like the rest of us, he was stateless. He was still the old, easygoing, pleasant Viennese "of the earth," as we used to say there at home. Like the rest of us, he had rediscovered his mother tongue and the true Viennese dialect. That was totally natural. Prior to the war, we all spoke exclusively French. Now, we were interned as Germans, and in defiance spoke German.

Once while chopping wood, the camp sentry spoke to us. "You claim to be three-fourths French. Why do you only speak German?" He came to the right place. Furiously I redressed him, "Can't we be left in peace? We are locked up here as Boches, aren't we? As long as we are treated as enemies, don't expect us to behave as French." He understood. He withdrew in silence. I spoke German from pure spite and fought with those internees who through strictly speaking French sought to demonstrate their convictions—as if someone in or outside the camp cared about such proof.

Sertorius, the coachman, another countryman, and I often emptied a bottle in the evening. Gustav was a teetotaler. One day the coachman received a money order for fifty francs. And on the same day, with telegraphic speed, we boozed the money away. In those days fifty francs represented an imposing number of bottles. We all participated valiantly, particularly Sertorius, casting aside his onetime lieutenant's dignity; in the end he crawled around the barrack on all fours to the great dismay of his sleep-deprived barracks mates. For naught, the barracks head thundered, "Silence!" Sertorius grumbled happily, "What's a once former Legionnaire against a once former Prussian lieutenant?" The "once former" were all represented: here a doctor, there a chemist, engineer, and at the door slept a genuine baron. The war brought us all to a common denominator, the denominator of wretchedness. The canteen had long closed, and all around the lights had been extinguished, while thirst still tormented us. Sertorius and I staggered out past the sentry, under the protection of the guardian angel of the imbibed, crawled to the canteen, and pounded on the door with our fists, demanding entry. Finally, someplace a beneficial slumber engulfed us. The next morning, the gracious head of the barrack ordered us to three days of emptying latrine buckets. That didn't bother us.

There were more severe punishments. One day one of my companions was notified that his wife was waiting outside. It wasn't a visiting day, and the man had not seen his wife in over two months. She had traveled over two hundred kilometers to see him and would have to return prior to the official visiting day because her letter of safe conduct was set to expire. Then, no one should be surprised when her husband goes AWOL. And no one should be surprised that the captain arrested him and imprisoned him for twenty-four hours. Regulations and order demanded it.

* * *

One day we were all summoned to the camp office, to declare our religion. I had a bad feeling. While never in my life have I observed Jews treated better than others, my Jewish companions were convinced of a different wisdom: "Jews can't be friends of Hitler. That's what it is."

The office head also worked in a silk factory. We were vocation companions. Following the example of Mr. Troiville, I was favorably disposed toward him. As I came to him, he whispered to me, "You are Jewish, but that doesn't matter: Mr. Troiville has taken care of you."

At first we didn't know why the declarations were needed. But in a few days, we were called again, and with few exceptions, the Jews were transferred to a special camp. Those with a definite job stayed in Chambaran: shoemakers, tailors, cooks, and so forth. Certain people in the camp leadership couldn't bring it upon themselves to send away the tradesmen who worked for them for meager compensation. It's nice to have one's shoes resoled or coat altered for a pack of cigarettes. I could stay as well. My God, a Jew I befriended stood next to me and said, "Only those above suspicion are being transferred. We won't be guarded so strictly. It's the first step in the selection of those to be released." I stayed only because of the intervention of a well-respected man in Chambaran, and therefore I knew the camp for the Jews could only be worse. I kept on going in silence.

Several others thought along the same lines. The point of view was not without certain logic, but what did logic have to do with our internment? Pure "Aryans" declared themselves Jews in the foolish belief that the Jews would be treated more leniently. I had to bite my tongue as a handsome, blond, Nordic youth, a type of rolling stone with a flowing mane and lute in his arm stepped to the Jews. Several hours later several Jews baptized as Catholics were transferred to a camp for Catholics. They picked out the Austrian Catholic immigrants. Besides those with steady employment, only Reich Germans—the most likely to come under suspicion of being National Socialists—remained in Chambaran. And yet we were those who fared the best. On the other hand, in the Jewish internment camp, strict leadership prevailed; it was very cold there, almost entirely bereft of homeliness; they adhered so painfully to the visiting rules that the poor Jews yearned for the once reviled Chambaran. That's what the treatment of the suspected and unsuspected "elements" looked like.

* * *

During the night following the evacuation of the Jews, I had an unusual vision. I dreamed about the Last Judgment. The trumpets blared so that people rose from their graves; they pressed in front of heaven's gate, craving to enter into the heavenly home. On a powerful cloud throne sat God, and the little people went past him in a never ending line. All kinds of notepapers lay in a golden bowl to the right of God, and God's hand reached incessantly for the red, black, brown, and green little pieces of paper; he moistened them with his breath and stuck them on the poor humans' shoulders, who with the celestial touch shyly drew closer together. I stood behind the throng and strained my eyes inquisitively forward to see how these colorful tags were used. And then I read: Jews, Catholics, Protestants, Muslims, Buddhists, and so forth. I asked a guardian angel the meaning of the colors, since God was anyway separating us according to our beliefs. The guardian was a chubby-cheeked angel with barely more than twenty heavenly stripes on his angel wings. "Ha-ha," he laughed. "You don't know? And yet you lived in the twentieth century, as I can tell from your square eyeglass frames." "Well, yes, you lay in the earth long enough, and you forget a lot of things." "Those are the party colors: Socialist, Clerical, Fascist, National Front, and so on." "Excellent," said a skinny little man with an emaciated face next to me. "That's just how imagined heaven to be when I gave up my spirit in the concentration camp. I also came from the twentieth century!" In that moment I woke up.

* * *

When we sat together in the evening, on our sacks of straw, and sang the old customary songs of our country; when our old homeland, which we had not seen for a long, long time arose before our eyes; when we thought about our homeland, where we voted and intended to serve with so much love; when we thought about our vanished freedom and the barbed wire surrounding us, then we often hummed the Buchenwald song[2] of our companions who were interned there and also made their home in Chambaran:

> Oh Buchenwald, I can't forget thee
> Because thou art my fate
> Whoever leaves thee, can only then measure
> How wondrous freedom is
>
> Oh Buchenwald, we don't want to complain,
> And whatever our future holds
> All the same, we want to say to life
> One day the day will come, when we are free,
> We want to say to life,
> One day the day will come, when we are free

Years later my heart still convulses when I hear this little song, this melancholy expression, which with such few words means so much. No, Chambaran was no Buchenwald, and the French were no SS. But only in freedom can man live and breathe. And were the cage made of the purest gold, providing the most exquisite nourishment, it would still be just a cage.

* * *

2 A well-known song with lyrics by Fritz Loehner-Beda and melody by Hermann Leopoldi, Buchenwald inmates. See for instance page 46 for English lyrics, *K.L. Buchenwald, post Weimar* By Jürgen M. Pietsch, Edition Akanthus, 2002, ISBN 3000107762, 978000107764

Oh my good Prussian lieutenant, how often our hearts were heavy; how often we no longer knew what to say or how to carry the shackles of the camp. No, I don't believe that you belonged to the fifth column; you were just another unfortunate one like so many, many thousands in our ill-fated times: a searcher in the whirlwind of ideas, a man lost in the jungle of life.

Poor Sertorius was at his end. His thoughts always returned to his wife, who without means was ill in Grenoble. And he, powerless, locked up here could not see or help her. In his over-irritated condition, he fell into acting as a spiritual medium. As his favorite pastime, he dealt cards and predicted our future. In the manner he did it, when he pointed his index finger in our direction and with his hollow voice foretold our fate, no one dared to doubt his word. After such a session, he was spent and incapable of uttering another word. Silently, he reached for the wine bottle he commanded as wages for his service and emptied it in a few moves. He prophesied his own violent death. Where is he now?

As for me? Almost all of his predictions came true. But then, I tossed his well-intentioned advice into the wind. He had no confidence in France. He showed me the harbingers of dissolution evidenced everywhere: the scarcity of precautions taken, the fear of spies in the wrong places. He considered Hitler and Stalin as the big winners of the war. The totality of the German military apparatus, which he had seen for himself, imbued him with fear and deep respect. The French gave no credence to his beliefs; no one wanted to admit the reality of the weak preparedness of the country. He begged and beseeched me to emigrate as soon as I was released and go as far away as possible from France, where nothing but disaster awaited. I didn't believe him, for to believe him meant to consider a victorious Germany. Oh, had I only obeyed him.

* * *

November: the first snow covered the field. Like white giants, the fir trees seriously reached toward the sky. In the magically transformed countryside, we continued with our unreal life. Again I stepped into the camp leader's office to inquire of Mr. Troiville if my release were not just a figment of my imagination.

Surprised, Mr. Troiville looked toward the door. "What Adler? You are still here? You were released a long time ago."

My legs weakened. I groped toward the door handle and stammered with a dry voice, "But you see...I'm here?" Mr. Troiville calmed me. "I'm a member of the screening committee. We decided to release you. Most likely your file got stuck someplace. One phone call and everything will be set straight."

At the morning muster of November 9, an unforgettable date in the course of this war, I was called to collect wood. Suddenly Gustav came running and hailed, "You are free, Adler. Come quickly into the camp."

Oh, how I liked dropping my bundle of brushwood, and ran back. My release document was ready within an hour.

I went to recover my house key from the office. I was handed a box containing over a hundred key bundles in total disarray. I found mine. As a result of my luck, I boldly asked about my fountain pen. The sergeant said, "What do you want? They disappeared a long time ago." He laughed unabashedly. "War booty."

Then came the good byes to my companions. As the Postbus was full, Mr. Troiville kindly took me in his vehicle. The moment the car drove through the gate and we left the barbed wire behind—I felt again free.

As in a stupor, I leaned into the car's upholstery and let myself be chauffeured through the autumn bedecked region. Woods and fields flew by. Suddenly, I saw in the distance a thin spire that quickly loomed larger. That was the steeple of Fourviére of the Lyon Cathedral, the city's symbol. Tears welled in my eyes; my throat was tied closed; I could neither speak nor think.

I was free—that was all I knew. As in a dream, in thanks I clasped Mr. Troiville's right hand and climbed out of the car and into the streetcar. And then I arrived at my apartment building. The concierge nosily pushed aside the curtain and spied through the glass door as she heard the heavy steps of my boots. "You are back again, Monsieur Adler?" she said in great surprise. I gave no reply.

With shaking hands, I rummaged the key from my pocket and opened up. Little Paul jumped at me. I was home.

4

GOLDEN FREEDOM

Nothing had changed in our apartment, but in the evening dark, blankets hung in front of the windows, and now and then the shrill whistles of the anti-aircraft defense, enforcing the darkness, frightened us awake. Silver threads appeared in my wife's black hair, and often I heard her sob. The future made her tremble.

In just a few weeks, how the city had changed its face. Most of the men had enlisted. The green of battle uniforms dominated the streetscape. Even women walked about with gas masks on their backs. Life had become oppressive; the carefree cheerfulness of the French had disappeared.

Business life rested. Trade and commerce had not yet adjusted to the war, neither did people understand that the war meant an increase in business and for some a great increase in "earnings."

Where should I start? Naturally, I thought of my old firm. I always got along well with my coworkers, and why not now? I thought of applying for my French citizenship, since I had persuasively demonstrated my good will. As a Frenchman I wasn't bound to a particular weapon, and with it qualified for military service. Under the present circumstances, the resolution of my application would only take a few months, and in the meantime I could stay in my previous employment.

The next morning I went to my office. I will never forget this event. How much of this war was permanently embossed into my brain. How often have I already said, "That I will never forget." Also, this passage belonged to the hardest experiences of that bitter time. Even outwardly, the firm had changed. We cleared the lower floor and transferred certain offices higher up in order to save on coal. The male colleagues, with a few exceptions, were in the service, and even the female contingent had left some holes. New fashion colors had appeared. On the wooden shelves, I saw silk fabric dyed khaki, the war fashion. Quiet prevailed, and not a single customer came to interrupt with business.

Two months had passed since I had to suddenly leave my coworkers. I was happy to see them again and relate my experiences. However, the reunion joy was not mutual. On my entrance, everyone bent over their desks or scrutinized some goods. Only now and then, a stealthy glance was cast upon me. No one looked at me directly, and no one returned my greetings. I felt a peculiar sense of emptiness; my steps became uncertain. Who in our midst had ever run the gauntlet? I didn't receive any blows, but I evoked that terrible image as I went from room to room and my appearance was greeted with icy silence. How is it that when you extend your hand in greeting, the greeted buries his in his pockets? I know. Soon I gave up searching for a friendly face, as no one granted me even a single word.

What did that mean? Had I done an injustice, or had I befallen an injustice? I crept to the director's office and knocked quietly on his door. "Oh, it's you, Adler?" He took off his horn-rimmed glasses and cleaned the lenses awkwardly with a silk cloth. "You look good. Take a seat." A confusing moment developed. I heard the ticking of the wall clock and watched a mosquito crawl on the window. "What are you thinking of doing?" I gave no reply. "Well…" the director hemmed and hawed, and slid back uneasily in his chair. "You know, business is at a standstill, and we were forced for the time being to even send some of the women home." Anticipating a possible objection, he went on, "You will respond that you are engaged in different work than the women, and that the men are away. But you must understand that we can't keep you since we had to furlough French women."

Now it was in the open. The director chatted on with a song and dance. "Who knows when business will pick up again? If that were the case, I could bring back all my furloughed employees…but this way?" As if everything were told and he had dropped a load off his mind, he got up, cheerfully lit a cigarette, called in the bookkeeper, and paid out my wage that in his eyes was certainly the last one. "We will send you the testimonial by mail." He added in passing, "I just realized: don't you want to go abroad? We have customers in New York and London that could be helpful."

Yes, so there I stood. I stuttered, "I'll have to let everything go through my head," and left.

Like a drunk, with heavy steps I staggered down the stairs and sat down on a bench along the banks of the Rhône. The sky was draped with gray clouds; the water currents flowed gloomy gray; gray was in my heart, and my eyes saw only gray. I spent just shy of eight weeks in the camp. That was enough to destroy our small and quiet life. Or? Could I still rescue something? What should I tell my Martha? How could I explain everything to her?

Finally, I collected myself a little. I needed to find out what actually happened. I waited until closing and approached two coworkers who were previously good friends. Perhaps they could now talk and provide some answers. And I heard how everything came to pass.

As my absence became more prolonged, my coworkers began to spread rumors: there must be something suspicious about me; the police would certainly not intern me without reason.

Just the news that I was declared unfit for military service in their eyes explained everything. Why unfit when the military doctors declared the weakest men, even cripples, fit to carry weapons? Lies—nothing but lies. I had fixed to feign my patriotism in order to stay in the backcountry and make money while the French put their life on the line. This dirty foreigner must be shown what it means to live at the expense of France. What gall to request the firm to step in on my behalf. The door will quickly shut tight on him. An intermediary of personnel demanded from the director that at the time I should not be rehired. Forgotten is the comradeship of almost ten years. Who thinks about making people breadless and pushing them into misery, people who were always decent and upright toward them and their country.

In one fell swoop, everything was suspicious about me. Gossip exaggerated every little thing. Why did my wife spend so much time in the Ardèche? I must have a secret stash of money. Oh yeah.

In short, in the eyes of my coworkers, I was a Boche, and a shirker besides that. So it was.

* * *

I went home. I will spare you the sad scene, as I admitted to my crying wife I had been fired. We decided to turn to Mr. Troiville; perhaps he could advise us.

Certainly he said, "You are going to have it tough. No one wants to hear about enemy foreigners. Why don't you want to emigrate? By the way, did you know that the War Ministry has enacted new regulations? Austrians and Germans may now enlist in the Foreign Legion for the duration of the war."

There again was the Foreign Legion. But I was now mellowed to push toward this army of the homeless. I was fed up with my French friends; I didn't want to see these false people, these petit bourgeois. We had become strangers. My place was with the stateless, the undesirables of life and society. There I could be Austrian and a Jew.

Only France dealt so harshly with refugees. England behaved more humanely. How my parents were comforted, though they had been there only nine months. Internment was practiced only within the confines of war borders. England accepted my sister in May of 1939, and as a result of following up all job opportunities, she received her work permit and reported to be doing quite well.

Maybe we should emigrate? No no no! I had been living in France for ten years; I wanted to continue living there; I wanted to conquer this dumb world, and I had to prove myself stronger than a faction of narrow-minded people. I did not want to admit that I had applied myself for ten years in the hopes of establishing a new homeland and was defeated. After the Anschluss my sister had beaten me over the head with these words: "We are the emigrants of today. You are the refugees of tomorrow." Was she right?

And one more thing: if I left France, subsequently everything that certain of the French had thought about me would be justified. Should it be said that this rotten foreigner enjoyed all those good years in France, and the instant the country was in need, the coward fled abroad? Wasn't it the guilt of Judaism's call, our unfortunate societal destiny, to remain in place with feet on the ground? If I'm doing right, God will stand by me—the wisdom purports.

Forgotten was the well-intentioned and pointed advice of Sertorius. I wanted to nonetheless forcibly extract something from the world. One should never do that.

* * *

At the same time, I was well acquainted with three other immigrants who had also been released. I looked them up and asked them their plans.

They all had difficulties and complained. "We would most like to join the Foreign Legion. France again gave us our freedom. We owe her that, to voluntarily do what the French are obligated to do."

I still have to smile thinking about the lofty patriotic sayings of these people. "Just today we went to the recruitment station, but there are my parents, who will next travel to America, there is my wife, expecting a child, there is that and there is something else." And whoever didn't have a convincing reason, served up an excuse.

I'm not asking anyone to be a hero. I'm not one, and I doubt if under a hail of bullets, I would ever become one. But nothing is more loathsome as when men preach water and drink wine. Only he is a man who asks nothing of others except what he himself is willing to do. The patriotic trio repulsed me. Not because they didn't have the courage to join the Foreign Legion. That was their business. But didn't they have the sad convictions to behave so patriotically in the camp as if they couldn't wait to get to the front? Didn't they demonstrate their love of France by speaking only in the French language? Hadn't they talked constantly about the obligation to serve France and the particular obligation of Jews? Now they contrived cowardliness. Everything turned out to be empty rhetoric. They chatted on, declared the four of us should

cooperatively enlist; such a loyal expression would benefit Jewish refugees. Certainly, I didn't question it. But cooperative enlistment…well,
don't hold your breath. I soon became convinced that they were more
concerned with words than deeds.

Later in my Legion days, I met many, many other Jews who wore
their uniform with honor. Many weren't particularly articulate; many
weren't as well connected and were much more reserved. But they were
upstanding, showed their sense of duty and courage. I must emphasize:
not all Jews were so.

Since then I have learned to comprehend better the attitude of the
three cowards. In this world, sometimes the gloss means more than the
deed. The world wants to be deceived; you must pretend in order to get
along. So much the worse for those who can't.

* * *

I alone took the path leading to the Foreign Legion. The very first steps
were to an opticians shop for without spectacles I would be unfit. The
eyeglasses made me fit within ten minutes.

Further, I had to verify that my next of kin had the right to military
assistance. One would have thought this obvious. But it wasn't so. Two
months after the outbreak of war, families of foreign volunteers had yet
to receive financial support. Only on November 20 did the prefectures
receive the corresponding directives. The compensation in any event
was a mere pittance.

Again, I went to my firm. I made no effort to speak to my former coworkers. At most, the behavior of the other foreigner with whom I worked hurt
me. It never entered his mind to volunteer for war service. Quietly and without a care, he pursued his work. Naturally, he was not interned because he
had the luck to have a valid passport. If anyone, he had the duty to recognize
my situation, and yet he shunned me as if I had been convicted and sentenced. The good man might suffer if he returned my greeting. He ducked,
so the others wouldn't take note that he too was a foreigner. War can make
humans so small and characterless. Civil courage, where are you?

I shared my resolve with the director and showed him the glasses to underline that it was not my fault that the doctor had earlier rejected me.

The director wished me well. "You can be certain that I will treat you just like the others. Our syndicate issues a small monthly supplement for the children of employees in the service. We will put you on the list. I have always been satisfied with you. At the end of the war, God willing you will return here." He was visibly pleased with this turn of events. That made me happy.

Mr. Troiville wrote a recommendation for me to the Foreign Legion examination commission. I still have it today. He did it at my request, for after all that had happened, I must serve.

* * *

The Foreign Legion had several recruitment and reception centers in the motherland. The nearest recruitment depot, Fort Vancia, was an hour from Lyon. I first made my pilgrimage there on a friendly autumn day. The last beautiful days of summer are unjustifiably called *old women's summer*[3], when the foliage lovingly shines in rustic reds, when little animals crawl into the sunshine and spiderwebs sway in the autumn air. My lungs expanded as I hiked on the long country road with my light rucksack. I was still free, if only there were no war. I clung to happy dreams, invigorating myself with nature. But for the people, the mountains and valleys had become a military landscape.

On the way I happened on a dust-covered fellow with a bundle in his arms that seemingly held his few possessions. After we marched for ten minutes side by side, I asked him where he was bound, and it turned out that he too was looking to join the Foreign Legion. So we hiked harmoniously together. My Hungarian travel companion had already spent five years in the Foreign Legion and, as a tailor, didn't have a bad time of it. He had worked in a Legion workshop and had no need to beg for an assignment. His master tailor had dismissed him, as no one was having suits made since the state was giving out fashionable uniforms

---

3 *Altweibersommer* in the original, more commonly translated as "Indian summer."

free of charge. And so this jobless man was searching for shelter in the Legion. I was strangely touched listening to this fellow, directly from a clothing workshop and from the Foreign Legion. Until then, I had thought of Legionnaires as raw soldiers; I had to discover for myself that the Legion was a haven for all stranded individuals. My companion advised me not to enter the fort until I had put all my affairs in order. Whoever signed up could no longer go outside, a precautionary measure against recruits attempting to leave the country as soon as they received their bounty. Only in Africa, after the clothing distribution was leave into the so-called city granted. A hundred years ago, King Louis Phillip founded the Foreign Legion and established the rules for service that still apply today. Only at the beginning of December were certain easements for war volunteers introduced.

In Vancia I learned further that a new recruitment station would open in Sathonay. I turned around. I could well wait.

In Sathonay, a village at the edge of Lyon, the Foreign Legion was set to receive a flood of volunteers. They were expecting thousands of applicants from our region. A barracks town had been erected on the formerly peaceful meadows. The needs of war necessitated that the sheep and oxen withdraw from their earlier play area, replaced by two-legged animals. The barracks remained empty at first. After wandering about, I happened upon an officer who was busy tapping away, filling out forms at a brand new desk. He was not at all pleased to me. "Don't you have any papers to spend the night in the city?" He asked me. "Oh yes," I replied. "Then come again in a few days, after the initial confusion passes and this operation runs properly." I had no objections to the delay and went home again.

* * *

Three weeks went by. My wife and I knew that our days together were numbered before I would take leave for a long, long time. We sought to live as if the outside events were of no concern to us. In the midst of this out-of-joint world, our home became an island, untouchable by the evil of humankind. We found the burden of life bitter enough, and often we failed at our attempts to think beyond everything befalling our lives. We lived in total isolation—so profound—as one lives when fate has permitted one last holiday. We belonged together, Martha and I and our Paul—the most beautiful fruit of our union. Truly for this cute tot blabbering his first words, I had to prove I was a man.

Early in the morning, on November 29, I left my loved ones.

Wild confusion reigned in Sathonay. The volunteers surged in hordes toward the military service examination. They came from the internment camps, with soldiers guarding them. Alone, I was about to exchange my freedom for the insecure lot of a soldier. The scribe looked at me scornfully as I pulled my recommendation from my pocket. "M. Adler is in a hurry to become a Legionnaire." The doctor asked me if I ever played sports and if I thought to be up to the strenuous exertions. His aide added two kilos to my weight to make sure the measurement was correct.

They still used the old forms. The phrase *For five years* was crossed out, and above it written in ink, *For the duration of the War*. The scribe stamped a large *A* for Africa on my contract. And then I could swear to serve France with honor and loyalty and follow its flag everywhere, and was permitted to leave. I could finally say, "I am a Legionnaire."

5

I AM A LEGIONNAIRE

In the bright, roomy barracks assigned as our sleeping quarters, quite a commotion was taking place. We made clean piles of the straw sacks to use as table and bed. We harkened eagerly to the tales of a former Legionnaire recounting his African adventures. What he expressed was not particularly encouraging. He bitched about the strict discipline and the superiors. After serving a long time and with much effort, he was promoted to corporal, but a drunken episode and a fight cost him his stripes. "Why did you volunteer again?" wondered a wise guy. "Well, the war and the camp." I found an isolated place to avoid listening to the lousy chitchat.

In the evening, I was assigned to my first KP. I had to clean the pots and pans. The sun had set, and only a dim light from the kitchen illuminated the patch of grass in front of the fountain. I did not have any practice in washing. The big boor, proudly playing the part of kitchen chief, twice rejected kitchenware. "Can't the pig Jew get the pots and pans clean?" I quaked with anger and yelled back, "The pig Jew has washed the kitchenware more than enough." I let the pots alone and left.

In the Legion, you can't let them walk all over you, otherwise you invite misery. I didn't have to wait long to convince myself of this. A sergeant ordered me to stand guard. I was to be relieved at one o'clock in the morning. The clock struck one, one-thirty past and finally at a little bit before two o'clock, the boy who had the next guard shift showed up. He had been in the neighborhood with girls. "We're buddies," he yawned sweetly as he finally came before me looking very tired. Nice friendship. Now I couldn't do anything about it, but the next morning I pounced on him and beat him up. Soon the two of us rolled like two hedgehogs, wrapped up in each other on the floor. I had to cease and desist as the sergeant threatened me with lockup.

We stayed in Sathonay nearly three days. We were photographed from all sides, as if they would enter our pictures into a criminal records book. They again examined our papers most accurately, using clerks from the Intelligence Service, and kept our identity papers so that no one would chance to run off.

In the meantime, my wife came to visit. I received two hours' vacation and could leave the military site and eat outside. But what are two hours when your heart is heavy and you can hardly speak.

* * *

After completing the examinations, we were marched to Vancia. The place was so crowded that they put us up outside the Fort, alongside peasants. My group, about twenty men strong, was quartered in a roomy barn close to the town square. A sergeant asked who spoke fluent French. I stupidly responded and was appointed barn elder.

My assignment was to lead the group in three columns to the town square, be responsible for order in our quarters, and report in the morning and evening. Not a big deal, but I would have my grief. Toward the beginning of December, the weather became noticeably cold. The barn door did not close, there wasn't much hay, and we had grabbed only a single thin cotton blanket. The night wind blew through the half-open door, and we froze pitifully. The next morning two of my companions had all the signs of a hefty cold. As no one to whom I could give a report came for the day watch, I went to our company's office after breakfast. I was attacked with a hell of a verbal flogging. "Couldn't you say that at the report?" the office orderly responded crudely. "No one came," I replied truthfully. With the many off-site quarters, the on-duty corporal overlooked our barn. The sick could see the doctor; the corporal received a reprimand and decided to pay me back. Green as I was, he found that not too difficult.

In the evening I lay peacefully in the hay and dozed off, when unforeseen the door opened and the spotlight of a signaling lantern glaringly stung my face. Our corporal stood in front of me.

"The report," he said curtly.

"Nothing to report, Corporal, all is in order."

"So nothing to report. And the report form?"

"Never heard of a report form, Corporal."

The corporal's mustache stood on end at my audacity. "Get up, you jerk!" He wanted to make fun of us. "March! To the guard with you." He put his foot into the straw to make me get a move on. For better or for worse, I stood up and followed the corporal to the office. He made me lead, he sarcastically remarked, so he could anytime permanently imprint his boot sole into the lower neighborhood of my back. I would soon see the stuff he was made of. We dealt with all kinds of people there.

In the guard shack, I thought I'd fall through the floor. There were prisons in Vancia for all sorts. "What do you think, you little dirty pig?" the sergeant berated me. "You'll see what it means to be disobedient. Here, you'll obey or die. I'll beat it into you, why you have an ass."

I silently let the sergeant's verbal assault pass over me, as I had the corporal's prior angry outburst. It left me speechless. In further passing of the oriental picturesque word stream, I heard how the cheeks of my ass would soon grow together and exactly how my teeth would march out in double columns and much more. Certainly, I should have filled out a report form, though I, the novice, thought it unnecessary as nothing had happened. I expected nothing less than to be placed here and now into the brig. But nothing of the kind happened. After the office personnel caught their breath, I was permitted to leave the shack.

In the meantime my companions in the barn held council. It was clear that camaraderie and the will to help got me into this mess. As I, accompanied by the corporal, again was with them, they extended friendly greetings, and one of the men went out to speak to the corporal. I don't know what he told him. I assume that everyone declared himself in solidarity with me. In any event, for me, the matter was closed. I was relieved of my position and breathed easier.

* * *

One day we were in the main square, as we frequently were, waiting for orders; I suddenly saw a familiar face in a passing unit. I rubbed my eyes. It was no illusion; it was really Eduard Wolf, a classmate from my school days. Suddenly I saw in front of me the sturdy stone walls of the high school, the somewhat dusty classroom with the ink-stained desks; I heard the droning voice of the Latin teacher: "Sit" and "Quickly with a thundering crash, our butts touched the benches," as one of our parodies went. "Pst, pst," I heard quietly whispered in front of me. "Slide over your booklet already." "Wolf Eduard," thundered the raging teacher, "you wish to copy, aye? Wolf Eduard, I'm giving you fair warning."

During a break we spoke with each other. His family fled first to Italy, but as deportation threatened, they fled to Nice in a boat. As if the poor things hadn't suffered enough, the illegal border crossing brought with it prompt punishment: expulsion from the department. Protest. Another expulsion. Appeal and expulsion. Edi and his family had to stay in France. They had no other choice. War came and the camp; without any prospect of release, finally the recruitment drum called the interned to the Foreign Legion. Yes, so we met again. We had been together in Vienna for almost two years, young people awaiting everything from life; we truly never thought of seeing each other again like this. We looked down at the shabby military coats that covered our civilian clothes, regarded the kepi, his too wide and mine too tight, nodded seriously yeh yeh, and then a happy smile covered our faces as we were happy to see each other again despite everything. Unfortunately we had to part company the next day as Edi was listed for transport to Africa. We met again later. In the unbearable days of basic training in Khenifra, he again became a good and trusted companion.

In a general way, things were not bad in Vancia. Although the nights were unfriendly, the sun shone during the day, and we had relatively little to do. The food was excellent. At noon and in the evening, we had a big portion of meat with ample vegetables. A quarter liter of pleasant tasting wine was served with every meal: no Legionnaire without his wine. Black coffee after meals, just like at an inn. It was still the golden time of excess in France.

All ranks from corporal up to sergeant major used the "raw but cordial" Legion language. *Shithead, pig, bastard*, and the whole litany that we soon accepted as our daily rations. In Africa we learned additional terms of endearment such as *queer, whore bag*, and many more. In addition every superior had his own special expressions at the ready. But even the most unflattering curse words lose their affect in the long run. Soon we became immune. If only the rudeness served some purpose. We still hadn't come to appreciate all the elegance of the Legion.

* * *

Every day at noontime, I sat on the country road leading to Lyon and longingly looked for Martha. Why didn't she visit? In three days I was slated to leave for Africa. My companions teased me; a Heine expert recited melancholy love ballads to the amusement of our little circle. They were nice young men, Germans and Austrians. We became good friends.

Our little Paul had caught a cold, and my wife couldn't entrust the babysitting to anyone to free her up for a visit. People were so busy with their own affairs; my wife had to be totally self-reliant. Finally she succeeded in convincing the wife of a refugee to look after the child. Oh, how happy I was to spot her silhouette in the distance. I sent her right off to the captain, so I could go home with her. The old but gallant gentleman customarily didn't deny the ladies a small favor. Without difficulty, he immediately authorized a twenty-four-hour leave. Had my wife seen him earlier, she could have extracted a lengthier leave, but now I was on the transport list, and nothing could be done.

My wife had to smile as I seriously saluted the captain in my strange garb and smartly did an about-face, turning on my heels. The captain must have thought that the buttoned coat, in very unmilitary style, that covered my civilian brown trousers didn't promote the prestige of the French army. He put me into the hands of the store clerk to outfit me properly. I grabbed a brand-new, gorgeous uniform that gave me a well-tailored military look. The Legion's stockroom was crammed full with supplies of top-notch workmanship. Based on this stunning abundance, I felt confident in the reality of a superior French material advantage. Whether reprovisioning functioned properly was another question.

Proudly my Martha accompanied her soldier home. My heavens—of the many German and Austrians refugees living in the skyscraper quarters, I was the first Foreign Legionnaire, and until now the only one who had signed his contract while living on in full freedom. Within twenty-four hours, everyone knew: "Adler joined the Foreign Legion." Well, even our little enclave was no better than the French petit bourgeois of the French. The gossip blossomed and flourished. How many nosy visitors did Martha have to deal with? I could have slapped their faces, these impudent interrogators. Their senseless comments just upset Martha. "As a foreigner you won't get any service reimbursements and so on and so on." "Did you carefully examine what you signed?" frightened Martha. "You are so absent minded; imagine if you have to serve for five years?" "As if everything is on the up and up." A good acquaintance put these worries into her head. "What are you thinking," I consoled the disheartened one, "of course only for the duration of the war." On that day the mailman brought a letter from my brother Dolo in London. "My dear Milo," I read, "you are joining the Foreign Legion. You have been living in France for ten years. Couldn't you join a French regiment?"

I can't recollect my reply. What should I have responded—that the war had made us outlaws and outcasts, but still just good enough for the Foreign Legion?

The stupidity of man is only surpassed by his evilness. As if wearing a uniform somehow promoted one to hero status, freely and in advance the masses bestow the laurel wreath upon the soldier. Any coward can put on khakis and yet remain a bed wetter. And what does it mean— *can*? He *had* to put on the uniform; the law forced him, and woe to him who ran away. He may well have originated the little song, "Oh What Joy to Be a Soldier." One thing is certain: its composer didn't live in the era of the *total war*.

Now I discovered for myself the respect that heroes earned. Everywhere, as with other soldiers, I was offered a seat in deference. In the streetcar, I paid no fare. Presumably, the "shirker" didn't dare demand from the conductor to collect money from those defending the fatherland. I made an agreement with the landlord regarding the rent and went to city hall to request a military supplement for my family. Everywhere, I was appropriately accommodated. I experienced the biggest satisfaction at my firm.

With my dear colleagues everything changed after I donned the gray field uniform. I was no longer the dirty foreigner, but one of them. "How are you Adler?" "It's courageous of you." "You will do our colors proud." "Off to the Curly Tail—we want to drink a toast." So it reverberated from all sides. If they only knew how annoying and ugly I found them at that moment. Hadn't I always been the same individual? Didn't I always have the goodwill to enlist? Wasn't it natural that I should have preferred a French regiment to the Foreign Legion?

After a quarter of an hour, I made myself scarce. After all, I only came to make sure my wife would be well received during my absence. I owed my colleagues nothing. I have not forgiven them for the icy reception I received upon my return from the camp. I think I shall never forget how war can make people so awful, how small and dangerous they can become in such instances. I noticed no patriotic exuberance, only much worry and woe, jealousy and envy, and most of all fear. If only all of humanity had experienced and understood such things, then certainly "No more war" could be made real.

I spent the afternoon in our den with Martha and Paul. Amid knocking and ringing, we didn't open. This last hour before the awful separation belonged to us—and us alone. I exhorted Paul to be good and listen to his mother. Martha made every effort to be steadfast; I was thankful to her for that. She didn't make any useless complaints. We really can't say we surrendered to fate, as we shaped it ourselves. Whether it was in our best interest lay with God. We had to put our faith in him. We spoke of the gloomy near future and the anticipated better postwar period. We felt in us the certainty we would survive the war. And then a new era would arise—for us Jews also; we would again have a homeland and be fully valued humans. We would insist on it.

Suddenly the hour of departure arrived. We went to the streetcar. Once more I looked at the trusted buildings, waved to my Martha, standing, as it were, lost in the faraway avenue; then the bell rang jarringly, and the beloved view disappeared into the distance.

* * *

I was lucky to be in an express car, or else I would never have arrived in Vancia on time. In view of the impending departure, after supper we were confined to the fort. But I still had to take care of several things prior to that. Most of all I needed to collect my first wages. Staying longer with Martha, I could have done without the pay, for after eight days of service the twenty-five centimes per day to which we were entitled wasn't even sufficient for a pack of cigarettes. Gauloises cost four and a half francs. *Tabac de troupe*, the so-called soldier cigarettes, were not available at the fort, at least not for us. Pay distribution occurred at five o'clock, and the office guy impressed upon me to be there at four o'clock, or else. Per regulation, the recruits traveled to Africa in their own clothes. You can see what dependable customers the old Legionnaires were. The state didn't even entrust them with one garment for the crossing. It was enough when a runaway relieves the public purse of its bounty money. Much to my regret, I also had to return my magnificent uniform. At this opportunity, the stockroom clerk pinched my absolutely perfect sandals, which his eyes coveted at the uniform issuance. I totally wore out my hiking boots in Chambaran, so I was forced to wear my sandals; I couldn't sacrifice my own good pair of shoes to the state. In short, the stockroom clerk lied to me about keeping the army boots and thanked me for the sandals. What blackmail! He kept the sandals, and the boots were army property. At the time, I was still too green to counter effectively, and I put up with the barely disguised theft. Neither did the stockroom clerk have the right to let me have the boots. He was by no means the only one that took military property for his own.

After the meal we moved into the fort. Many such structures surrounded Lyon and once made the city into a real stronghold. Situated on a hillside, Casemates and other chambers were buried deep in the ground. Since Vauban's time, the French have been master builders of fortification structures. The Maginot Line was never penetrated: encirclement and the general collapse of the French defense caused its demise.

We put away our meager baggage and went into the canteen. An old, weakened piano stood there. A comrade attempted to banish the tenseness of departure with several pop songs. The barkeeper bestowed upon us his schnapps and cocktails to forget our troubles. I had a "Legionnaire," accurately named for its pungent mixture with which most of us invigorated ourselves. It heated the throat and muddled the brain. We drank ourselves into a stupor; nothing really mattered. Only God knew what was ahead of us. Just don't think—this first commandment of the soldier, we already began to understand it there. A men's bacchanal, a raucous loudly crowing crowd on unsteady legs wavered amid thick, heavy cigarette smoke. Singing and screaming until the rotgut had its effect, we senselessly staggered behind the old Legionnaires into the sleeping quarters. Taps sounded, and then quiet prevailed everywhere.

6

CROSSING TO WHERE THE PEPPER GROWS

Military organization can transform a flea into an elephant. Our train was supposed to leave the Lyon Parrache train station at eight in the morning. But already three hours earlier, the bugle tore up the stillness of the night. We were pressured into an incomprehensible haste. Soon we were assembled in the inhospitable courtyard. Lanterns weakly dispelled the darkness. We shivered. An eternity passed as we answered the roll call, standing in formation in the dawn until all the names were called. Finally the canvas-covered trucks rolled in. Through the gaps, I tried to capture one last picture of the city. We were not surprised that the residents were spared the unmilitary image of our swarm.

We sat in the train long before the train station came to life, this snorting train about to carry us in new directions. Adieu Lyon.

I occupied a compartment with a well-loved collection of companions. The soldier lives for the moment. Left to ourselves, we relaxed and stretched out comfortably, chatting as we observed the picturesque landscape of the Rhône valley. After a long stop in Valence, we arrived toward evening in Marseille. Through dirty, narrow lanes, we marched to the far, outlying Fort St. Jean on the sea. St. Jean is the big citadel of the Foreign Legion on the Mediterranean, the last resting place before the crossing-over to the designated land of the Legionnaire. Located on a peninsula penetrating far into the water, it connects to the outside world only through narrow spans. We scaled the steep steps under archways up the fortress structure. The heavy and massive gray stone walls rose, encircling the spacious courts, which even in December offered anticipation of the African sun. The fort's interior had its own imprint. Its rooms were not just barracks, but also a home for the homeless Legionnaires. They were bright and cheerful. The tone of the people giving orders there was crass, but do they know any better or another way? And would the Legionnaires obey otherwise? The whitewashed canteen, with its terrace looking out over the unending sea, invited many visitors. Leaning against the parapet, we followed our thoughts until the bugle announced night rest. The roar of the waves crashing against the stone walls soon lulled us into a dreamless slumber.

The next day the friendly impressions vanished. Senseless servitude began.

We were assigned work tasks. We could not be idle; we had to work. I later heard, according to other Legionnaires, that the stones we brought up into the fort, they later dragged down again. If only the stones weren't so damn heavy. They told us it served as fortification work. Fortunately, I managed to snag a saner job, playing roofer on an addition to the fort. High over the sea, we passed up tiles and improved the roof. After a while, the work leader thought, as light as I was, I could lay tiles on the roof. A Legionnaire can do everything. I climbed up and from the dizzying heights of the gables gazed at the sea. It was glorious. The fresh breeze caressed me; I felt free and strong. Below thundered the sea, and above the sun shone brightly against a clear blue sky.

At the noon whistle, all hands rested. We climbed down. The meal didn't taste bad. Weren't there heroic inscriptions all around the mess hall to what purpose we were fed? A telegram for example from General A—— to the minister: "Give me a thousand Legionnaires, so I can die in dignity." Another more modest commander requested in a similarly troublesome situation five hundred men. The life of a Legionnaire is cheap. *Honneur et Fidelité, Valeur et Discipline.* "Honor and loyalty, courage and discipline" demand the inscriptions and remind us of our pledge, which for some means death. We are destined to be heroes. And if hero consciousness had yet to fully permeate our being, it would surely have by the end of basic training.

We passed our time with all kinds of diversions. The lad next to me would certainly have had success on the cabaret stage. He aped the officer of the internment camp recruiting for the Foreign Legion. With what strange solutions they sought to win us over. One had the feeling that—as if they were a little embarrassed about this army corps—it might be difficult to drive us into the Legion. "Here, gentlemen," blared the fresh and lively recruiting officer, "is no longer the Foreign Legion. Here is the Legion of the Foreign, standing with France." Truly, they were legion, the foreigners that declared themselves for France. Their compensation was a concentration camp in the desert. And this happened at the same time that "Work, Family, and Country," replaced "*Liberté, Egalité, Fraternité.*" "You may not have family," said the men from Vichy to the stateless, for you also have no country. Yet we give you work in the Sahara until you perish. Those were the patriots and pioneer fighters for a "united" Europe. But enough.

They explained to us for a long time the difference between the old Foreign Legion and the new "Legion of the Foreign." To our benefit, our war-weakened brain could not fathom the difference.

* * *

In the morning twilight on December 8, we were brought to the harbor, where the *Sidi-Brahim* awaited us. This ship transported many Legionnaires to Africa; not all returned. Many lost their lives there, true to their vows, and their bones bleach in the hot desert sand.

We were shown our sleeping places deep in the ship's bilge. The room was confining, but we could move freely everywhere because you can't desert ship on the sea. The food was ample and first-rate for soldiers. We had beef with rice. We emptied the bowl clean to the bottom. Besides that, for very little you could buy African grapes, sweets, and Algerian cigarettes at half the price of those available in Marseille. In the afternoons we made ourselves comfortable on the upper deck in the tangle of ropes; the wind blew about our heads; we gazed back to Europe. Quickly, the coast totally disappeared. High above in the sun-warmed air of the south flew a formation of birds.

It was stormy. The wind drove high waves against the ship's hull. We held on tight to the ropes. Most of us were crossing the sea for the first time. Many soon discovered the ship's rocking disagreeable to their stomachs. They leaned on the railings with pale faces.

At night we squeezed together like sheep, for it was noticeably cold. But the wretched smell of sweat wouldn't let me sleep and drove me on deck. The sky was gloomy, veiled in gray-blue shreds of clouds. The waves stormed against the hull. Without a trace, their foam dissipated behind us while new waves attempted to scale the ship. So passed our lives. We arrived, emerged into the time that receives and extinguishes us, and no trace gave evidence to our existence. I was captured, with yearning for France making my heart heavy. Why hadn't I stayed in Europe? Belated regret is useless. I could have tried to stay in Vancia. They were looking for help with the administration of the steadily growing military machine. Mr. Troiville would gladly have given me a recommendation. But Europe was expensive, and the soldier was poor. Our meager savings had to secure the livelihood of our family, because the compensation for service was limited. Life in Africa was less costly, and the colonial wages higher. Besides, we were promised that after basic training we could be assigned to the motherland. They sent us to Africa, not just because we came from enemy territory, but also because in France there was a shortage of training facilities. Basic training in the Foreign Legion had the reputation of being the toughest but also the most thorough. The colonial units, always deployed and battle ready, were France's pride.

But also the lust for adventure drove me there. Never again would I have the opportunity to see so many mysterious foreign lands, to hear and experience so much new. Boyish yearnings stir in man romantic dreams to escape the striving and the everyday life. The magic of the far away enticed me. Oh, there will always be time to squat in front of a warm stove when you have become old and tired, I thought. I wanted it so: no gloomy thoughts. Forward and boldly into the future!

The *Sidi-Brahim* carefully followed the coastline of Corsica and Sardinia. Even there a German submarine could be reconnoitering for bounty.

The end of the voyage drew close. It was my tough luck to be again made head of ten men and responsible for the eating utensils. Sure enough, two pieces were missing. Where could they be hiding? I delivered the utensils to the noncommissioned officer and reported the loss.

His forehead vein swelled up. I stooped in anticipation of his outburst. But what wonder, his face smoothed over, and I regained my courage. "On a ship it's easy to lose things," he said rather friendly. "Look for them, and if you succeed in getting everything together, you'll get a pack of cigarettes." With that he graciously dismissed me; I must have made a very childish impression.

Blockhead that I was, I ran and churned up the dusty corners inboard the ship, searched behind the ropes, the life vests, the blankets, and finally found the missing utensils in a pile of all kinds of other ship property. Even the missing tin plates of the neighboring ten-man unit strangely found a hiding place there too. Proudly, I showed the sergeant the find. "Good," he praised. "And the cigarettes," I dared to remind him. "What?" he thundered into my ears. At my audacity he turned beet red. "What do you think, you moron? Cigarettes. Be happy I don't get into your shit…you rogue, you. About-face, march! I don't want to see you ever again."

I didn't have to be told twice and disappeared at once because for less than that fellows were put in the brig.

A sharp line appeared on the horizon. The trip's destination, Oran, came into sight. The coast descended steeply into the sea. The high cliffs were naked—nowhere a green patch—as if the arid arms of the desert were seeking to encircle the city. Here, the white stone buildings glistened in the intense sunshine, and where the red-brown earth glimmered, no tree or bush gave any shade. Even the blue brightness above could not lessen our apprehension triggered by this foreign image.

Ships and men filled the big harbor. Loading cranes with steel claws reached into the opened bilges and tightly grabbed the crates and bails and then with a deft rotation carefully placed them on the dock, where indigenous long shoremen mightily grappled the wares. On naked backs they dragged the loads to their place. They slaved away in dirty rags, their skin dark and leathery; guttural sounds whirred strangely through the air. The harbor bustled with activity.

Unfortunately, we had seen little of the city, for hardly had the *Sidi-Brahim* anchored and we marched directly to the base of the Legion, which lay at the city's edge.

Slender columns supported the arches around the square courtyard of our new quarters. Moorish and European influences combined to fashion the modern architecture of North Africa. The broad court at the center of the building, the stately columns encircling the hall, and the flat roof were of Arabic origin. The small fountain that adorned the garden court was also Arabic. The inner construction of the multistory building and the staircase with its wide stone steps were European.

The rooms were meticulously clean. The quarters in Oran were endlessly scrubbed and cleaned. I spent the night there twice, then and on the return trip to France. The walls and barracks were whitewashed both times, and both times we had to clean away the white drippings from the lime sprayer. We went at it with pails and scrubbers. The work detail leader, a sergeant, leaned against a column with folded arms and watched us with a critical eye as we poured pail after pail over the stone floor and scrubbed until our arms ached. He obviously wasn't happy with our efforts, for unforeseen he tore away my scrubber and began to forcefully work the stones until the bright sun reflected from the polished surface to his satisfaction. At least he led by good example. Out of his narrow and egg-shaped face, his inflamed eyes peered at me with derision and superiority. "Another two or three years in the Legion and you'll get the secret, you assholes." He was right. Others taught me how to clean and scrub too.

Several trees with odd leaf formations and exotic seedpods grew in the courtyard. I foolishly asked an old Legionnaire the name of a tree. "Peppertree" was the prompt response. And even if it wasn't literally true, so it was figuratively. We were there, where the pepper grows.

7

SIDI-BEL-ABBÈS

A few days later, we traveled to Sidi-Bel-Abbès. This city was the principal garrison of the Foreign Legion, ancestral seat of the First Foreign Infantry Regiment. Here, the new arrivals were once again carefully examined and once and for all accepted into the bosom of the Legion.

How romantic our exotic existence appears when you read the adventure-filled songs and books about the Foreign Legion. "Il était beau, il était fort, il sentait bon, le sable chaud" ("It was beautiful, it was strong, the warm sand smelled good") Madame Dubas sentimentally sang forth in the sultry atmosphere of a nightclub, and the customers were shimmying in their elegant evening clothes, their breasts heaving under silken blouses. Lost in dreams, they sipped from champagne flutes and admired the triumphant, strong, mysterious Legionnaire. Oh, he doesn't exist; this Legionnaire never existed, only in the imagination of the writer, next to the hooker, the pimp, criminals, and other characters of the underworld. Literature.

Legionnaire: synonymous with work—hard, harsh, dangerous work—combat and discipline. *Basic training*: to drill until the poor devil loses every vestige of his individuality and is made into a spineless machine. A robot of the war trade, for whom nothing is too difficult or impossible; who equally well builds streets in the blazing desert as continuing combat against all odds under the command of his fearless officers; who equally finds his way in unrecognizable, unexplored terrain as in the sandy infinity of the desert; who fears nothing, because the drill has erased all fear except possibly fear of his superiors. The enemy can't be worse than the toughness of his own military machine. The daredevil adventure of war is a welcome change from the pressures of rebellious people. And death? Isn't it a deliverance from a failed existence into which only woman and wine offered short escape from a destitute inner life? The Legionnaire is feared. He is stepped on inconsiderately, and inconsiderately he steps on others.

* * *

We were led into the so-called small quarters under the scornful eyes of the "elders." Guards with rifles stood in front of the passageway to the big quarters. The elders and the greenhorns were not to talk with each other. It's an unwritten law of the Legion but now with the massive war transports difficult to enforce.

For over a hundred years, haircuts for new recruits had been another venerable regulation. One after the other, we entered the barbershop and left bald. The buzzed heads were to prevent lice and escape. In that region a sheared scalp betrayed the Foreign Legion's recruits. My friend Bartel looked in the mirror and was furious. "No more will I be able to look at a girl," he lamented. "Girls? Where are girls?" fat Walter burst out laughing. "We have to make do with whores." In the stockroom we grabbed a uniform, shoes, underwear, and a scarf. They were second-hand goods of inferior quality. Walter led the store clerk into a corner and stuffed a bill into his hand. A little later he appeared in a gorgeous, full-length field coat. "You have to know how to speak with people," he boasted. Then the kepi, which looked similar to a mail carrier's cap, topcoat, and cover flourishes—and the Legionnaire was complete.

The Legionnaire was not allowed to keep his civvies. We would have liked best to send our clothes home, but Europe was far, and for us the shipping costs, expensive. The arrival of new recruits meant a booming business for the vendors of Bel-Abbès. The Legionnaire didn't sell: for a pittance he dumped everything not absolutely necessary or anything that could be converted to money and drunk away or spent on loose women. We were not like the old Legionnaires, and our superiors didn't care. The master sergeant completely wrung his hands as he heard we wanted to send our baggage back to France. First he declared, bald-faced, that it wasn't allowed; as we didn't fall for it, he found a thousand difficulties and used all the chicanery at his disposal, such that we became convinced he was in cahoots with the vendors. Finally he relented, but not everyone dared to make use of the consent. The junk dealers came, and a repulsive haggling began. The vendors in their pleated robes looked like Arab bandits. They appeared to be a consortium; no one raised their first offer. For a few shabby francs, the owners of perfectly good valises were changed. A well-maintained suit brought thirty lousy francs. I sold my worn-out pants but also had to sacrifice a new canteen, for the dealer bigheartedly approved the twelve francs I needed to cover the freight. Bartel squandered in youthful recklessness the rest of his belongings, and with the clinking coins, he disappeared into the canteen.

Now we were finally Legionnaires, accoutered and with light baggage. The canvas bags in which we stowed our possessions flopped from our shoulders as we left the small quarters. We had to free it up for the next transport, for every four days a new ship arrived with fresh freight. There were enough homeless in Europe.

The big quarters made an overpowering impression on us. A white-washed wall enclosed the area of the Legion. And inside: what a great variety. Tidy little houses with flat roofs, shaded with tall palms, revealed everything we needed. Offices, bedrooms, mess halls, and canteens—everything planned for several hundred to a thousand men, stables, trucks, and arms. A self-contained city, with well-maintained streets and squares—a pleasing setting for parades but also the place where recruits were honed until they were worn down. In the background rose the sports palace, with a spectators' gallery just like in a theater. The expression "palace" was not an exaggerated description. Adjacent was a huge swimming pool. These weren't bare barracks. One felt, it gave people a home. But was that possible? Could a coercive community become home?

The Legion also owned the property beyond the highway extending alongside the quarter. That's where they put the hospitals. Each specialty occupied its own building and was provided with the most modern resources. The physicians, particularly the surgeons, enjoyed an outstanding reputation. They equaled the boldness of their patients' methods and enjoyed wide popular acclaim, for always somewhere the Legion was engaged in combat, and the daredevils were always beset with mishap. In Oran we happened upon a disarmed Legionnaire who suffered a skull fracture traveling recklessly fast in the desert. The native drivers were bold, but imprudent like children. Speed was everything to them, the equipment nothing; and with respect to danger, they were fatalists. How the victim was found twenty-four hours after the accident, unconscious, brought to Bel-Abbès, and kept him alive by trephination borders on the miraculous.

In this neighborhood of the Legion's quarters, the officer's casino and noncommissioned officers' the mess hall were also located. Here, the central command, under the leadership of the colonel, the commanding officer of *Le Régiment Etranger d'Infinterie* and depots for recruits, resided.

* * *

Bunk beds were erected in the sports palace to accommodate the strong influx of recruits. This was where recruits that were not yet undergoing basic training were billeted. Several comrades who had been declared unfit for service after the second examination were now waiting to return to Europe.

The examination was more careful than the one in Sathonay. Nevertheless, the doctors had recently received orders to not be quite as strict in their selections. Man is only matter for the insatiable Moloch of the army. In peace it devours material of the best sort; in war it is satisfied with lesser goods. Except for a few, whose disabilities were obvious, we were declared suitable. A peculiar act of Providence once again called on me to remain civilian. At the eye examination for acuity, I failed again. I lost my patience. I hadn't traveled this far to be turned back. From my pocket, I pulled the note of the Lyon optician from whom I had purchased my glasses and presented the findings. The incompetent aid couldn't come to terms with my two different eye strengths, copied it word for word, and I was declared fit.

Our quarters were afflicted with inadequate security. Our belongings lay in the open and invited outright theft. There was no shortage of pickpockets, and they never passed up lucrative opportunities. One day, I was about to put on clean socks when a fellow spoke to me. I turned around, and we exchanged a few words. The whole thing took less than a minute, plenty of time for the thief to make the socks his. He must have lain in wait for the opportunity.

A thieving raven made off with all of fat Walter's possessions, including his canvas bag. By happenstance, we found the things on another day on a bench, but without discovering the thief. Walter was delighted, but he rejoiced too soon. The thief liked his English electric razor and the hand-knitted full sweater much too much to relinquish them. The next night he repeated his prank, and this time all searches failed. We couldn't count on the help of the superiors; they just laughed when we told them such things. A Legionnaire was responsible for his possessions under all circumstances. It was, by the way, fortunate that we owned so little and didn't have to suffer any great losses. Money we carried on our person and even at night when going to the latrine. The pickpocket fraternity was ever on the lookout, and as soon as someone left his sleeping place, they were sure to ransack his clothes.

Losses made you clever. Walter bought a belt with an inner pocket and carried his cash on his body. I was inadvertently reminded of my Martha's cousin, who as a Czech served in the previous world war in the Foreign Legion. The Legion appears to be an inescapable fate of our family. Now, this cousin owned a valuable gold watch. In 1916, his division was deployed for an assault. The night before, he overheard two of his buddies. "When his lights go out, we inherit his watch," said one of these brave fellows. Fortunately my cousin survived.

* * *

All nationalities of Europe were represented in my unit. Half were Jews from Germany, Austria, and Poland; the rest, a polyglot of others. Many spoke only a small smattering of French, as for example the Spaniards. They recently arrived from the internment camp Gurs, a name synonymous with hunger and suffering, where they had spent twenty months after they had fought two years in the civil war in the anti-Fascist brigades. The poor devils were starving, and with animal voracity they attacked the food buckets. Besides that, they didn't have a single centime in their sack and were totally dependent on the penurious pay. We received fifty centimes per day, not even enough for cigarettes. No wonder that many Spaniards couldn't resist the temptation to pilfer. What did they think of a world that treated them this way? Among them were fine and educated humans. They were good to each other, but isolated themselves from strangers. And most of all, they were driven by hunger and need.

The group I had lived with since Vancia had slowly shrunk. Originally we were seven. The friendship eased our service. Soon after completion of the examinations, three were assigned to a cavalry company. They were already in basic training while the rest of us, without anything proper to keep us busy, roamed about. Even fat Walter abandoned us. He disappeared without any training into a typing pool—an exception without equal. Of course he possessed the great capability "to speak with people." A filled wallet eases your way of life even in the Legion; master sergeants and sergeants would never spurn an invitation to an extensive feast and be appreciative of the opportunity.

So I decided to hang out more with Bartel, a really nice young man, who at twenty-one years of age had seen much of this world. He was enraptured with England, where he studied hotel management. He liked France. The Legion? Service is service, he thought, and better here than in Germany. A tasty meal, good drinks in a circle of comrades, dancing with girls who weren't protected by their mothers—that's all he wished. At least in his company, no gloomy thoughts were raised. I, on the other hand, tried to rein in his youthful foolishness and teach him a more serious attitude toward life—a laughable challenge in the Legion.

* * *

We future infantry soldiers were to leave only after Christmas for basic training in Saida. In the meantime, every day we were assigned different duties. What *didn't* we do. What concerns the sweeping and cleaning of dusty and dirty streets, I could challenge any street warden; also the honorable occupation of a cleaning woman holds no secrets from me. I even learned how to pluck chickens (unfortunately Martha never brings poultry into the house—but why?). For the officers' Christmas dinner, three of us plucked a dozen feisty turkeys.

One day we brought mules to the veterinarian. I was handling a rather stubborn animal. I tried kindness and petting, but it didn't respond to that. I finally lost my patience. To quote Nietzsche: "You go to your woman, forget not the whip." I whacked the reluctant mare on its buttock. Under no circumstance would it accept such roughness and bounded off, and I after it caught it by its reins. A comrade helped me capture the unruly beast. In his knowledgeable hands, it became tame and trotted behind him. The animals were beautiful, clean, well groomed, and well fed. They sparkled with freshness. The animals were better cared for than we were. Rightfully so, they were more valuable than we were, as the influx of volunteers had no end.

As soon as our duties were done, we hid in a secure place so as not to entice a sergeant by our inactivity. The soldier quickly learned: once a deed was done, disappear; and most importantly, cross the barracks square with deliberate speed as soon as a field coat appears.

In the evening, we frequently went into the city. Since we had not yet had basic training, we were not officially permitted to leave the base premises. Because of the massive influx, we were still housed in the small quarter. With the mass of people, the inspection couldn't be that exacting. And Bel-Abbès tempted with the magical allure of the Orient. Among us, who had ever been to Africa?

Our barracks were close to the European district, spreading out unevenly. You came across undeveloped tracts of land only two to three hundred meters from the main street, with native settlements on each side. In this area was also located the so-called reserved quarter, which was primarily intended for Legionnaires and otherwise only sought out by low-class rabble and the indigenous population. Legionnaires held watch at the entrance and roamed through the unsafe areas to be on hand in case of disturbances.

We used the first opportunity to acquaint ourselves with African female beauty. My God and Lord! Such filth and excrement, such baseness and depravity, I have hardly ever seen. The love paradise of Bel-Abbès: a snarl of confined, crooked, unpaved lanes, narrow door arches, dilapidated houses, whose walls had been consumed by leprosy, through which open doors and windows a nauseous smell overwhelmed us. In front of these, squatted on bare dirt repulsive creatures, fat matrons in the deepest stuffing of a mat, with puffed up bodies, and young girls hardly past childhood with narrow shoulders and hollow cheeks. Garish red lips, a smile in the made-up face, solicited with spread knees for customers. The places stank more of bitter and neglected poverty than from sweet idleness. And yet many Legionnaires, as long as their pay permitted, sought this scum of hookers. Bartel and I were repulsed; we did not even want to drink a glass of wine in this disgusting place. We hurried back and breathed easier as the nightmare of this sex realm disappeared into the night behind us.

Finally we were again on the main street with its clean houses and modern shops just like at home. Electric lights illuminated the street on which European-dressed people strolled about. This was our world. This was where we belonged; here we had the feeling of being humans. We entered a pastry shop. A petite waitress hurried by and asked our wishes. We ordered coffee and cake. The girl carefully placed the aromatic cups on the table, and we thanked her indifferently as if we were accustomed to being served and didn't tremble the whole day in front of a corporal. Bartel winked at me. "That tastes better than from a bowl," he shouted, and relaxed with a cigarette. The clock struck nine, the excursion into the civilized world at an end. With a noble gesture, we gave the waitress an ample tip and went on our way.

Another time we roamed through the Arabic marketplace, the colorful boutiques of the natives, in which patriarchal figures, merchants from *A Thousand and One Nights*, displayed all kinds of junk. Honorably they debated with their customers the praiseworthiness of the wares as if dealing in precious objects. I saw on the shelves thin inferior materials in screaming colors with which our factory lords sought to make the African customers happy; I would have preferred to see the handmade oriental weavings, but these were apparently only available abroad.

The Legionnaires' quarters were a very tolerable place; on Sunday, when no duties were assigned, we sat under palm trees and enjoyed the noonday sun. As cold as the nights seemed, the sun always shone at noon and chased away gloomy thoughts.

* * *

"You hit it just right," said the old Legionnaire, "Christmas in Bel-Abbès lacks nothing." The Legion festively celebrates Christmas—not from devoutness, because the church and priests have no place in the Legion. The men for whom the Legion was their last resort would have rejected an invitation to a church service with scornful laughter. For these displaced, did God exist? Yes, perhaps they believed in a devil who maliciously fractured their lives and cast them here, to have them all assembled when he one day would call them. They knew nothing of divine Providence or of God's goodness.

The Germans, having been well represented in the Legion for eons, transplanted the custom of the Christmas tree to Africa. Once a year even these failed humans remembered that a mother once loved and took care of them and told them about the Christ child. As small children, they looked forward to Christmas, blissful in the light of candles. And so the holy day signified a retrospective moment and melancholy until the light Algerian wine, which goes down so well, numbed their distress.

The Christmas celebration was carefully prepared. Bel-Abbès had an outstanding jujitsu and gymnastics group, who could easily compete with professional athletes. The presentation was a pleasure to watch. Also the orchestra accompanists were artists. Everyone in France remembers well the Legion Band that on July 14, 1939, scored an intoxicating success. The leader of the Legion orchestra was not at a loss for choices, enough musicians were in the Legion. To be a trumpeter at headquarters was an honor bestowed only on the best.

The midpoint of the program featured a play with patriotic content. An unfortunate set of mistakes, the presumed unfaithfulness of a physician's wife, whom he loved passionately, drove him to join the Legion. Friends investigated his whereabouts, cleared up the misunderstanding, and hatched a plot in association with his wife so that the doctor, who bitterly regretted his rash decision, could make possible his escape from the Legion. The lonely life of the Legionnaire far away in the desert, the toughness of his service, the distress that pursued us, was accurately portrayed. The piece ended with the doctor, after a heavy inner struggle, rejecting the suggestions of his wife and friends. The duty of the given word triumphed over love; the doctor volunteered for the frontlines in France, and as the orchestra played "La Marseillaise," the curtain slowly lowered.

The performance took place in the neighboring movie theater of the Legion. We marched four abreast into the cinema under the command of the corporal, who even on this evening reprimanded us in the usual manner. Even this entertainment didn't spare us the Legion's military coercion. This circumstance rubbed several others and me the wrong way, and we promised each other to forgo next year's celebration and not fall into formation. At least in his free time, man is entitled to escape the pressure of soldiering. No, at least in the evening we wanted to be free and not be surrounded by corporals, whose mere presence spoiled any pleasure.

The giving of Christmas presents took place at midnight. We had to stand for hours in the open until the gifts were distributed, and in the meantime the rain poured down in buckets. The day was tiring, and we were tired and sleepy for the evening; before the celebration we still had to thoroughly clean quarters. One of the fellows suggested forgoing the gifts and going to bed. But that was not possible. Celebration is celebration.

Finally we were allowed to enter the flower-decorated and light-flooded hall. The presents were raffled off. I drew a toothbrush; Walter, a shaving soap, which he gave to another fellow who exchanged it for a glass of wine; lucky Bartel drew a bottle of red wine, which we consumed on the spot. Oh, that was good after the cold soaking rain. At two the merriment came to an end, and we sank into bed; the tiredness closed our eyes, and I doubt if anyone of us thought on this evening that Christmas was a celebration of the birth of a savior in order to bring peace to humanity.

The day after, we sat in the canteen. One of the comrades, a man of middle years, who had left wife and child at home, spoke with a gloomy face to the wine, thinking of his kin. "Hey, today we are supposed to be merry; toss the corporal over your shoulders." Bending over, he saw the picture another one held in his hand. "Do you think about your old lady?" He laughed boisterously. "She will be sleeping with someone else."

* * *

After Christmas, a newly trained company from Saida returned to Bel-Abbès. Most of them were so-called five years. Nonetheless, there were volunteers for the duration of the war among them because some of the local French authorities had already at the beginning of the war permitted internees to commit for the duration of the war. The company proceeded to demonstrate their exercises. They executed their drills splendidly. They aligned themselves in a perfectly straight line, the human component of a windup toy. Every foot was raised in the same instant, all the gun barrels formed a single wall, the provisioning sacks dangled in the same spot, and the ammunition pouches were all at the same height. The arms moved back and forth in perfect cadence.

It looked marvelous. They presented a splendid image, marching into quarters from field maneuvers. No ballet could have been better choreographed. Certainly, no infantry troops could surpass the Legion's. At least as far as drill was concerned; with conditions in France, the knowledge of weaponry unfortunately remained limited.

We often watched our comrades, but we could not enjoy the splendid image of these precision acts without mixed feelings, because we knew the great chicanery our comrades had to endure. As the proverb goes, "More haste, less speed." These first war volunteers were posted to Syria. And that meant far, far away. They were still better off than the next group, who completed their basic training four weeks later. Many of these were transferred to Indochina. Three years in Indochina! Well then, we thought, it would be "only" for three years. Today we know that they had to stay there for the entire war. The Legion reserved the right to fight against the injustice of Japan's occupation of Indochina. The battles lasted only a few days, because Vichy gave the directive to submit to the occupation. The Vichy slogan "We are defending our colonies" was invalid against those in a pact with Germany.

* * *

How far had our three weeks of training progressed? They taught us only the absolute necessities from the school of soldiers without weapons. We could salute, right and left face. When humans still ran barefoot, there were no standing armies. When finally the bombs—which a never tiring technology is so valiantly perfecting—hereafter destroy the last shoe and uniform factories, then the wars will be over. What would happen if instead of prohibiting the manufacture of war means, we simply banned the production of heavy shoes and boots and also uniforms? If you couldn't wear stately uniforms or solidly click your heels, then even the most ardent militarist would lose the desire to be a soldier. What would it be like, if for the sake of beloved freedom, we all decided to go barefoot?

Foremost the corporal taught us per regulation how to knot our kerchief. Our shirts had no collars, and the kerchief replaced the collar and tie. It took a long time until we could tie a perfect knot. It was war, people fought and suffered death, and we spent hours knotting a piece of cloth.

Before our departure, there was a big parade at which we were presented to our colonel. The corporal taught us how to say our names to the colonel. In civilized life it's a simple thing to present yourself to someone; for a soldier it's totally another matter. After the ritual, when the formidable came close, we had to stand erect, strongly click our heels, look the colonel straight into his eyes, and with a deep manly voice call out the name: *"Adler, mon colonel."* Luckily we didn't have any rifles yet, for such a thing complicated matters considerably.

What panic for a soldier—the first parade. Long before the preordained hour, we fell into formation, marched in place, until the colonel arrived. He praised our smart looks with pithy words and expressed the hope that we also, as our predecessors, would do the Legion proud. I thought of the general who requested thousands of Legionnaires to nobly descend into the shadow realm (today I think about the hecatombs that preceded the Nazi leaders in death). The idea of retinue and fealty lives. Strange that humans are capable of gladly sacrificing themselves for others or causes, and particularly those people who would not otherwise make such a sacrifice for humanity for peaceful purposes. And so humanity is chided as a collection of egoistic beings.

After the address, the colonel strode past the rows. Next to me stood a good Alsatian; he was so nervous that instead of saying "*Gack, mon colonel,*" he thundered at the colonel in a true stentorian voice, "Colonel, mon *Gack.*" We had trouble biting our tongues. The colonel remained unmoved.

And then we went "out the portal" and through the small city to the train station. Several cattle cars awaited us: eight horses or forty men. Some of us would have liked to declare ourselves horses.

* * *

Dozens of millions of men made all kinds of trips in the war. Crammed together, entwined, head on the feet of a neighbor, or your boots in your own face—we rolled hours on end in an oppressive grassy air, amid an unbearable smog and stink, through the countryside. The cattle-to-slaughter–like destiny tormented our conscience. It wasn't just the discomfort of the trip that was irritating, but also the abasement, which we perceived as our descent to meaningless pieces of meat with one goal: the battlefield. The trip was a little more tolerable during the day with open doors, but at night it was a nauseating mixture of sweating, tossed bodies.

That's how I emotionally sensed it at that time, and I can remember it well. We knew nothing then about the deportations and gas chambers. There are things so gruesome that the mind is incapable of imagining them. We have only now discovered how the inventions of nihilistic minds far surpassed any norm. Certainly there are more awful experiences than that of the war volunteer, but if more powerful sensations are demanded, they are easily found. I want to show nothing else except that even in our civilized world humanity (not just the stateless) has been degraded. What good is the fight? Don't we recognize that even with us—not just in Germany—total and wide-reaching reform is necessary.

8

SAIDA

What Legionnaire doesn't know Saida—its dusty old garrison with thick walls through which moisture oozes; it is like a jailhouse, but could well pass as a monastery in whose rooms monks oblige their penance. A fine, cold rain drizzled down on us from the winter sky. We shivered from internal and external uneasiness. Tiers of gray clouds passed on high without an iota of blue in the firmament to promise warm brightness. Our superiors missed no opportunity to rub in the worthlessness of our existence. There we were simply raw material: kneadable clay. No, not even that—for the potter has sensitive hands; in Saida, there were only drill instructors without souls, who suppressed us until the human in us made space for a Legionnaire to their liking.

Even the food was mediocre. No efforts were made for the novices. After lunch we disappeared into the canteen for coffee to boost our morale. Coffee in Saida? Who are the Legionnaires that ask for coffee? "Who the fuck sent me these Legionnaires?" the canteen chap bellowed at us. "There are no church ladies here. Here we drink wine."

* * *

We were organized into platoons. So far I was lucky. Our lieutenant was a good man. The company, assigned to the "black" lieutenant got off easy. The lieutenant, a Negro, had the well-proportioned body of an athlete, fine-drawn features, and clever bright eyes. However, possessing skill and endurance like no other, he didn't always grasp that his recruits could not measure up to his capability. In contrast, the group quartered in the so-called Camp des Chasseurs was not so lucky. There, the most notorious drill instructors gave orders. Well, if we only had to deal with French officers...But fundamentally, noncommissioned officers and corporals were in charge of our training.

In the Camp des Chasseurs, a sergeant let one of my buddies with a 102° F fever crawl from the garrison to the exercise square. A favorite sport in Saida—war exercises in the worst filth. The recruit had then to clean himself up and make sure that the next day no dust particle was visible on his field coat. A recruit had to sweat blood. Sick? My friend lay unconscious in the square. Only then did the sergeant hospitalize him, after he had threatened him with jail on the previous day if he didn't march with the others.

The rooms were full of bugs. We discovered them prior to dusk as we claimed the unused hooks. As we removed the iron piece from the wall, the little unappetizing animals streamed in a procession from the wall. "Good thing it's winter," exclaimed Bartel, whose lively imagination was always at work. "What must it be like here in the summer."

A corporal taught us to make the beds and arrange our baggage on the shelf by our heads according to regulation. Making beds was a skill that the beginner had to learn with great effort. The covers had to span the mattresses, as taut as if boards were underneath them and not the soft sea grass filling. Everything had to look hard and angular just like the movements we were taught on the drill place.

Now the baggage...We acquired more things, particularly underwear. A misfortune—the more you owned, the higher towered the hated baggage, the so-called *paquettage*. The military coat, the second uniform, yes, every shirt (fortunately we only had two uniforms) had to be folded into a rectangle using a small board. The board was the length of a bayonet and ten centimeters high. One piece after another was wrapped on the small board and stacked on the shelf. The base layer consisted of the green coat, and the second layer was the light brown of our summer outfit. Next came the shirts and the underwear. The construction of the paquettage reached seven layers. Every piece of clothing was reduced to the form of a book, and the front board acted as the bookbinding. On top of the structure of his effects, which the recruit cherished like life itself, rested his steel helmet. The canteen stood to the left of the paquettage; and to the right, the metal bowl with spoon and fork: to the left, the fork; to the right, the spoon; the two crossed in the handle of the mess kit. Bread bag, ammunition pouch, and other leather items hung on nails over the bedstead. A small tag with name and number informed all which poor sinner slept in that bed.

The Legionnaire regarded the finally completed work with worry. Everything was organized; just don't touch anything. In the evening the sergeant stepped through the rooms, peered with critical eyes into the farthest corners, and inspected the paquettage. Woe if a little corner stuck out or a little fold spoiled the board. Then the mighty stretched out his arm. "Lederer, naturally, that swine," he thundered through the room. One tug and everything was on the floor. Timidly, Lederer folded the items anew. Then the mighty bent over the bed. Triumphantly, he pulled a book from under the covers. "This will be confiscated," cracked the sergeant. Nothing could be placed on the shelf aside from your baggage; nothing could be hidden in or under your bed. The Legionnaire was graciously allowed a small trunk that held the bulk of the paquettage and rested under the baggage. Therein we stowed our personal possessions. A dependable lock secured the contents against theft.

Seldom did we have a free moment. After the day watch, with coffee barely gulped down, we began our duties: cleaning all the rooms, making the beds and the baggage. Everything had to be done by roll call, leaving barely an hour. There were so many steps, so many rooms and windows to scrub, that we hardly had time to swallow a piece of bread. Five minutes before roll call, the corporal would chase the unit out of the room. We crowded together in the halls and, on the whistle, we all plunged downstairs. In one minute we had to stand in formation. Lateness at roll call resulted in eight days in prison—that was as certain as *amen* in a prayer. And barely had the morning drill ended and we had put our things in place, then the whistle blew again: line up for peeling duty. This duty lasted a half an hour at noontime and in the evening. It was a fundamental part of basic training, like the saddle and the horse. I had heard that there was a machine in Meknes to peel potatoes. But it was never used: for why were there Legionnaires? When the peeling was done, we fetched the meal. Each section provided four men. After the meal we quickly washed the mess buckets and bowls, and immediately the whistle blew again: line up!

* * *

Between the training, which demanded all our strength, and the remaining duties, our days passed in deliberate haste. If that were not enough, we suffered spiritually. Scolded in unflattering terms, we trembled and feared that a sergeant with malicious delight would draw a bead on us, that the laboriously folded baggage would be thrown from the shelf, and more. In the evening we sank tired into our bunks, happy to know from nothing.

At the end of the second week, we were issued our rifles. At this point, we had obtained a certain expertise carrying out our duties and constructing the paquettage. The rifle remained in the magazine, picked up before line up. Earlier, when the weapons were kept in the sleeping quarters, a curt fellow might have grabbed his rifle to settle his quarrels.

Initially, basic training mostly emphasized strengthening the body. For this was rightfully the fundamental prerequisite for a good and useful soldier. The physical exercise, *éducation physique*, (*éducation Frühstück*[4], as our German sergeants called it) endeavored to tone the body. We ran, jumped, and crawled. The exercises had a military emphasis: you ran or crawled up a hill and on top briskly jumped over a wall. We practiced arm swings, which later became exercises for tossing grenades, as well as knee and stretching exercises, to become familiar with kneeling or lying prostrate for protection.

The discipline was tough, yet if you were reasonably equal to the task, it strengthened and developed your capability. A twenty-year-old who played several sports had an advantage. But who among us was so

---

4 Breakfast

lucky to have counted only twenty summers? Barely a third of the volunteers were under twenty-five. Most were in their thirties and forties. Old Kermisch and his two sons served in our unit. The youngsters were about twenty and did well. The old man was well into his late-forties and panted heavily during drills. Another chap was fifty-two. Well, if we had ever previously been in the service, a lot of things would have been easier, but very few of us could make that claim. Most of us were from Germany and Austria, which since 1918 had only a small professional army. We never served and hoped for "no more war" in our lifetime. We came of age in the epoch when a world bled dry swore peace. And yet there was war again, and we were wearing the field coat.

To fully understand our situation, you have to think about the fear-saturated atmosphere that prevailed in our barracks. The corporal was a demigod, who of course let us suffer the same trials and tribulations that he himself endured when he was a recruit. His superiors beat the same into him: that only the worst drill and shock make the Legionnaire. Woe to the Legionnaire who didn't promptly salute the corporal everywhere. The corporal had served a long time and, to be promoted, partook in a strict course of study. He had know-how that could not be matched by any other noncommissioned officer of another country. No Arab could measure up to a Legionnaire's battle worthiness. He was a professional soldier and proud to stand over the mass of second-class Legionnaires. He got irritated at the novice's least show of incompetence and meted out punishment at the least provocation.

And how about the sergeant? What was said about the corporal applied doubly or even triply to the sergeant. Not too many Legionnaires could boast of having ascended to the rank of corporal. They considered themselves happy to close out their military careers after twelve or fifteen years, with the rank of senior corporal. What did noncommissioned officers have to offer in such an environment? First, the sergeant was a simple Legionnaire for a few years, then corporal for a while; he fought in Morocco and Syria and served three years in Indochina. He had no understanding for heart and soul, and he didn't understand that you could build a life outside the Legion. The sergeant dedicated the best of his abilities in service to France; he demanded as much as had been demanded of him.

The inconsolable bleakness of a professional soldier's life was devoid of any spiritual inspiration—women and wine helped only for the short instances of inebriation that chased away the distress. In the isolation of his situation, worlds away, his mind was inevitably seized and never set free. The professional Legionnaire had as little understanding of the civil environment as it had for him. His life was forever misspent.

* * *

There, you were just a cog in the machine; it was bend or break. Rebuked and harassed, without a minute to ourselves, in constant fear of imprisonment at the slightest suggestion of suspicion, with threat of insubordination and robbed of every last vestige of human dignity and essence of who we were—we suffered. Fear and hate gnawed at our nerves. That in a nutshell was the Legion. We could ultimately deal with the physical demands, but we could not deal with the destruction of every spiritual emotion by uneducated ruffians, who through the circumstances of war became our masters.

Our superiors sensed full well that we were poles apart. We were not from the circle of people from whom the Legion drew its young blood in ordinary times. We were not men with an utter addiction to a dangerous life or a failure in a civil occupation, but a collision with the law forced us to the enlistment officer. We were not finished with our existence, willing and pliable raw material for the artisans of war. In our struggle for life, we had conquered a place in society and had no need of the particularly hard precautionary machine of the army; somewhere there were people who depended on us, women and children who lovingly thought of us. In short we called that our own, and what the professional Legionnaire did not have but would so very much have owned.

This contrast could not be bridged and explained why we took our treatment particularly hard. In any event, our treatment appeared so unbearably difficult just by way of the human beings into whom they partly transformed us.

84

And that wasn't just insofar as the service was concerned. We received letters from France, statements of affection from our relatives. Someone worried about us. In the weeks after we arrived, the postmaster in Saida had to deal with unprecedented amounts of mail turning his usual life upside down. There he lived, the long-serving soldier with sparse earnings, and suddenly recruits showed up to whom the mail transmitted an impressive amount of information. By the end of the war, these people would stand once again above his rung on the social ladder. But now we were in his hands. Our presence humiliated him. No wonder that he and everyone else of his rank succumbed to the temptation to let us feel his instant power in every measure.

* * *

One day, Canadian airmen visited. The local commander, who was also our commanding officer, made them most welcome. How we envied their freedom and independence, these masters of the sky. How much would we, stepped-on earthworms, taken on all dangers to be just a little bit more human so that we wouldn't have to hear "you shit," "bastard," and "asshole" all day.

The big hall of the garrison was shining with festive decorations in honor of the guests. White plates and goblets were set out on white tablecloths, and candles bestowed their light to the happy gathering. We pressed up against the windowpanes to see it all, as in life, just guests on the fence looking in, when a sharp look and slight gesture chased us away. My friend, Bartel, who spoke fluent English, approached the guests. They weren't arrogant toward us for they didn't live in a death-threatening world hierarchy, and they amply presented us with the good things that the Canadian armed forces supplied them.

* * *

With my friend Bartel, the last of the Mohicans from our small group of Vancia, and other companions of similar persuasion, we moved into a small room with a capacity for only fifteen men. With fewer roommates, comradeship drew closer, and the possibility to talk openly and to ease our suffering became more certain. Still, in the evening, when the sergeant on duty crossed through the bedrooms, he usually felt the need to mete out severe reprimands; we hoped that having unloaded his fury elsewhere, we would escape his wrath. Though none escaped, Bartel was a magnificent companion in this regard. He was young, and the nastiness of our seargent rolled off his back.

One of my best acquaintances in Saida was Dr. Grünwald, a German physician. After the Dachau concentration camp, where he spent several months of "penitence," the Legion seemed to him a place where life continued. He had a visa to America in his pocket and still opted into the Legion, a hero ready to suffer and sacrifice as many Jews did in that war. Owing to the complications of his escape from Germany, he had been separated from his spouse for quite some time. I dared not think what fate awaited these humans. Perhaps after the armistice, he would successfully find refuge in the United States. Dr. Grünwald understood me and didn't dismiss my complaints as petty whining; but in retrospect, when considering the suffering of millions, that is exactly what my behavior appears to me to have been. The war had displaced such masses of people that spiritual agony, besides the physical torment, paled into insignificance. Dr. Grünwald attempted to teach me to shutter myself, so as to repel all evil. He didn't succeed in changing me.

Again and again I was outraged, and with all my strength I wanted to be free. The devilish drilling had nothing in common with our love and desire to take a stand. I wished I could have just eradicated my name from every contract that bound me to the Legion. In the first hours of instruction, the lieutenant spoke to us about the essence of assault. He said, "On ne fait pas d'omlettes sans casser des oefs" (You can't make omelets without breaking eggs). We were the broken eggs. Certainly every conflict fosters sacrifice. We were the fast, expendable raw material of the battle. We promised to give our lives in service to our country. Service to our country! If only we had a country to call our own. But we were all certainly destined to die without being sure to have fought for a homeland, for our homeland. Where was the ethical posture that would have helped us to bear the hardship of basic training?

Nonetheless, the lieutenant did teach us one rule that I subsequently always followed, whether in the Legion or the several refugee camps that I later passed through. "When faced with approaching enemy aircraft, there is only one thing an unprotected infantryman can do: disperse and camouflage." When opponents (men in uniforms with patches and stars on their arms and collars) came near, I always followed this golden rule, and even today I am thankful for the lieutenant's instruction.

* * *

Our basic training was to take three months. I bade Martha to seek Mr. Troiville's assistance, so that I could be transferred to France. There the Legion could not be so inhumane. The garrisons and drill squares, in the vicinity of the enemy, lose their terror. I didn't even dread the front, though not for heroic reasons. But there the enemy lurked only in front and not behind and beside us, as we used to say with bitterness. If only my ulcer would have acted up again. In vain I pressed on my abdomen, where the duodenum was located. I was totally healed.

Then already I dared considering to make myself ill through a preparation and spoke to Dr. Grünwald seriously about it. In the evenings, when we were tired and degraded by swear words, we sat on our bunks and discussed our future and our awful, inconsolable slave existence, robbing us of every will to live; then it seemed to me totally reasonable to take my life. A terrible hatred came over me when I thought of the three acquaintances whose patriotism was all talk and who were now sitting comfortably at home.

Meanwhile, I could never think of portraying our condition to my dear Martha in her own totally bleak situation. Besides the censorship, it would have been evil of me to add my own woes to Martha's. The poor thing toiled with great difficulty. Prices had climbed; the military support including the family supplement was insufficient to feed Martha and Paul. Martha was reluctant to work in a weapons factory, like others with a similar fate, for we had no one to whom we could entrust our child with peace of mind. Many of us thought that the government purposely set the spousal support low in order to force women into the factories. Be that as it may, Martha's only alternative was to knit socks and other wool items for the soldiers. Home piecework: so pitifully compensated after much work, she often cried upon receiving the pittance of a wage. She also rented out one room. Yes, the fatherland, fatherly cared for the families it was defending. Economizing was essential to conserve savings as the war could last a long time. I, too, urgently needed a subsidy, because the wages were hardly enough for cigarettes, not to speak of our yearning to go out for a coffee, eat a piece of cake, maybe even take in an entire meal just to escape the constant sight of the tiresome meal bucket. The meal bucket along with the tin bowls and camp barracks was one of the most depressing signs of our time and our degradation.

* * *

After eight days, we were allowed to go into the city for the first time. We carefully cleaned the field coat, the buttons, and spit shined our shoes. If the tiniest bit of dust lurked on your uniform, if the buttons didn't glisten like polished gold, the boots didn't shine like patent leather, then you could forget about your pass. There was a small board with several holes into which you could insert several buttons at once and polish them. We spent a major portion of our wages on shoe paste and metal polish.

We conferred over who would be the first to chance going by the sentries and the eagle-eyed observing sergeant. "You take three steps forward, sharply about-face, take three steps back, and again about-face. If you are lucky, the old man will let you by, otherwise you try climbing over the wall." The sergeant never let you know on what grounds he refused your exit. We had to discover for ourselves what was wrong. How often did we again polish our already lacquer-glossy shoes, when it was a button that didn't sparkle sufficiently or a pocket that wasn't open or closed per regulation?

Finally outside, our gang quickly dispersed. Where were they all—or almost all—going? To the bordello—the others and myself. Curiosity drove me. The place barely passed as a pub. Several half-naked girls sat at the bar, with solicitous smiles in caked-on, overdone makeup. They didn't mind showing the wares that they had been offering for lease on the sex market for years. Some of the stalwarts threw themselves upon those who had gone for so long without "the sex." The word "fair" won't flow from my pen in the face of these pathetic prostitutes and whores servicing the Legion. Drunk, with glassy eyes, trousers half undone, a fellow staggered down the steps that led from the girls' chambers into the lounge. Quick turnover of tricks was the rule. Love was carried out in business fashion. Here the act alone counted and never an affectionate word exchanged. The girls didn't deceive with love, and the Legionnaire sought no deception. He was a drunken animal in heat. For these venal fellows, even these girls were too good. Our oldest bunkmate, a strange creature named Kowalski, who had already served once in the Legion, was wild about the Negros of Morocco, whom everyone heatedly yet shamefully embraced. Prior to the First World War, he served three years as a Russian citizen. That was the usual tour of duty. Then came the First World War, and Kowalski re-enlisted. He spent five years in the Russian Army. Then in the Polish-Russian war he fought in a Polish uniform. When peace finally came to his homeland, the good man had spent a total of twelve years soldiering. What wonder then that he could no longer fit into civilian society, was incapable of finding a job, and finally, after many wrong turns, slipped into the fighting uniform of the Foreign Legion. He spent five years in Africa and Indochina. Only in 1927 did he return to civilian life. He was however destined to be a soldier. In 1939 the cannons again did the talking. He was betting on a long war. He knew no other. With equanimity, he signed on for five years. He was right. What else could become of this man who knows only how to fight and destroy and never learned any peaceful work?

Dr. Grünfeld and I invited him once for a glass of wine. In the pub, Kowalski told us about his time in the service, beginning with Morocco, the Legionnaires paradise, where he was feared and revered like a god. The low stone walls surrounding the camps of the Legion of Morocco were easily scaled. There in the hot arms of a woman named Fatma, Kowalski found the blissful pleasure of love. I could picture the tavern in the marketplace, the red polished table, the wall mirror, and Kowalski. There he sat, tall and dry like African soil, his cap had slid half off, his bald head shone brightly under the electric lamps, and his face beamed blissfully as the wine, like a lively brook, gurgled down his throat. His nose protruded red like vermillion from under his happy twinkling eyes. With a strong Slavic accent that gave his broken French a peculiar ring, he described the allure of dark-skinned girls. We could hardly hold back our laughter when we pictured the scrawny Kowalski in the ecstasy of love in the brown arms of a Fatma.

His weakness for women and wine did not hinder him from being a good companion. Through his experience in the service, he shielded us from many stupid actions. We repaid him by writing his reports, since he was at loggerheads with French spelling.

* * *

Toward the end of the second week, we received triple inoculations against typhus, diphtheria, and tetanus. With each set of inoculations, we received three days of rest. We gladly would have accepted more immunizations just to be able to stretch out quietly on our beds.

But then the struggle began anew. I didn't think I would survive. Time and again, I was up against the rigid regulations. I was like a captured bird that flapped its wings to no avail. There was no escape. I could not tolerate it any more. I could not tolerate the service, the offensive speech of the crude characters, the many thefts that made every companionship in wider circles impossible. Just think: when we simply washed a few handkerchiefs and put them out on the line to dry, we had to have a change of guard. The pressure from above, the shortage of companionship—it was too much. It was not considered theft when you "acquired" a missing piece of equipment from the nearest pack. How could you yourself escape the threat of imprisonment if in an emergency you didn't decorate yourself with someone else's belongings? We called this self-help "decoration." Now the equipment set had to be complete as we were always subject to inspections. So a single missing item, a single theft, initiated an unending chain of "decorations." In the end, one of us had to buy, or in exchange for a glass of wine, get the missing piece from the stockroom. Once we had to exhibit ourselves with open clothing. "What can that be about again?" we asked ourselves. "They want to be certain that we are not spreading any gonorrhea," a fellow guessed. "To see if we are wearing clean underwear," Bartel innocently wanted to wager. None of these guesses were the case. They just wanted to see if our packs were complete. Whether clean or dirty, the powers that be could care less.

And yet again, as in all my life situations, when in the depths of despair and with hardly any remaining faith, and with the last ounce of strength beseeching God for assistance, there came unexpectedly, suddenly rescue. After scarcely two weeks, we were recalled to Bel-Abbès. All recruits left Saida. What happened? We knew nothing about it, but there must have been important reasons, as recruits who hardly knew how to hold a rifle were suddenly withdrawn from basic training. A rumor leaked from the noncommissioned officers; we were going to Morocco. We didn't care why we left Saida.

Cheerfully we returned the things that they had given us, and we packed our haversack. It sufficed for our few belongings. There was a great exodus in the evening. Dr. Grünwald and I celebrated our departure from Saida in a charming, newly opened pastry shop. A petite French waitress served us. After the hookers in the brothels, she appeared to us as the epitome of female beauty. We made ourselves comfortable in the deep wicker seats and savored the tasty sweet pastry with hot chocolate drinks. It was a delight. For an hour we forgot that a crude fellow, who perhaps was promoted to corporal by dint of his seniority and who could hardly read and write, became our master.

How gladly we accepted the dreadful trip in cattle cars, even if we did go only to Bel-Abbès. We had conquered a small piece of our service—the most awful, we thought.

9

MEKNES

The rumors were confirmed: we were transferring to Morocco.

During peacetime, the Legion fielded six infantry regiments. The first one was in Algiers and the Sahara. The second, third, and fourth were located in Morocco, with bases in Meknes, Fez, and Marrakech. The fifth was in Indochina, and the sixth in Syria. In addition there were two light cavalry regiments with light tank armaments, one of which was stationed in Algeria and the other in Morocco. This distribution made apparent the significant influence of the Legion upon life in Morocco. In peacetime, it numbered about twelve thousand Legionnaires. In Bel-Abbès I received the registration number 89,233, and in the course of the war, those numbers climbed toward 98,000. In total, about one hundred thousand volunteers were placed into the African regiments. Yet we were only a fraction of the foreigners that France put to the disposal of the war. The majority of volunteers served in proper French army units, and they were awarded at the same time rights to French citizenship. All who originated from a country directly bordering the French lands—Italians, Belgians, and Spaniards—as long as they had the proper residence permits, enjoyed this preferential treatment. German and Austrian refugees were naturally exempted even if they had lived many years in France. We could only serve in the

Legion and were trained in Africa. Assignment orders were determined according to situation. Furthermore, France made an agreement with the representatives of Poland and Czechoslovakia whereby subjects of those states could serve in their own national units. Full membership into French units, therefore, was out of the question, but they could sign a contract with the Foreign Legion, which anyone could join. Many Polish Jews, who understandably wanted nothing to do with a country that stripped them of citizenship prior to the war and then graciously recognized them as citizens at the start of the war, did so. The Spaniards in the camp also could join only the Foreign Legion. Several marching regiments of the Legion were established in mainland France. In the few short weeks of the German offensive in the spring of 1940, they were deployed in the most dangerous places and suffered terrible losses.

I cite an example of two companies of three hundred men of which only six survived. The survivors, one a friend of mine, all received the Military Cross with Palms. The list of meritorious service put out by the Vichy government, which certainly didn't express any fondness for Jews, honored names such as Kohn, Levy, and Bloch. Most of those so recognized were at the time of their honor no longer alive. It is expected, that a special publication will record the Jewish participants in the battles of 1940 and in the liberation of France in 1944. Not because we as survivors want to claim any fame from these sacrifices or make capital from the human suffering. But I remember how it filled us with such bitterness when the newspapers of the Vichy regime, Hitler's mercenaries, accused Jews of cowardice. The shadow government may well have disappeared, but much of the poison spread by the fascist propaganda has remained. We must defend ourselves and promulgate the truth if we want to fight against anti-Semitism, the worst enemy, not just of the Jews but also of all humankind.

The posting of march regiments in France offered the advantage of trained forces. Good portions of the career Legionnaires were transferred here. At the time we were recalled from Saida, the Moroccan regiments lost half their men. This gap needed to be filled, and so we were ordered in to reinforce the Moroccan regiments.

* * *

The few days we spent in Bel-Abbès prior to our departure to Morocco were among the most pleasant of my service. We were no longer considered green and were therefore treated better. We also knew the subterfuges, how best to avoid duties and or hide from a sergeant.

We again were subjected to a medical examination, the fourth since our enlistment. We always had to strip down for them to ascertain our fitness to take the lives of others or to serve as a sacrifice of battle. The examination was a mere formality to fulfill regulations. Surely, it can be understood from these portrayals, that several of my companions lost their joy in the Legion. The training had made them aware of all sorts of weaknesses that were perhaps suited to relieve them of further service. Some of my colleagues had the audacity to demand that the head doctor see them. But the sergeant, who vigilantly guarded that access, threatened the foolhardy with prison. Woe, when the doctor didn't diagnose the professed ailment. The sergeant didn't use polite words, and his crudeness disheartened not just those wishing to avoid service but also those who really were sick. The night prior to the departure, a Spaniard with a heart condition suffered an attack and died. His body was added to the Legion's cemetery. And yet he was fit.

After a last parade in front of the regimental commander, the lively tunes of the Legion marches accompanied us to the train station. This time we traveled in fourth-class cars. These were native cars with crossed wooden benches of the simplest type, but after the cattle car accommodations, we appreciated this deserved comfort.

* * *

We were certainly near a thousand men on that train. Each of the three Moroccan regiments received a reinforcement of several hundred recruits. The word was out. Bartel and I were going to Meknes to the second regiment. Bartel envied the comrades that had been commanded to the third regiment in Marrakech. He read in some paper that a Danish prince served there. Supposedly, things were quite plush in Marrakech. Corresponding to the princely presence, so the rumor went, the

Legionnaires wore white tennis coats: fashionable, in other words, the knightly noblesse of the Moroccan south. His talk cheered us up. What honor to serve at the side of a prince. "I would rather be together with my Kathy," commented Lederer calmly. The Prince of Paris, pretender to the French crown, enlisted in the Legion for the duration of the war under a false name. As if people didn't know who he was, he didn't enjoy special treatment from his superiors.

"I heard disturbances broke out in Morocco," Bartel continued to whisper. "It is feared that Spain will declare war. We will be taking over the security of the borders." The good young man had the gift of a terrible imagination. I, for my part, gladly forwent the white uniform. And as to the meaning of our reserved assignments, I was skeptical. I was satisfied to leave Algeria and could ask for nothing else. I was sorry that Dr. Grünwald remained in Bel-Abbès and I had lost his pleasant company. Supposedly, the war volunteer physicians were persuaded to care for the sick and wounded. Later, a circular came out that dealt with this question. Our leadership strove against the release of the dirty foreigners from their power, and most of the physicians for most of their service remained privates second class. In the hospitals, they could at most clean toilets or mop the floors. Now, after Dr. Grünwald was forbidden to practice medicine in Germany, he learned shoe repair, and with this useful skill, he was assigned to the cobbler shops in Bel-Abbès. We promised to write each other, but the service left little leisure, and soon our exchange of letters waned.

* * *

In our eyes, the countryside was not always beautiful, but it was captivating. In Europe, we were used to a deeper green. The rocky, yellow tinted, parched expanses, rarely interrupted by trees, struck us as foreign. Where the land was developed, the uniform cultivation of large-scale land holdings of the countryside did not give the appearance of the multicolored pattern of the small land parcels of European peasant properties. How lovely our fields appeared: the deep green of a meadow, soon golden corn, soon flowering clover, and again a shady forest. And sprinkled between little farmhouses with their colorful flowering gardens, cows and sheep grazed, dogs pranced about, the entire animal world delighting children viewing the scene from their railway cars. Nothing from home was to be seen. A single fruit covered the fields, which had the proportions of a European settlement. At the train stations, silos stretched their white towers toward the dark blue sky. Natives were working in the fields. Their torsos were bare, straw hats reminiscent of Mexico covered their heads, protecting against the scorching heat. Everything was so broad and big, the countryside seemed to have no end. Brilliant light beamed down everywhere, no halftones and no shade to beneficially dampen the glaring colors. Abducted by the train, we glided farther and farther along, and the countryside hurried forward with us, always the same, unending and unbounded. We were but a small seed from a former earth out of which God formed us, nothing in the face of this peculiar, foreign, and exalted greatness of land. This space awoke in us a quiet uneasiness, somehow irritated us, and finally overcame us.

Only Tlemcen, located in outermost western Algeria, reminded us, with its decorated little houses and fruit gardens, of home places. Tlemcen was situated in a mountainous and forested area from which the brooks splashed happily and quickly into the valley as if they were fleeing the glowing sun. Unforeseen, border posts appeared. They didn't separate two different states but indicated the start of a different administrative territory of French colonial rule. The train stopped. We were in Morocco.

* * *

Oudja was the first station on Moroccan soil. Here began the true Orient. The French had been at home in Algeria for over a hundred years. Algeria belonged unequivocally to the home country; it was divided into departments, subordinate to the prefects, exactly as any part of French-European land. In Algeria, at least those living along the coast spoke French quite fluently. The cities, even if mostly in the building style of the previous century, carried a European stamp. Yes, exactly because many small streets exhibited only older construction, they instilled intimacy. On the other hand, the 1906 Algeciras Conference let France gain a foothold in Morocco, and by the 1912 Treaty of Fez, Morocco became a French protectorate officially under the control of the sovereign sultan residing in Fez. The conquests of European states were cloaked in different disguises: in one place they were owners, in another merely protectors; or they may have appeared as trustees. All forms of course had in mind the best interest of the native population, who didn't always understand this; they exhibited no understanding of the nuances of European legal scholars. Neither could the native peasant care if the soldier, who as punishment set his hut in flame, was his lord, protector, or even his friend. They were just people without culture—the natives.

But in Morocco everything was new and modern. The cities were young; the developments, American. Next to the untouched Orient stood tall commercial buildings and modern apartment buildings in radiant, unstained white. The country was being crisscrossed with broad asphalt streets on which autos sped. Even the remotest areas, the so-called Bled, without rail service, were reachable by highway. In view of the over-whelming developments of these settlements that almost shot up from the ground overnight, we often had the impression we were lingering in America. And this young world, in which we communicated not in English but in French, stood sharply apart from the Arabian world in the style of its houses and the clothing and deportment of the people. Every bigger city was divided into three parts: the European quarter with the fast-paced life of the here and now; the Jews lived apart and formed an impressive part of the city dwellers, for even there, their connections to the environment were not always the best; and the indigenous quarter in which life proceeded very leisurely as if airplanes and machines didn't exist. Here the weaver knotted artistic carpets with colorful threads in the fashion of their fathers; there the goldsmith bent over noble metals and finished sparkling jewelry; the saddler prepared leather; and all this splendid, colorful life played out in front of our eyes and cast us under its spell.

No one who has seen Morocco can deny the great accomplishments that the French effectively achieved in relatively short time. Casablanca was the white city on the ocean with exponential population growth and a harbor whose traffic increased year to year. All Moroccan French had taken it to heart; it was unique in its development and, apart from the New World, could be compared to the Jewish city of Tel Aviv. And it was not alone. European quarters were everywhere: garages, factories, businesses, hotels, and living places occupied by French families for whom Africa was their homeland, who couldn't live elsewhere and wouldn't want to, because after Africa's expansiveness, Europe would only hem them in.

Legionnaires were soldiers first and even more so mercenaries of France, and I often asked myself why this work evoked such notice by my companions and me. The Moroccan transformation was an accomplishment, and the recognition of an accomplishment could not be denied. The men who acquired Morocco for France were not just fighters, but men for peaceful and beneficent growth. In Morocco, the term *Empire Francais* was much better understood than in Algeria. And the technical and managerial achievements of a Lautey and his successors had to be admired so much the more as the French population policy situation in no way made their tasks any easier. Except in Tunis, where the Italians formed quite a proportion of the European population, nowhere else in Africa did you come across so many Spaniards, Portuguese, and Italians. They formed the masses of European workers of the lower echelons. Their children, often with citizenship rights, regarded themselves as genuine French and often behaved more chauvinistically than how the genuine Gauls were expected to. In general, the North African French stood more to the right than their European national comrades; this attitude could be explained by the fact that they were, to greater measure, beneficiaries of French rule.

Population-poor France could never have pacified Morocco without the deployment of the foreign regiments of the Legion and could never have achieved the growth and development without the influx of foreign workers. The French provided the management officials, and were the employers. Physicians, teachers, lawyers—the educated workers were French. The French also owned the agricultural production means, with an incredible output in our view, under the leadership and supervision of French employees who directed the physical labor of the indigenous workers. Wasn't it a remarkable achievement to place various peoples into the service of France and to assimilate them such that their descendants were proud to be French? Didn't that show the French genius in its ability to civilize in all its glory and power? If all French had spent several months in their colonies, if they had known what a great proud realm they owned, if they thought of the Empire as fervently as the English of theirs, then for France, the Second World War would not have come to a temporary end in the woods of Compiègne.

I don't presume to pass judgment on the right of colonization; moreover I know and affirm that every people have the right to live in its own acceptable manner. Didn't the French claim that right when the Germans wanted to impose upon them the way of life of the "new Europe." But it is impossible to speak of Morocco without appreciating France's great work, for it obviously contradicts all who believe in the collapse of this land. A country capable of such achievement still possesses much unused vitality. We would be ungrateful if we didn't recognize that the achievement of colonization, particularly in North Africa, also bore the fruits of the Axis capitulation. I must speak of it also, because Morocco and the Legion belong together. When, as Legionnaires, we strolled through the streets of Meknes, overspread with the magic blue sky, when we walked through the public gardens with its tall palms, whose wide treetop fronds gave shade and promised peace, then we discovered ourselves proud to be Legionnaires and to belong to the regiments that were first in line as France took possession of this land. Yes, then we were ready to forget what the old Legionnaires had told us about punitive expeditions against rebellious tribes, ready to forget how hard and undignified our life was, and that all these triumphs were bought with the blood of our—like us—homeless predecessors in the Legion.

* * *

A line of French power: below the surface of apparent peace still lurked the conflicts and quarrels. Now and then they flared up unexpectedly from the ashes as a reminder to maintain caution and vigilance. On the evening of our arrival, the alarm sounded. The riot squad quickly donned their helmets and grabbed their rifles. The trucks with the Legionnaires rolled into the old city where a disturbance between Muslims and Jews had broken out. Order was quickly restored. On the command "Fix bayonets," the streets emptied out at lightning speed. The people here knew what the Legion signified.

Might ruled. Even the most savage tribe knew the futility of attacking the French army. The Moroccans had reconciled themselves, and their hankering to fight was no longer directed against the French or blood-related tribes, but against the enemies of France. The natives satisfied their war lust under its leadership and flag. The security regiments and the Goums were the gathering places for these forces. But vigilance was always in place. It was always necessary to show strength in order that strength need not be used. Warriors used to battle, respect only the strong, and softness appears to them as a weakness.

* * *

The buildings of the Legion in Meknes far exceeded the quarters of Bel-Abbès in extent and beauty. Everything was new and conveyed vision and might. Of the many barracks in the city, garrisoning the nearly thirty thousand men, ours were by far the best. Lush gardens surrounded the quarters; benches were set on the gravel path as in a park. All that belongs to us, Legionnaires; our work companies had put a fence around this once desert country, put up the stylish buildings, made the ground arable, and laid out the pathways. Our comrades took care of the plush plants with their magnificent flowers that pleased us with their colors and scent. It was also our comrades who brought home the varieties of animals and funny monkeys from their travels and hikes in the Atlas Mountains, into whose cages we so curiously gaped. If we had our fill of all that beauty and entered into the canteen for a refreshing drink, it was roomy and bright. The canteen chap poured us glasses of smooth wine, and we sat down with friends and tasted reflectively. That was good. Sweetly the wine glided down the throat, and with pleasure we emptied glass after glass without thinking of anything evil until we suddenly discovered that our legs were swaying and we were hardly able to find our beds.

We were more careful the next time; we avoided the visit and went to the reading room, where all kinds of publications were available. There were also parlor games, and we could even borrow books and expand our minds, as long as we were still capable after the tiring day. Looking up, we saw displayed on the walls the honor roll that the regiment earned in bloody battles. Now they hung neat and spotless behind glass to challenge the newcomers to prove themselves with the same courage. There was no battlefield of the preceding one hundred years in which the blood of the Legionnaires did not mix with the blood of the French. All the wars of France were represented: campaigns in Africa and India, the conquest of Madagascar, the Mexican expedition, the Crimean War, the Italian wars of independence, and of course the First World War.

The Legionnaires fought as obedient soldiers, not asking the cause of the war, not thinking about which side was in the right. They were not permitted. On a panel, hung in a clearly visible spot, we could read that in this place politics and religion could not be discussed. The Legionnaire must blindly obey orders. Arguments about belief, perhaps even race, were preposterous in this colorful thrown-together company.

* * *

We liked it there. How could it have been different after the colorful days in Saida? It took some time until we were placed. We were again presented for medical examination—now for the fifth time. What a senseless waste of time. The results were always the same. After the doctor satisfied his thirst for knowledge, we were assigned to the regimental company units. Each received an allocation of future gardeners, mounted guards, mule handlers, shoe repairers, and typists. It wouldn't have taken much to put me at a desk in Meknes. The need for trained office orderlies was great. Before the war, only the French were employed in the administration of the regiment. Now they were assigned to the marching regiments, and the foreigners were tapped. But our colonel supported the incontestable standpoint that everyone must go through basic training. In the Legion, no one who did not previously undergo thorough training could be employed in a shop or office. Even the most confirmed writer, always glued to his desk chair, had to be able to toss grenades and service a machine gun. And if push came to shove, even cooks and bureaucrats had to join the front lines. The Legion had no place for shirkers.

The regimental command found reinforcing the so-called Companie Montée the most difficult. It was the one with the riding mule company. For each of two Legionnaires, one mule was assigned, which they rode alternately. The animal also carried the packs so that the unencumbered and rested Legionnaire could manage a fast pace. This company was uniquely qualified to carry out police actions in dangerous terrain. It could advance without difficulty seventy kilometers in a day. You had to be in good shape, even though sitting half the time. They picked the youngest and strongest. Those chosen made long faces, and our Bartel was threatened with assignment to the Montée; but the smart aleck succeeded at the last minute to pull the wool over the captain's eyes, and with a broad grin, he hobbled back into our ranks.

I was then definitively separated from my former buddies, assigned to the first battalion of the first company. I knew no one among the twenty whom fate had chosen to be my new comrades. The first battalion had its headquarters in Khenifra. We had never heard this name, and we did not care where we were being sent. We hoped only that we would be treated better than in Saida and that we would not be mistreated.

10

KHENIFRA

O ur bus sped on roads leading through fields and meadows and through desert. We traveled up and down mountains, through narrow gorges, past gaping precipices; and the tempo took our breath away. We stopped on a mountain pass to refuel. Snow had fallen. White flakes covered the torn flanks of the mountain. The winter scene reminded us of home. We were three thousand kilometers distant from our loved ones and going farther.

An inn on the pass seemed so petite and nice as if we were in Switzerland. We were touched in a peculiar way, approaching a European house in the strange world of a Berber tribe, amid their dirty huts before which ragged boys were scrapping. It was as incongruous as the classy ladies farther up the slope practicing their skiing—St. Moritz in Africa! The guest lounge served café au lait, white baked goods, and of course all kinds of drinks, without which modern sports would be unthinkable. We had nothing to do with this chic activity. After about a quarter-hour break, we again boarded the vehicle.

The trip continued. Now we found ourselves virtually surrounded on all sides by high mountains, enclosing a hollow at about an altitude of eight hundred meters. The slopes were bare and only seldom did the refreshing green of a wooded area break up the craggy background. The road hurried straight as an arrow toward a larger village along rows of trees seemingly planted by soldiers: Khenifra.

The native quarters stretched out on the right of our camp. Khenifra had five thousand inhabitants. Setting foot in the village was strictly forbidden. The town belonged to a not yet totally pacified zone. The tribal sheik, to whom the subjects were loyal, had not yet consulted with the imam, which meant he had not yet executed the act of submission. Though he didn't commit any hostile acts, it seemed advisable to avoid any contact with the indigenous population. Otherwise, it could have led to bitter confrontations. The natives were very sensitive to the manner in which they were approached, and Legionnaires were not people with any particular tact.

So we were limited to the European quarter. To it belonged predominantly the military administrative buildings and the many varied country houses of the civil servants. The government quarters were also off-limits to us. They didn't perceive much trustworthiness in us, neither grant us any respect whatsoever. So that left us: the two inns, right and left on the main street directly in front of our camp; the two stores offering for sale everything we might need in the middle of nowhere; farther away, the coffee house, The Post Inn, the three brothels—essential places for the Legion battalion and other troops stationed in Khenifra. We were seen socially in the brothel, not in any evil company, for our commander had a drink every day with the shrewd owner of the thriving sex business. We often emptied there a glass or two and danced to worn-out records with the girls, who tried to no avail to conjure up a steamy romantic ambiance.

All these houses were of the simplest construction, blockhouses surrounded by wooden fences, which somehow reminded one of a palisade. With the harsh landscape for a background, one could feel transported to the loneliness of the American Wild West, and we would not have been surprised if a band of unforeseen redskins on the warpath had appeared in front of us. Of course that didn't happen, but now and then a native mounted policeman would slink deftly from his saddle and tie his horse to the fence in front of the store. These policemen were dressed in pleated, white woolen robes, and when they were riding, their blue coats would flutter like wings behind them. In the evening, the moon eerily lit up the wild landscape. So strange—and yet everything fit together properly: the odd foreign place and the peculiar life we were dealt. If it weren't for the letters from home, our hearts would not have spoken so powerfully, and perhaps we would have totally surrendered to this world, as Legionnaires are supposed to—to have given up useless resistance and reconciled ourselves to our fate.

* * *

Our vehicles stopped in front of headquarters. We disembarked and lined up. With an examining eye, the commander looked us over. He truly had only one—for the other he lost in battle. He experienced quite a few, had fought in the First World War, then in the Rif War (helping to put down the insurgency led by Abd-el-Krim), and mostly in skirmishes and bloody expeditions, which since the French occupation of Morocco belonged to the Legion's daily bread. Our commander was a model officer, transferred there voluntarily. Only the boldest and most reckless, for whom battle is a daily need, choose the Legion. In Khenifra there was no getting bogged down in the dull rut of a provincial garrison; you had to prove yourself a leader of unbridled men. To be an officer in the Foreign Legion meant to be a whole man, not just a fighter, but also an administrator and even a diplomat. He had also to know and master the emotional being of the natives. The natives judged France and the French based on the officers. Far from home, dependent only on himself, almost without any contact with his counterparts to serve as examples or for advice, the officer had to dedicate himself to the task of convincing the savage tribes of the might and greatness but also the good will of France and to convert them to loyal subjects of his motherland. The reality bore witness to the fact that the French officers were up to the task. Also a sense of chivalry, long vanished from us, distinguished the Berbers tribes. In any event, stormy Morocco remained quiet during the war, as was also the case from 1914–1918; not only that, but the Moroccan regiments, as brave fighters of France, proved their loyalty and contributed an outstanding share in the campaign of Italy and later in the battles on the Rhine.

I made the acquaintance of several officers in Africa. By most of them, military curtness became the necessity to guard their distance, in the end ameliorated through kindness and humaneness. Even for those who committed body and soul to the craft of soldiering, the dulling grind of the service did not destroy the human aspect. A French officer attended a school that not only taught military science but also honored pure intellectual development. Unfortunately, in the Foreign Legion, slaves to war of a totally different nature, for whom being a human and a soldier meant two different things and had nothing in common, came between officers and soldiers.

* * *

My group drew quarters in a somewhat shaky barrack with clay flooring. The whitewashed walls had faded into gray. Iron beds were arranged right and left in meticulous order with a narrow aisle in the middle. A cast iron oven heated the room. We built our paquettage in the accustomed way on the board at our heads: the mess kit on one side, the canteen on the other, and the steel helmet on top.

We were fortunate to be housed in this dilapidated hut, where we could not be tormented so badly about cleaning during our stay, as was the case with other companies quartered in a modern building. Nevertheless, we swept the dusty floor several times a day, rubbed the oven with boot polish and the beds with oil, to make them shine beautifully; yet there was no tiled stone floor that showed every little dust particle and no steps to mop. We gladly declined the comfort of a new barrack, which for the new recruit only meant more work.

For me, this was the beginning of a life, which in the Legion could rightfully be considered fortunate. After two or three days, I was ordered to the company office. Chief Corporal Robert, our secretary, had received a homeland leave. That meant one month of leave and round-trip travel, amounting to about six weeks of holiday. I was to replace him and immediately become his apprentice. We quickly became friends. Robert was clever, cheerful, and held a positive outlook on life, as most French. He was certainly diligent; yet the work and the service and his responsibilities here, while forming a foundation, were not his life's objectives. In general, the Frenchman sees in his work the necessity, the method, to gain his subsistence in order to enjoy life. He will never let his work interfere with who he is, as a German might. Robert had done some foolish things and felt obligated to put the past behind him. And so he came to the Legion. That was by then a while back; he had atoned for his past long before, and the fortysomething was satisfied with his career. He was a bookkeeper; he didn't care if he practiced his profession in a private firm or in the Legion.

In the meantime, he was happy to return home again even if only for a month. The joy made him younger, smoothed his furrowed face, and he beamed from his dark eyes. Four years ago he left his native soil, shy, by the darkness and fog of night like an outlaw. Now he could again carry his head high and visit his old mother with confidence. What satisfaction.

Good Robert was a beneficiary of the war. During peacetime the simple Legionnaire did not receive any home leave. Now of course, the Legionnaire could not be denied the same benefits granted to other soldiers. What did four years in the Legion mean? The foreign regiments were quartered in zones that had not been deemed fully pacified and were therefore under military administration. There were no units of the Legion in the coastal cities like Casablanca. The chief military administrative places in Morocco were Meknes, Fez, and Marrakech, certainly beautiful places but they couldn't compare with the white pearl of Morocco. Only the headquarters remained at the main place, while the other units of the regiments wandered from one godforsaken place to the next. If we had lived in freedom and with people like ourselves, then we would have become as fond of Morocco as the French immigrants. But so, the Legion seemed like a dungeon, and faraway France like a star in the sky, like unattainable paradise. The letters we received from home did not quiet our yearning; they only increased it.

I didn't begrudge Robert his fortune and knew that he had served hard enough to earn it. And yet when he talked about his hometown and his mother, it was like rubbing salt into my wounds. My parents were very far away from me. We hadn't seen each other for a long time, for neither they nor I had travel permits.

The excess of joy made Robert almost childish. He showed himself off in his smartly tailored Legion uniform. The girls were said to be crazy about Legionnaires. Robert strutted about like a proud peacock. He made me smile. "How awful," he yammered unexpectedly, "that my separation papers have not reached the chief corporal's desk. Disgusting how the offices can mess things up. The most important things just sit there naturally. I'd like to know how the personnel cadre spends its time." The corporal's boss actually wore golden stripes and looked uncannily like a noncommissioned officer. The captain had for quite some time recommended Robert for promotion. I asked Robert if he didn't want to postpone his leave. The separation had to be confirmed within the following week. Robert gave me a look to kill.

* * *

As soon as he left, I moved into the small room adjacent to the office. Certainly, I felt connected to my companions and knew that their fate was also mine. What they experienced in basic training pained me. But I could not reconcile the happy feeling that came over me as I retrieved my pack from the ugly barrack and entered my room. When you had been housed in mass quarters for so many months and that rude environment had almost stripped away the consciousness of your own existence, then you had to be happy to become human again and have your own room. It was a modest stroke of luck. Nonetheless, for me there was no guard duty, no roll call, and no taps—and most of all, no basic training. And even my pack was no longer arranged as a paquettage but rested just like in civilian life peacefully in a closet. I needed only to make sure of satisfying Sergeant Major Albrecht, bookkeeper for the company. That was not difficult. For a start he let me only rule notebooks with straight lines. Later I titled his books in clean block letters.

Sergeant Major Albrecht was German—"a good German," as he always emphasized. On the other hand, he felt a profound connection to the French environment, thanks to his many years of service and through his marriage to a French woman. His wife was expecting, and naturally this child would be French. The very basis of human existence always remains the same: the impressions we receive in childhood and the way we were molded can never be erased. When later life forces us into different directions and a different model must take precedence, our being loses its unity and ails. That was the case with Albrecht. He wished France the best, but still dreamed of German might and greatness. The thought of "right or wrong" that so depressed a man like Sertorius was foreign to him. Albrecht was the same as any great number of Germans who, without knowing the extent of the National Socialist teachings, approved totally, declared themselves without thought in agreement with everything that was necessary in the opinion of the leadership for German victory and domination of the world—a flock of sheep blindly following the bellwether. But there is a blindness that produces guilt and gives rise to a crime not of commission, but of omission. One day Albrecht told me he dreamed Hitler had dug a subterranean passageway under the Rhine and the Maginot Line and would suddenly stand in the middle of France. Albrecht's conflicting essence was revealed in his words, more so in what he kept to himself than in what he said. He honestly tried, if not always successfully, to suppress the errant voice in his blood.

The departure of trained forces and the increase in volunteers brought about a sensitive shortage of corporals and noncommissioned officers. The regimental commander ordered all qualified personnel to Meknes for training as corporals. Even volunteers without basic training were admitted. The company captain wanted to ship me out, but Albrecht was against it and thought that I understood too little of the craft. I was happy to remain in Khenifra. The schooling of corporals far surpassed the toughness of generic basic training. In Meknes, we saw the exercises of corporals-in-training. The toughness of the movements bordered on the incredible. The manner of their rifle drills reminded me of a puppet play.

At the time a special unit was formed whose intended purpose was not familiar to us: they looked for Legionnaires who could ski. We thought it was about a terrain security force for deployment in the French Alps and would have eagerly applied, but to our disappointment only trained Legionnaires were being considered.

I would gladly have changed places with our office orderly, the small Jeannot. He was thirty-nine and father of two children. His contract was to expire shortly. Jeannot did not want to enlist voluntarily. After the end of his contract, in view of his age, he was counting on a transfer to the second reserve and expecting to arrive at a quiet little place. "In the last months of my contract, should I put my life on the line? God knows to where these asses will transfer us," he intoned, all worked up. The poor devil, his feelings didn't carry. Half of his light infantry brigade was shipped to Norway and fought at Narvik, suffering heavy losses. Despite his resistance, because of his job, he was posted there as a French citizen. Companions that had been in Narvik told me: One day we had to reach the coast of Norway in fast march. The participants: the Foreign Legion, the French Mountain Infantry, and an English regiment. The Foreign Legion covered forty kilometers per day, the French Mountain Infantry thirty-five kilometers per day, and the English regiment twenty-five kilometers per day. The Legionnaires arrived first and fought first. Jeannot was among them. He did his duty until some grenade shrapnel mortally wounded him. He got his quiet place in the distant north. Poor Jeannot, you didn't want to be brave, but became so nevertheless.

The forming of this brigade produced such a severe reduction in troops that the battalion commander decided to combine all remaining recruits into a single company. The remaining career Legionnaires could sufficiently and securely run the camp without any trouble. With a heavy heart, I retrieved my pack, left my comfortable room, and returned to my companions. "After basic training, I'll ask for you again," Albrecht consoled himself. "For now: good luck!"

11

BASIC TRAINING: KHENIFRA

The establishment of the new battalion was tough on me. I missed four weeks and had to start basic training from the beginning. My companions had in the meantime eagerly practiced rifle drills; they had stood before the targets and knew where specifically to place the rifle. In short they knew all kinds of things about which I had no idea.

And even though my superior knew that it was not my fault that I could not do as the others, I still had to absorb evil words of abuse. The superiors had to be crude and curse, as it was part of the service. I had difficulty readjusting to the demeaning treatment, having grown accustomed to the totally different approach when I sat in the office—then and there they needed me. Moreover, the initial well-meaning position toward the recruits had gradually waned. Before the war there were no centers in Morocco for basic training. The men and the graduates lived peaceably together, like humans with many experiences in common. But this solidarity didn't apply to the war volunteers. Like in Saida, always a deeper cleft came between us. After time, the noncommissioned officers developed a taste for training the green ones and took sadistic pleasure in our preparation. The tame Khenifra gradually became the gruesome Saida.

I can compare our drills only with Prussian barracks floggings. "You see there Waschke, the one with the neck of a bull," Robert told me one day, pointing to a noncommissioned officer who with overbearing words was giving my companions a dressing down. "Since time immemorial he belonged to the *Marinebrigade* Ehrhardt; after the failed Kapp Putsch, he fled to the Foreign Legion. Fine fellows—they certainly regret not to be with Uncle Adolf. I don't trust any Germans."

Now, concerning the roughness, the foot soldier mentality for many a sergeant appeared to correspond to the wild being of volunteer corps bands. At the outbreak of the war, Legion headquarters transferred the Germans, depending on their reliability, to Syria or Indochina. Several sergeants were retained for the training of recruits in the hinterland.

Our company consisted of about 40 percent Jews. I needn't emphasize that the German graduates didn't like seeing us. Certainly, making distinctions based on denomination or even asking about beliefs was banned. But if someone's name was Kohn or Levy, or if he had a bent aquiline nose, then race was no secret. Waschke certainly did not plague us because we were Jews, but to make soldiers of us. Waschke wasn't the only one. There was a certain Hinze, also a sergeant, and the two of them competed with each other to make our lives a living hell. Naturally they plagued the "Aryans" too, but they really liked raking the Jews over the coals.

Humans are not born poisoned by hate. The child searches for love, and where love is encountered, it blossoms like a flower in sunshine. Not for naught are the concepts of "human" and "good" closely related. The evilness of the world requires the hardening of human hearts, but even the hardened remain receptive of goodness. With admiration, we clung to our Sergeant Major Gerbault. He was like a father to us. You don't have to be a fiend to mold courageous soldiers. Gerbault recognized the capability of the German soldiers and did everything to make us equal to our opponent. When he pointed out the meaning of details and warned us of thoughtlessness, we sensed from his warm words his loving concern for us. We had him to thank, for example, when the captain once let us leave our packs in camp on one of our weekly marches. For this magnanimous man, we would all have jumped into the fire. But not all sergeant majors were like Gerbault. And it was not the sergeant majors that frightened us the most. The sergeant majors of the Legion are mature men with experience, but also decency. Career soldiers don't advance to sergeant majors very fast. For the most part, they were born French citizens, or at least naturalized; their selection, consequently, was predetermined.

But as said, sergeants were our first line of domination. The bad example set by a Waschke or Hinze also tainted the other corporals. This Hinze was the incarnate Himmelstoss that Remarque brought to sad renown.

Hinze put us down with devilish enthusiasm whenever we left the camp in the morning. We struggled through muck and undergrowth, constantly up and down, ripping our clothes, until we arrived, beat and disheveled, on the exercise field. This morning pleasure initiated the day, but only with the rifle drills did the day really come to life. After an hour we could barely hold our rifle.

As I think of Hinze, the image of my companion, Blauer, comes before my eyes. Blauer was almost forty; he had a weak build and had never been a soldier. He had a son in Palestine, from whom he had been separated for a long time. The trusting Blauer hoped that after basic training he would be transferred to Palestine or to nearby Syria. Inspired by fatherly love alone, he came to the Legion. Poor Blauer.

Blauer had taken apart his weapon; carefully he laid piece after piece on a cloth, with the objective that none would be lost. With a rag he cleaned and oiled each individual piece. Now the rifle had to be reassembled. A tough beginning—the pieces that before fit so well together, he could not now connect. A few small screws had slipped under the cover, and again others onto the clay floor of the barrack, driving poor Blauer to insanity—and, flustered, he rummaged through everything and made more disorder. Time pressed on, and Blauer was sweating and swearing, "Now in with the damn bolt." Finally it was in place, and Blauer breathed easier. At the next exercise, however, the weapon failed to fire. The others had long since fired their shots, but Blauer remained on the floor working on the trigger. Finally the irate corporal ripped the rifle from his hands and brought it and the shaking Blauer before the lieutenant. But he could not manage to make the weapon work. In taking the weapon apart, it turned out that the loading chamber didn't close because Blauer had lost one screw. Eight days in the hole. From then on there was always some kindhearted fellow who took apart Blauer's weapon and cleaned it. Whose knapsack was not packed per regulation? Blauer's! Whose pacquettage always stood crooked and brought Hinze into consternation? Blauer's!

You can bet that Hinze cast a sharp eye on the caricature of such a soldier. When the command "shoulder arms" was given, the cock, in French called *chien* (dog), had to rest squarely on the shoulders. The good Blauer made us laugh when he complained with animated sounds about this dog preventing him from becoming a good Legionnaire. When shouldering arms, Hinze loved to casually step in front of Blauer and to stare at him maliciously until Blauer began to shake and his rifle quaked like an aspen in a storm. Hinze's eyes turned red. "You shithead!" he thundered. Then he went into action; he grabbed his rifle and heftily pushed it repeatedly against the fellow's shoulder until tears came to poor Blauer's eyes. We had to watch helplessly.

Soon Sergeant Hinze became the most hated of the entire company. Woe to him, if we ever were supposed to leave the field together. His cup would runneth over.

Next to the drill square, we had prepared a so-called *piste du combatant*, a combat trail. It consisted of a water ditch, a wire entanglement, a wall, and all kinds of other obstacles that might greet the soldier in the field. It goes without saying, we had to overcome all the obstacles in full gear.

Hinze consciously turned it into a game of torment. One of our fellows, past the age of fifty, could not master the combat trail. Hinze took extra pleasure in persecuting him on the trail. The old man panted and clenched hard to the wall while Hinze, with his arms on his hips, smiled lasciviously and smoked a cigarette. Our blood was boiling. At that moment, the sergeant major unexpectedly appeared. "What are you doing?" he asked disapprovingly. Hinze stood there like a schoolboy. "Oh, we are all exercising," he said, attempting to excuse himself. "Sport is healthy." The combat trail was not on the daily program, but now we all had to step up.

I happened to be carrying a light machine gun, the ammo sack with the munitions and accessories dangled on my left shoulder. I did the circuit and came to the ditch, which had been filled with fresh water the previous day. Quickly, I estimated my chances of reaching the opposite edge with one leap. It wasn't a big one. If I slipped, I risked the danger to get the weapon and the munitions wet or even to lose one of the accessory pieces. So I went straight in. Most of the companions fared no better. When we all arrived back at the barracks, we took off everything: pants, underwear, leggings. We had to wash everything, and only on account of such a person. We all were boiling with rage. This brute, this slave driver, deliberately stole our free time, with the lust of a sadist. No, this had nothing to do with basic training. That evening he would not have left our barrack alive had we been able to seize him. For all this, Hinze was a weak, skinny little man with a decrepit face domed with a bald scalp, like a skull. His uniform hung unkempt over his scrawny body. He was more like a fidgety elementary school teacher than a well-tailored officer of the Foreign Legion.

Much to our chagrin, Hinze was also entrusted to the special training of the light machine gun (LMG) group. The LMG consisted of seven parts. We soon learned to effortlessly disassemble and to rapidly reassemble it. In the end, we could do it blindfolded. Every LMG marksman had to acquire the skill to rectify an LMG breakdown. Unfortunately, Hinze decided to make us into artists. Under the threat of punishment, we had to take the LMG apart and put it back together in less than one minute. To spur us on, Hinze promised a pack of cigarettes to the best one. We greatly feared the punishment because Hinze was usually true to his word. So we fooled him in that we blindfolded each other loosely enough to be able to see everything. The first one set a record time of thirty-nine seconds. Hinze was totally surprised at the marvelous performance, and with a smirk the comrade pocketed the cigarettes.

* * *

I had the greatest difficulties with the rifle grips. I had missed too much. Ignoring the scorn of my colleagues, I practiced in the evening with a broom handle. I was fed up with the continual berating of the corporal and had to finally come to deal with it. With blood, sweat, and tears, I finally learned all the grips. The disassembly of the rifle did not come easily to me, and of course I failed at shooting as I had never held a rifle before and had never been on a rifle range.

At the first shooting practice, I did so well that as punishment I was ordered to work in the vegetable garden on Sunday afternoon. Some of the other Sunday marksmen kept me company. The work didn't give us any trouble. We brought a couple of wine bottles from the canteen for the corporal to whom our oversight was entrusted, and he happily retired to the little garden house to partake of the mind-deadening drink.

In this war we tasted a variety of communal living arrangements. A soldier's life is one of those. It is the most severe, apart from the concentration camps, which occupy their own special place of honor on this earth. Now there are men who thrive in collectivism and really feel happy in its structure, find no fault, and have no other desires. Of course, it's open to debate if the Legion belongs to the most satisfying of collective life. We war volunteers didn't find it so, yet I knew career Legionnaires who could no longer adjust to life outside the Legion. They wanted out; they bitched a lot; they swore they would never renew their contract; and then when their obligation ended, they re-upped for another little year, and then still another little year, and so forth until they became unfit for a civilian vocation. I personally hold that one's fortune lies in obeying one's inner voice. In human nature, the most meaningful community is the family. It's no accident that in the oldest people—the Chinese, the Jews—it ranks above all others. Scholars claim that these people lead in the power to govern. Nevertheless, it is most of all the esteem for family values that best guarantees the continuance of peoples.

The punishment I sustained that Sunday wasn't severe. Also, I couldn't call it unjust according to the rules we lived by. It was simply an intrusion into my personal free time. They took four hours of liberty. After a week of the most difficult drills, a man was entitled to go out and breathe an air different from the abusive saturated air of the barrack. Sunday belonged to me. That was when I took the week's letters from Martha, left the camp, and sat someplace and read. There before my eyes was my home—the living room, next to me Martha—and we spoke to each other and in front of us the child played. But now I was under the dictates of the harsh laws of military discipline; they held sway over me and proved to me hourly that I no longer was my own person.

It was an ugly time—as ugly as everything arising from war and the mutual annihilation of people. Is trouble shared really trouble halved[5]? If it were so, then that war would have been a preliminary stage to human fortune, because millions of people experienced the same unending distress. To be able to bring friendly comfort and consolation to a loving soul—that is truly sweet. To pour out one's grief to a friend gives relief.

* * *

Fate was kind enough to bestow a friend to me. One day my old school colleague, Edi Wolf, whom I had met again back in Vancia, was transferred into our company. He occupied the bed next to mine. He was very thick skinned. In the worst of confrontations with the corporal, he maintained a stoic peace. He felt only coldness toward the Legion. He accepted the Legion from the most sensible standpoint: fatalism. Edi was built of hardwood. He stood up like a solid monolith, with wide shoulders, firm and unconcerned. Even if the war had uprooted him and banished him from Vienna to Morocco, it never robbed him of his lust for life. We often discussed the question of whether we did well by opting for the Legion. Edi said yes. "No man can make the fulfillment of duty dependent on outside influences, which in the end are only secondary considerations. We must take the path that we deemed right and therefore engaged to its end. What will be our lot after the war if we had not served? We must earn for ourselves a homeland, because it is man's need, because no one can live forever as a displaced person."

He was right. But no one can escape his skin. And I didn't have the thick hide of a Legionnaire. Time and time again, I beat my head against the wall that fenced us in. The uneventful battle pause gnawed at me. It ultimately would not bode well for us.

We no longer looked at the further course of the war with the same certainty as at the beginning. Why hadn't the Alliance engaged? So many

---

5 "Trouble shared is trouble halved," a German proverb.

of our fellows served in Germany. There was one, Walter by name, a perfect soldier. Even the strictest corporal could discover no blemishes on him. Walter was a deserter. Our drills made him laugh. "What does it mean in a serious engagement," he said, "when we parade around like puppets, march and demonstrate the rifle commands when we don't have any modern weapons." Indeed, in the entire battalion, there wasn't a single sample of the new gun models of 1937. "Look at this Negro rifle," Walter laughed. "That's from the year 1870. Do our superiors think that the German are Bushmen?" What was the use of cleaning our cudgels so thoroughly that the lieutenant could put his white-gloved hand into the barrel of the rifle without getting it dirty? What use was our proficiency in handling the light machine gun, when of the dozen in our magazine, half were so worn out that they failed to fire? What were we supposed to think when firing practice was postponed because the ammunition didn't arrive on time? At the front, would it matter if the buttons of our field jackets were polished to a high gloss? We never learned about modern weapons at all.

To our distaste for the drilling and violent tactics of the Legion was added our vivid doubt of whether the subordination of our basic selves could pay for victory, whether the emasculation of our person, transforming us into mere tools of the military, could achieve a necessary contribution. It was not just the question of whether this worst school for the disregard of man was too high a price to pay for victory. They sought to make us into amorphous foot soldiers. But modern war is not decided by mercenaries, but by men rich in ideas.

We were not particularly impressed with news form France, and it did nothing to motivate us. The service law that obligated stateless foreigners to service without weapons was finally enacted. They wore uniforms and were perceived by the French civilian population as soldiers. Certainly they remained under definite restrictions. But what kind of freedom did we enjoy? Right: we could visit the brothels at night. In our miserable state, we would gladly have switched with those serving in France just to see our relations from time to time. If they would finally transfer us to France, even if they sent us to the front! Oh, if they treated us like French born. But that was and would never be the case. The contradiction between our readiness to sacrifice and our awareness of our statelessness, from which everything arose, gave us no rest.

* * *

One day we practiced close encounter battle with bayonet. They taught us the best method to stab the belly of the opponent and to pull the bayonet out again. Stabbing was only the first part of the job; the second part consisted of placing the foot on the dead person or perhaps to brace yourself against a man writhing in agony to pull out the bayonet. Several others and I, in whom the war and prewar events had not yet choked off every emotion, became nauseated. For the moment we did not think of our opponent as a being who hardly deserved to be called human, who perversely tortured our brethren in faith and millions of other humans. We found the handwork of battle degrading. Close encounter fighting is the most gruesome manifestation of modern warfare. In vain, we searched for a little chivalrous remainder of battle from an earlier time. But it was just pure butchery, in which crudeness and toughness alone were learned. Only a stupor can so rob a human being of its feelings that it treats another in worse fashion than an animal. Or is it the air over the battlefield that intoxicates us with the stupor? Is the death-impregnated roar of the defenses and bombers, the flaming lights, the horror of the last judgment enough to stir the animal in humans? Yes, it has been stirred, and yet we still wonder that it threatens to devour us.

* * *

Everything gnawed at me, so that I thought only about the possibility of getting away. Every Legionnaire has rebelled against fate during basic training. During peace, a great number tried to desert. But we were at war. Desertion could not be considered. Even self-mutilation was not too big a price to relieve this torture. I thought I might succeed in bringing back my ulcers. To get back home I was ready to undergo an operation. An old-time Legionnaire told me about a substance proven to make you sick—simply swallow several of the strongest cigarettes. This would result in such an inflammation of the intestines that hospitalization would be absolutely necessary. I hoped that such an experience would bring back the ulcers. I can still see today how I secretly whispered to Edi when we went to bed, "Tomorrow I'll be in the hospital." Edi laughed, "How are you going to accomplish that?" I convincingly said, "You'll see."

With great revulsion I forced down two cigarettes of strong tobacco and awaited the results. The fever was not forthcoming. My intestines remained in order. Edi teased me but changed his attitude when I confided to him what I had done. At the same time, I began to feel a hefty pain in my armpits. A few days previous, I again had to work in the garden as punishment and developed blisters on my hands. They now became filled with puss. In my state of mind at the time, I was convinced that the cigarettes poisoned my blood and favored the conditions for developing pustule sores. I wasn't totally in possession of my faculties. Wide reddish stripes appeared on my right forearm and on the back of my hands. My arm felt almost paralyzed. What to do? I dared not see the doctor. So many stories abounded about Legionnaire doctors. Many sick colleagues reported that the doctors considered us inferior beings and treated us that way. I believed only too willingly that they wished to waste no time with us and from sheer joy loved to perform operations and amputations even when not absolutely necessary. Again, I was not of sound mind and believed all the gossip. Blood poisoning appeared to be in the offing, and the doctor could cut off my finger or even the entire hand.

Edi was outraged and struck his hands together. "How could you do such a thing, Camillo? You're making an invalid of yourself. Aren't you thinking at all about your family?" He was right of course. As I went to bed that evening, I folded my hands like a child, prayed fervently, and beseeched God to forgive me just this once. I called to him, not as to a heavenly being, but as to a generous Father graciously ready to forgive a remorseful child. And so strong was the power of the prayer that my pain diminished, and I fell asleep consoled. I vowed to consult with the doctor if there was no discernible improvement within twenty-four hours. I had been foolish enough to tempt fate, so now I had to endure the consequences. My regrets were so sincere and my prayer so profound that God heard me. The red stripes disappeared, and the immediate danger of the poisoning had passed.

In contrast, the septic wounds had spread quickly. Big wounds formed on the inner and outer surfaces of both hands. The medical assistant made copious incisions with scissors to the extent possible. Poking around with the sharp object in the exposed flesh, he asked me if it hurt. "No," I replied, because a Legionnaire could not admit pain.

Thick bandages covered my hands. I could not wash myself and festered in filth. However, the worst part, despite everything: I still had to participate in all the rifle drills. The firm grasping, the hard slapping of the weapon with the hand was a torment, because under the light gauze, the infection burned. The effort to have the doctor excuse me from the rifle drills failed. The medical assistant gave me no access. He claimed, "If you handled your weapon properly, you would feel no pain."

Fortunately, the sergeant major was more understanding. He permitted me for a time to appear with the light machine gun. So I stood quietly while my colleagues practiced their rifle positions.

Slowly, the wounds began to heal. Yet it would take another two months before I could remove the last bandage. I was already happy, when after three weeks, the one hand was totally healed, and I could finally clean myself thoroughly. I still remember how good this washing felt. I played with the water and splashed about like a little boy at the fountain.

12

ON THE EDGE

My illness so stirred me that the everyday hardships now seemed trivial and secondary. I was so thankful to God for his forgiveness of my rebellion against my fate and the self-inflicted misery that I was happy to carry out my daily obligations. So the sinner must expect to happily meet every pain because it gives him the opportunity to prove the sincerity of his regrets. I had become worn down. I no longer gave things any greater importance than they deserved and carried out my duties with sufficient equanimity, and gradually became a useful Legionnaire.

No one can assert his will forever against the relentless drill. I had seen many a Legionnaire with exceptional write-ups, who at the beginning of his service tried to desert. Captured and sentenced to prison, he comprehended the futility of rebellion. Such strongly endowed personalities, later, often became exemplary Legionnaires. No robot can take the place of a self-assured person.

My colleagues included all sorts of people who enlisted because there was no other possibility to escape internment. Several, anointed with all of life's experiences, thought that after a short detour into the Legion they could return to civilized life. Rubin belonged to this type: a middle-aged man, a little portly, and comfortable. As basic training began, he pretended to have flat feet. The sergeant thought his behavior suspicious and even the doctor thought Rubin feigned the condition. He obstinately refused to march. So for the time being, he was left in the barrack and was assigned the housekeeping and cleaning duties. The clever one thought he had won the game, but that just became his undoing. The sergeant had him observed and caught him walking briskly and with pleasure about the barracks, without the slightest hint of the tired steps he had always found characteristic of a flatfooted person. Of course Rubin was immediately put into prison and thereafter so mistreated that he lost all urges to revolt. A few months went by, and Rubin became an outstanding Legionnaire.

* * *

Soon I became one of the good marksmen of the company. As soon as I could again take up the rifle drills, I discovered that they were not that difficult. With time, everything became part of the flesh and blood.

At marches, I also had the resolve to show I was a man. The practice marches began at about ten to twelve kilometers, with hardly any backpack. We marched each week, and each time the distance increased, and more pieces of equipment augmented the carrying load. So the marches slowly lengthened to thirty-five kilometers, and at the end we carried all our gear, including a second uniform, underwear, a second pair of shoes, blanket, tent canvas, two field bottles each with two liters of water or coffee, and of course rifle and ammunition—a considerable load.

One of the most tiring marches was the ascent of the Table de Zaians. Goose-stepping along the hardly recognizable mule track, we plodded forward with powerful steps and heavy panting. At ten o'clock in the morning, the sun burned down upon us in full heat. We loosened the neckband and loosened our collars. Even so, sweat flowed out of every pore. We carried our full gear on our back and had to cross a ridge at twenty-four hundred meters. The trail climbed steeply to a pass. I thought I would never scale this last piece. My lungs labored like a mountain locomotive, and my heart thumped as if it wanted to blast through my breast. The sweat ran down the languished faces of my comrades. It was useless to explain to the corporal that we could go no further. With crude invectives, he took the rifle from the tired soldier, and if he was about to break down, he also took his knapsack. But then no one cared about the exhausted soldier. For that reason, we had to move forward, we gave it our all and our best. The relentless "we have to" whipped us forward, pulling our unwilling legs high. We wanted to stay back on the sunburned rocky slopes without nourishment, soon without water, alone in the middle of the indigenous people, who may have been hostile toward us.

Small, fat Schreier sobbed like a child. For naught, the corporal gave him a dressing down with crude words and threatened him with punishment. The most defamatory crudeness had no effect—Schreier was done. The words no longer penetrated his hot head. Just another fifteen minutes…just ten minutes…No, he could not; his legs no longer supported him. A long time before a corporal had already relieved him of his rifle and backpack. Slowly Schreier dropped to the rear. Apathetically, concerned only with oneself, the column sauntered past him, who with an unusually tear-drenched, disfigured face, mechanically and half consciously tarried about. How much farther could it be to the pass? Fear struck me that I might not reach it. The clear visibility gave the illusion of reduced distances. Only a small gap seemed to separate us from the heights, which after every gain retreated anew. The pack pressed. The straps cut sharply into the tormented flesh. Another hundred meters… another fifty meters.

The first ones had made the top. The lieutenant let us stop. We made it. With one move, I threw the monkey off my back, and then we mechanically stacked our rifles into pyramids. The cramped faces loosened up. We sank into the grass, wiped the sweat from our brows, and breathed deeply. Relieved, I opened the bottle. It was filled with coffee. What a savoring moment as the quenching liquid moistened the parched palate. I looked around. And who sauntered in totally spent yet happy? Fat Schreier. His full cheeks were black with dust, crossed by white channels carved out by his brook of tears.

After the effort of the climb, the way home seemed easy. With renewed strength we descended. We were proud of our accomplishment. We rested once more in front of the indigenous quarter from where the "trainards," the incorrigible latecomers, were sent via a side route directly to the camp. We others arranged our uniforms, buttoned the neckbands, and cleaned off the dust. Drum and trumpet led the formation. With proper posture, in columns of four, to the tunes of the music, we marched through the city. When the noisy street crowd saw us, they fell silent. The natives left their stalls and planted themselves on the curb as we marched past in the slow cadence of the Legion. The crowd gazed on us with respect. They knew we had a difficult march behind us and were returning as lively as if we had just left the barracks. With satisfaction, the commander reviewed the recruits. Dismissed! We put the rifles away and hurried back to our barracks. We fell on our beds. On this day there were no more exercises.

Those were our marches. Each one called on the highest capabilities of our bodies. We learned to always demand more of ourselves, to squeeze out the last bit of strength on demand.

* * *

Soon the sun burned so hot that it was no longer possible to march during the day. At two or three o'clock in the morning, we broke camp. We had to be familiar with this land even in the dark, for woe to the Legionnaire who lost good judgment.

On one of the nightly outings, I was the intermediary between the lieutenant, who rode at the helm, and my section. We lost the trail in the dark. Very weakly, its rocks glimmered in the indistinct gray. We had to maintain contact. Time and again it was necessary to make sure the troops were behind me and then catch up with the lieutenant. Several times I thought I had lost my way, until I rounded a hairpin turn and the light buttocks of the gray horse popped up in front of me. Finally it dawned. The red sphere hung over the naked rock stratum and lit up the craggy mountains. The trail wended through the morning-fresh fragrant pine forest. Thick bushes, overgrown with giant ferns grew in the shadows of the tree trunks. Now and then we came upon a storm-uprooted tree with all kinds of secret life rustling under its branches. At a clearing, the lieutenant rested his horse. I reported that our section was completely in place and everyone accounted for.

We left the forest behind us and marched along a brook beside a meadow with sparse growth. A flock of sheep grazed under the watch of half-naked boys. At a settlement of many dark, low, clay huts, we halted. Ragged children crowded curiously around us, while the old folks looked us over with unmoved faces. We had no idea what they made of us, as we couldn't read their expressions.

Always, whenever possible, we rested at some village. The march was exercise and police patrol at the same time. If it weren't for the war and maintaining a readiness for unforeseen transfer orders, we could have moved ever farther into the mountains. The Berber tribes had to know that we were on duty. Our presence guaranteed the tranquility of the country.

When we returned, we took off our shoes and socks, and the sergeant major personally inspected the condition of everyone's feet. Woe if any one professed not to be able to march. We did learn to maintain our feet. Instead of sacrificing our last pair of socks—during the entire service time, we took only one pair of socks—we wore rags and rubbed our soles and toes carefully with grease we obtained from the kitchen. The "Russian" socks proved their worth for the best.

Slowly, the drill also became routine and no longer terrified. We practiced rifle drill for only one hour per day. We spent the rest of the time on combat exercises. The new sergeant major was a reservist and himself not up to the most rigorous strain. When we fanned out for an assault and had to throw ourselves on the ground, we remained in the grass longer than necessary, before we continued with the next leap, which brought us closer to the enemy position.

* * *

Spring had moved into the land in full force. Its wonder lasted only a few weeks, as everything flourished and faded so quickly in the fast-moving life of this southern climate. Yet in this short time, what beauty to behold: in extravagant abundance, the precious flowers covered the newly awakened earth, and over it floated the unblemished blue sky of the south. We wandered frequently with rifle and pack through this impetuous, intoxicating creation, yet hardly anyone noticed this beauty. To our ears, all that mattered was the sergeant's whistle, the crude words of a corporal; our heavy packs rested on our backs, and yet we had to be careful to fulfill every order. Unaffected we moved through the dew-freshened meadows with a small bit of sleep still in our eyes.

At five each morning, revelry tore us from our slumber. We quickly made ourselves ready, shouldered the rifle, and went off into the field. Were it not for the dilapidated huts and tents of the Berbers and the scrawny cattle of the Moroccan peasants, the gentle fragrance of the morning would have transferred us home.

As most of us spoke German, we usually sang songs in our native tongue. "Annemarie, where does this voyage lead?" we intoned almost every day. It was our commander's favorite. Well, where did the voyage lead? When the singer then asked, "Annemarie, what will your child be?" We replied grimly, "I'll only give my child away as a Legionnaire." Mild mockery—the only ridicule of the Legion the sergeant major allowed. When the bastards didn't want to sing lively, the sergeant major ordered us to march in parade fashion with "shouldered arms" until we were worn down and sang. So it went day in day out. We were caught in the Legion's cogs and would be freed only when we forfeited the last breath of our being.

Exercise, shooting, marching...The marches stretched ever longer; the targets moved farther away. We threw grenades at alleged enemies, learned to deal with the gas mask and breathe artificial air. Murder handiwork had become multifaceted and demanded diligence and skillfulness.

Maneuvers included night exercises, in which we had to creep up on the enemy without being seen. If the scout was discovered, he was greeted with a hefty artillery salvo. Once the corporal had me disassemble the LMG in the dark, and a screw fell under the tent cover into the grass. A terrible fright came over me. Nervously I groped along the ground. Ten anxious minutes passed until I found the thing.

Another time, we demonstrated rifle grips to the captain. "Fix bayonet!" We had to mount it quickly onto the rifle barrel. I was a little too hasty; at the next command, it suddenly became loose, flew point-first through the air within a hairsbreadth of my neighbor's head and sped into the dirt. The sergeant major gave me a singular look. If looks could kill, I would no longer be alive. The earth did not do the furious drill-master the favor of swallowing me up. The incident passed so fast that the captain, inspecting another group, didn't notice the accident.

* * *

A three-day field exercise in the mountains ended our basic training. After a lengthy hike, we made camp on a meadow surrounded by wooded slopes. Four men were assigned to a tent; one of them was responsible for order. You had to be careful for the oversight was very strict. A painful cleanliness ruled the camp.

Each of us brought a blanket. Two men slept together. We spread one blanket on the ground and wrapped ourselves as well as we could into the second. On top of that, we placed our field jacket and coat. The nights were cold, and we shivered with the frost.

Stiff and frozen through, we arose from the hard bed. We were no match for the Bedouins, whose bodies were used to the abrupt temperature changes from the sun's heat to the night freeze. A wadi forced its way through the steep rock face a few hundred meters from the bivouac site. We wended our way there to take a refreshing bath in the frothing water. As we went about our business on the sandy bank, a nomadic Berber brought his flock to drink. I paused, awestruck by the strange scene. The shepherd, supported by a knotty walking stick, slowly advanced at the head of the animal train. A pleated robe fell from his tall stature, and a long white beard bestowed on him an aura worthy of reverence. In the middle of the sheep, a young woman of unusual beauty and charm swayed on a donkey. The animal, as if conscious of the honor, rocked its precious cargo with care like a mother its child. Like a scene from the Bible, the strangers passed us. They hardly glanced at us, the intruders in their land. My thoughts strayed to the Jews of the once promised land. I thought about my ancestors, who certainly once wandered through the countries of the Middle East, through the bestowed blessings of their gracious God, laden with all their possessions.

In the wild, you had to constantly remain on guard. Not too many years ago, hostile tribes overran the nightly field camps of the Legion. We put our rifles into rows and secured them against theft with chain and lock. A guard stood at each campsite. Rifles were greatly sought after, and it being possible often to acquire them free-of-charge justified cultivating one's thievery know-how. The men of the desert are masters in the use of weapons. A European doesn't know how to deal with an old ironside in whose hands it turns easily into a tool of death.

In such a place, where all forces had to be unified, the consequences of insubordination were much worse. My companion Lederer, to his own chagrin, discovered corporal punishment. During the march, he stepped out of line to rest and had the audacity to talk back to the corporal urging him on; he wouldn't take orders from an idiot. We had hardly arrived at our destination when the unfortunate one was thrown into the desert jail, a low, narrow one-person tent. The imprisoned had to lie on the bare earth under the tent canvas. The meager space didn't permit pulling in the knees. The canvas was stretched taut and hindered every movement. You had to relieve yourself there and then. The prisoner was defenseless against the pests of the desert—tarantulas—and left to the mercy of scorpions. Lederer had to spend twenty-four hours in that jail until the lieutenant mercifully released him. The poor devil squinted complainingly as he stood in the bright sunlight. He was covered with a rash and had need for medical attention.

The adolescent Berber boys, the *mutschus*, accompanied us even here, carrying an impressive store of lemonade bottles in their pannier. There was no canteen in the field camp, and their trade prospered. The officers had the foresight to take along a small wine barrel; the refreshing drink streamed from the spigot into their cups, which we had to observe with thirst. Finally, though, the lemonade and the Arabic tea did the job.

The mutschus were not independent entrepreneurs but worked for an older youth. He, a resourceful lad, established a profitable business caring for the thirsty and hungry Legionnaires. At the exercise square or on marches, the rascals always surrounded us, offering their wares for sale. "*Beni, beni, tschai, tschai*," (beignets and tea) was their battle cry. The beignets, honey fritters, were not to be scoffed at. Naturally, a Legionnaires stomach was of the constitution to digest the indigenous low-quality goods, baked in rancid oil by this unwashed social order. The *tschai* was a rather cheerless drink, served in glasses that were never rinsed. Fortunately, the Legionnaire is not spoiled.

The sale of baked goods and drinks was only one branch of the multifold enterprises of the mutschus. Once a week we went down to the river on which Khenifra was situated to do our laundry. The mutschus, who knew our schedule better than we did, were already there and ready to do our wash for fifty centimes. They had their own unique method. The wash was dipped into the water and rubbed with soap, then stacked on the flat rocks of the river's edge and stomped on. That took about fifteen minutes whereupon the boys rinsed the wash and spread it out to dry. The sun did the rest and bleached well, not a brilliant white, but usable. The mutschus further sold the cleverly leftover soap to increase the profit they gained from our comfort. But it was nice to lazily stretch out in the sun.

In the evening, when we went into town, the unavoidable mutschus dogged our heels and tried with all their powers to drag us to a "fatma." "Cheap and a real beauty, sir—a flower." This trade also brought profit.

* * *

On the last evening of the bivouac, we kindled a huge fire and sat around it in a circle. The flames roared brightly into the night sky while the forest secretly rustled. The crackling sparks flashed in the darkness. The lieutenant asked us to sing songs of our homeland. We sang them and were filled with bitterness. Homeland—how long had it been since we had one? We dreamed of home and peace and were given war and desolation. A breeze from the woods stroked us, and the breath of wind touched me softly. It was as if Martha stood next to me. I turned my head, but only another fellow sat there and, lost in dream, wiped his eyes.

Pour the wine, let us sing rowdy songs proper for a slave, let intoxication wash away our sorrow so we can become men again, Legionnaires in Africa.

* * *

This night, I stood watch. Above me, the night sky formed a golden, star-spangled dome. Inaccessibly far stretched its dark blue blanket. I raised my eyes, and in the middle of the gleaming splendor, I spotted the shining polar star. There was the north; there was Europe; there lived Martha and Paul. Lost in thought, I strutted back and forth before the entrance to the camp. Fifteen paces to the side and fifteen paces back; and again fifteen and once more fifteen. My heart ached; I was lonely, and on my shoulder rested the weapon. They gave it to me because there was war. I was a foot soldier among other foot soldiers. They put a printed paper before me, and I signed it. I traded away my earnings, my life—and for what? Now I wanted to go home but couldn't, because somewhere in an office lay that paper bearing my name.

With my right hand, I once stroked my child. That night it rested on the strap of a loaded weapon. Should a human approach in enemy clothing, I would shoot him—for that is the order. They took my intrinsic being and taught me obedience.

Again I paced off the fifteen steps. I said a prayer and calmed myself. The world lay in a deep sleep. I buried myself in its nightly splendor to totally call it my own when the sudden steps of the sergeant making the rounds tore me from my captivation. In the nearby stall, the horses whinnied, their massive bodies waltzing in the rustling straw. The chains jangled against the wooden post. Then everything fell into total silence.

* * *

How often did I look up toward the heavens on those starlit nights and steer my thoughts, seeking clarity and composure, toward God in the glory of his creations. Humans feel small and insignificant in the face of the solemnity of the African night. What are we before God and his omnipotence? A piece of dust on an unworthy planet. Are we destined to be crushed by world events, like pebbles that the torrent sweeps away and grinds into sand particles? And yet, in those nights, my heart yearned for God. He must be there; he must exist. Doesn't the well-ordered movement of the worlds attest to that? Prayer gave me strength and hope.

* * *

We often guarded the prison of the Legion, which then held two Frenchmen. They deserted because they could no longer tolerate being in Africa instead of on the front. I felt strange seeing them. They were French; I was stateless. They carried shackles; I carried a rifle. Six months before, I was a prisoner myself, and French soldiers guarded me. Now it was different. I had given up solving the puzzle of life, because I was a soldier and not allowed to think.

* * *

Our basic training ended one day in the middle of April. One by one we reported to our captain. He asked each of us if we wished to volunteer for the front. We all said yes, and we all said it willingly. More than 90 percent of the company voluntarily renewed their vow. Would it have taken courage to stand up for one's beliefs and say no in that moment under the strict eyes of the captain? I won't deny it. But we, who said yes, said it from the heart. We wanted to fight, true to our promise.

The company's record attested to the honor of the volunteers. It didn't matter to us if we were not permitted to fight like our companions in Europe.

13

RECOVERY

Soon they announced the new assignments. Most of us were transferred to companies headquartered near Meknes. Again the groups, connected by common experiences, were torn apart. I said good-bye to my dear Edi, and did not see him again.

Khenifra was designated as the development center for recruits. The training method, proven out on us, was made a model by the higher-ups.

At the same time, a new course for training corporals began in Meknes. Our sergeant major asked me if I preferred becoming a corporal to taking over the office affairs in the training company with him. The choice wasn't difficult. Having just survived first training, I had had enough. Military ego didn't plague me. I was a good soldier, a natural advantage even if I decided in favor of a desk and balancing the accounts. A scribe ran the danger of being looked at scornfully by his superiors, as a bureaucrat, if he didn't also show his manhood on the drill square. At any rate, we would all leave Morocco sooner or later and be relegated into a fighting unit. Administrative personnel with military grades were not exempted.

So for the time being, I remained in Khenifra. Typists sat glued to their office chairs like flies on honey and through patience, industriousness, and business acumen earned colorful lapels and golden braids. The timid soul of the bookkeeper concealed itself behind the smart uniform of a courageous fighter.

* * *

In the office, I again came together with my old friend Robert. He had been promoted to chief corporal. His leave home was a thing of the past; only once in a while, in the quiet of the evening when we made ourselves comfortable, Robert would speak of it and reflect on how nice it was to be home: how happy his old mother was to see him, what eyes the neighbors made, and how life went on unhurriedly in the town except that the men had all enlisted. Morale was high, and everyone hoped for an early victory.

We spoke often about the Legion. Robert had much to tell. He too had been in Saida and didn't think he would make it through basic training, which then took nine months. If he weren't French, he surely would have deserted. "But so? I could never have returned to France." Poor thing. A real Frenchmen will never quit France; Geneva and Brussels are French, but otherwise, for the French petit bourgeois, people who don't know how to live inhabit the world.

The Jewish question didn't exist for Robert. We were all humans. To him, the Germans naturally seemed barbaric and in general unusual and strange sorts of beings. Robert came from the north of France. In the First World War, he had already become familiar with and learned to hate the cold German militarism, devoid of any morality, and its way of treading on humanity. "National Socialism," according to Robert, "is just the last expression in a striving for power unconstrained by any moral considerations. I was sixteen years old when the Germans broke into our home and dragged me off to forced labor. My father was enlisted and served on the other side of the front; I was alone with Mother as the soldier took me away. Do you think I will ever forget that? And then a comrade said to me we should refuse to work, because its war work, and we should not help the Germans. And civil law forbade the misuse of citizens of an occupied area. So we all stopped working, whereupon the cold-hearted

Germans let us go hungry until we were all worn down. The war ended; the Germans appealed for world compassion and explained that they were human like others and were dealt a bitter injustice. Whereupon the victors yielded. Had we been asked, the north French, the Belgians, we who had been tormented by the Germans, we would never have given the barbarians the opportunity to reap ruin upon the world a second time. How can two people understand each other when one aims to live life in peaceful bliss and the other lives for the arrogance of power? One considers the creation of the individual a crowning achievement, and to the other the individual appears only as a valuable member and tool of a racist society. They will always be foreign to me—these contemptuous humans who feel appalling joy in others' pain." Robert continued, "Look around you: who mistreated you recruits the most? Didn't you breathe easier when an Italian or French noncommissioned officer was put in charge? You're wrong. Observe Köbel and Schlechter more carefully, those two that work in the magazine—closet Hitlerites. I once overheard them sing the Horst-Wessel song or whatever else their hymn is called."

Concerning Köbel and Schlechter, I also had the impression that they regretted their rash decision to leave Germany and to be now in the service of France. Even among the Legionnaires of German origin, who after the expiration of their contract settled in Morocco, there were those, according to Robert's opinion, who inwardly stood with Nazi Germany and could deliver Hitler a fifth column should he ever find a footing in Morocco.

"Thank God," as Robert customarily emphasized, "no danger threatens us behind the Maginot Line. We will vanquish the Germans with our blockade."

Oh, it was still the time for song to break out steadily in the Post Café: "Nous iron prendre notre linge sur la ligne Siegfried" ("We will hang our wash on the Siegfried line"). Everyone sang this song on the hit parade, from the captain to the simple Legionnaire. Three months later, these words became horrible scorn. Do they still play the song "When the Cowslips Blossom" in Germany?

* * *

There was plenty to do. Old and new regulations unleashed a stream of paper for deployments, account settlements, extracts, requests, and letters. Measured by our use of paper, we had the best organization in the world.

At the start of every month, we reported to regimental headquarters how many men, horses, and weapons we had, and further provided the names, nationalities, previous experience, and educational background, and training of the troops. In addition, there were reports about illnesses, accidents, and quite a lot more. Particularly important was the records book, where all the service agreements were noted. From time to time, we had to generate an extract with a person's pertinent dates and determine if the person needed to renew his contract or to where he eventually wanted to be discharged and so on and so on.

The individual service notebook contained the inspection notations and descriptions. A majority of the inscriptions pertained to penalties. Every misdemeanor, written up according to law, with verdict and cause, was noted in the company books and personal records of the Legion. Some Legionnaires with lengthier service time had so many penalties on their accounts we added additional sheets over previously added sheets in their service notebook. Typing the penalty extracts was no small matter. Most concerned disorderly conduct resulting from intoxication, an offence that brought no harm to the honor of the offender.

We were paid every two weeks, a simple matter for the war volunteers. We received the colonial pay of fifty centimes, also a Morocco allowance of fifty centimes, and a tobacco subsidy of twenty-five centimes, for a total of 1.25 francs, or just enough for one pack of cigarettes. The pay of career Legionnaires was indexed to their age and was substantially higher. In the evening, after payout, the bordellos were at maximum capacity.

* * *

At the beginning of May, new recruits arrived. More than half were Spaniards and came from the concentration camp Gurs. They could hardly speak a word of French. In addition there were representatives from the witch's pot of Europe. We counted twenty-five nationalities in the company: Russians, Poles, Lithuanians, Dutch, Rumanians, Hungarians, Portuguese, Italians, Germans, Austrians, Czechoslovakians, Belgians, and many others. Even a Syrian, two Chinese, and a Japanese served with us. Most of these people had lived in France for many years and were duty bound to serve.

From time to time, they inspected the military pass books. We had to report to the lieutenant and present our service notebook to him. That was usually triggered after a futile attempt by the lieutenant to communicate with a recruit—the good man might not even understand a request for his name—who would sobbingly burst out, "La liberté éclairant le monde" ("Freedom will light the world"). All these people who couldn't even read or write in their mother tongue loved freedom. For them, France was the symbol of all human rights; its sparkle drew them on, and they fluttered to it like moths ready to burn in its flame. Millions of people from every country highly valued living happily and fighting for France; Germany was feared, France loved. It should always be the country in which the unfortunate could lift their heads high with trust.

* * *

But war prevailed, and from the barracks square, we saw France from its bad side. The new recruits didn't get along well. In my time, the troops were less diverse. My companions came for the most part from the internment camps for Germans. These camps had now been emptied. In the new arrivals, only those of a single nation found ties for friendship. At meal times there were sometimes such ugly confrontations that the lieutenant finally entrusted the corporals with the distribution of rations. To the many insults we had to endure, a new one was added: we joined the Legion because of the food. From "Engagés pour la durée de la guerre" we went to "Engagés pour la durée de la gamelle."[6] The poor Spaniards, who starved in Gurs, pounced with total greed on the mess

---

6 From "Sign up for the war's duration" to "Sign up for the duration of the food bowls."

buckets. That was understandable. As the saying goes, don't mock the afflicted.

* * *

One week we did the usual march. A couple of crude fellows flushed out a tarantula and a scorpion and set them upon each other. After a lengthy battle, the scorpion vanquished the tarantula. Not satisfied, the animal torturers built a fire and threw the scorpion into the flames. Confused, the animal tried to escape, but always the fiendish boys pushed it back. It is said of scorpions that when danger of death threatens, they will commit suicide[7] by stabbing themselves. The two chums wanted to be convinced, and they didn't rest until the tortured animal reared up and turned its venomous stinger upon itself to end its life. The fellows watched the drama with cruel contorted faces as the scorpion writhed in pain. The tips of the flames crawled through the grass, and the woods threw strange shadows around the fireplace. It was as if ancient stirrings forced their way, as if evil spirits were sacrificed here. I turned away and before my own mind's eye there emerged, in an unending line, pyres of flaming wood and humans with pained expressions on them. All around stood humanity—we all stood, you and I looked on, fanned the flames and gloated over the torture. Cries rang out: "Oh, the witch! Oh, the heretic! Oh, the enemy! Oh, the Jew!" Humans died, and others who also called themselves human applauded loudly. When this drama ended, drinks were passed around for refreshment and strength. The townsfolk drank and ate and went home satisfied and spurned on from the delectable theater; they gathered up their wives and bred children just like them, human beings, and they thought it good.

Could I be a partner to fornication, a companion of injustice? And what was I when I went with them? Well, we were like animals and subject to the law of the jungle. I obeyed it myself. One evening, I met

---

7 Scorpion suicide is a myth. See for instance "The Myth of Scorpion Suicide: Are Scorpions Insensitive to their Own Venom?" *The Journal of Experimental Biology* 201:2625–2636.

a Spaniard in the washroom. We didn't understand each other because he spoke only Spanish, and I but German and French. He looked at me, and I at him. Then he said something I didn't understand. I replied curtly he should get out of my way. I did this because we lived under the law of the fist, and I could not retreat from anyone. The Spaniard didn't understand my words either, but he knew that per our law only brute strength held sway. So he pounced on me; we became entangled and beat each other. In the end a sergeant entered and threatened to arrest us for disturbing the peace, yet I managed to get away in the dark. While undressing, a chain with the Madonna fell into my hands. I must have torn it from the Spaniard's wrist and hadn't realized it. My lips bled, for my opponent bit me like a wild animal going for the throat of an enemy, and on my hands I carried the deep impressions of his teeth.

Another time, a fellow had cleaned his mess kit at the fountain. A second one came by, and without a word he punched the other away. The hook to the chin broke three of the unfortunate one's teeth. The lieutenant locked the ruffian into the prison. Was prison really a punishment for someone who previously was a pimp? Lenzi, as he was called, was never on the drill square, so much the easier to find him either in the hospital or prison. He had a venereal disease, as many there did. In the first months of the war, the company consisted of only career Legionnaires; in Oued-Zem, where life was "easier," half the troops had syphilitic lesions or gonorrhea. A visit to a bordello with healthy, perfect, medically supervised "material" cost five francs. On the other hand, you could sleep in an indigenous hut with a fatma for nothing. The fatmas would give their bodies for a piece of bread or bar of soap, which you could get at no cost in quarters. Those were my companions at the time.

* * *

I didn't like going into the so-called city. The permitted quarter measured barely two hundred meters. We constantly ran into ranking officers, whom we had to greet with a snappy salute. In addition, we had the duty, even on the hottest summer days, to wear the waistband. We pushed the field jacket into our shorts like a shirt, and then the three-meter-long blue sash was artfully wrapped around the hips. Over that we placed the leather holster for the sidearm. These duds lent a smart, though operatic impression, which I would rather have done without.

I preferred therefore to escape the camp after work by a back gate and, in the company of a friend, enjoy the coolness of the evening, ambling through the meadow of Oued. One day, we went for a walk, when suddenly a screeching woman's voice, interrupted by the halting French of a career Legionnaire, penetrated our ears. We went closer. There stood a woman with dirty skirts folded up over her head and fighting hard against the lecher, who harangued her in a hoarse voice. When he saw us, he let her go. The woman fixed her clothes. What a disgusting sight. The woman had no nose. An intolerable rash covered her face. The bare nose bone protruded from a leprous, festering, eaten-away hole. We staggered back. But the woman, seeking protection, clung to me. I pushed her away; I couldn't do anything else.

* * *

Not all fellows stood so low. But didn't they throw all of us into one pot? While the worst swear words bounced ineffectively off the hardened fellows, there were others twice as sensitive to the rude tone of the barracks. True, I worked in the office and no longer participated in further training. I was approached politely, and the unflattering words were not intended for me. But my soul was tied to my fellows and suffered with them.

As office orderly, I often visited the residences of the noncommissioned officers. Several of them, particularly those of higher rank, were married and some even had children. I took it as a favor to be able to idle away fifteen minutes in a home. The houses of the noncommissioned officers were of the simplest construction, more like summer huts passing as houses. They stood on pilings and were covered with corrugated iron. A company remained in one place no more than six to nine months.

And so the furnishing was appropriate to the frequent moves and consisted of very few solid pieces of furniture. But just the presence of a woman brought a certain hominess to the unadorned rooms. I hadn't been in a home in over six months, having only resided in the mass quarters of the army. It was a celebration for me to be permitted to enter these houses, to talk to a woman—who was also a housewife, sometimes even a mother—and not a prostitute. Fortunate was the man who could still call such a humble home his own, who had a small place for himself alone, who had a person to live with who understood him and for whom he wasn't just a number.

Our need for a woman whose home wasn't in a bordello manifested itself in odd ways. Indigenous cleaning women, who sold their favor at higher prices, made their fortune by us. We fooled ourselves and talked about buying living creatures, which in the end were available to everyone, to an allure and exclusiveness available only in our imagination. Most people paid no heed, and values vanished in this sad environment.

The submission of a woman for money in Morocco is not measured by the same values as in Europe. It's an achievement that in certain circles has no contemptuous connotation. I knew a cleaning woman who in an easy accessible manner earned her dowry this way. And she forged very civil plans: marriage, purchase of a business, children. She would have been very surprised if I said to her that her plans were highly incompatible with her current trade. Yes, we lived in a strange and for us disconcerting world, and we yearned for ours.

Our yearning for France steadily increased. It lived in us, unreachable, endowed with all the magic of a dream. Our souls flowed into the letters we wrote home; the few words hid the nightlong desires and churned within us, not for what we wrote, but more for what we failed to write. We dreamed in the disquieting dark, of the bedroom of home, in happiness stretching side by side, sharing delicate words whose breath quietly dissipates; their murmurings alone indicating sweet caresses. And then we sat in front of the empty paper and wanted to entrust it with our true feelings. And our hearts, having disclosed themselves only to the innocent night, were ashamed of the unseemly trend, and we write totally drily that we were well and hoped to hear the same from there.

At the end of April and into the beginning of May, the vacation lists were drawn up. The front was quiet—so quiet, we hardly thought about it. In a few weeks, the first of us trained Legionnaires would be permitted to travel to France. We could hardly contain our joy at our good fortune. I was among this group and hoped to be with Martha in July.

* * *

All of a sudden, the fierce war turned hot. The fronts mobilized. Vacations were put on hold, and we no longer thought of leave; unexpected, misunderstood, crazy circumstances forced the ban.

Waves of German successes reached higher and higher. The enemy army was like a storming sea of victories, breaking through every dike and now flooding over everything. Soon, Belgium and Holland were overpowered. An unleashed torrent of German masses rolled into France through the breach of Sedan. We listened with dread to the shattering reports. Could this overwhelming force be stopped? Would there be another miracle of the Marne? But there were no miracles. Events happened fast and furious; Paris was evacuated. Worries about our loved ones accompanied concern for France. The mail stopped coming. We were cut off. The postal clerk irritatingly pointed to the slack mailbags. What would happen to our wives and children when the enemy occupies all of France? Which persecutions would ensue? With the fall of Paris, the last hope of resistance faded. If only they could succeed in maintaining a European bridgehead from which to attack again.

And we sat in Africa, incapable, and could do nothing to help our kin. We couldn't fight. We could only look on with senseless fury, as we were robbed of home, homeland, and hope.

It was mid-June. The campaign in France neared its end. Robert no longer shed tears; no words crossed his clenched lips, which had suddenly become so narrow. The furrow between his dark eyebrows deepened and crow's feet had developed on the corners of his mouth. We decided to have wine so that the intoxication would drown everything, and to help forget the disgrace of our defeat. Italy had sided with Germany to secure its share of the bounty. It was said we would be sent to Tunis.

It didn't happen. Who had spread the rumor France was laying down its weapons? That couldn't be believed. It could not, it must not be true. Should we have believed, we Legionnaires, who had been taught to fight to the last bullet, to the last breath? Six weeks previous, in remembrance of the brave and loyal Legionnaires, we celebrated Camarón[8] Day.

The French troops protected Emperor Maximillian and even in Mexico fought in the front lines. Camarón was a hacienda near Palo Verde, Mexico. In April 1863, a small infantry patrol defended it against an overwhelming enemy force. No one capitulated. When the battle ended and the enemy overran the Legion's last defensive position, the enemy found only dead and heavily wounded on the battlefield. No Legionnaire survived unscathed. And Camarón was no longer.

On June 25 we pressed against the wall of the noncommissioned officers' barracks and listened to the radio within. We heard Marshall Petain's speech. An ice-cold vice squeezed our hearts. It took our breath away. France—the great France, the hope of Europe—bowed to the Germans. We dared not look up. Tears welled up in my eyes and rolled down my cheeks; I was not ashamed to cry. Our world collapsed; the war appeared ended.

---

8 For the Battle of Camarón, see for instance, http://en.wikipedia.org/wiki/Battle_of_Camarón, accessed September 2009.

147

14

ARMISTICE

Now the worst time began. The war had ended, and we were no longer needed.

A crippling, stifling air floated over our camp. Legionnaires were foot soldiers, useful only for combat. Suddenly, we were just plain stateless foreigners, an undesired burden for a country that had to take care of its own sons. For a few days, we thought the war would continue in Africa. Our officers wavered between Petain and attachment to England. General De Gaulle had many adherents. Our officers were not used to laying down their arms.

In the meantime, French troops landed on African soil. The air force had been moved for safety to Morocco. With the fleet that had left France's harbors prior to the armistice, there came exceptional weapons systems, large artillery units, and tank divisions that intensified the resistance possibility in colonial territory.

Then, the Moroccan headquarters for Petain were formed. The will to fight was further extinguished. The army, used to following orders, followed the orders of the leadership. Then the British attacked the French war fleet that lay anchor in Mers-el-Kebir. The newspapers seized on the opportunity; an unbridled propaganda campaign unfolded and began to agitate against the allies of yesterday. Humans are such inconstant beings!

To be at pains to speak one's tongue on the great event, a Legionnaire has no opinion of his own, only the will to convince himself. For the sake of this worry, he denies today what he said and thought yesterday, and will stone tomorrow those whom he obeyed today. Our officers, who only yesterday spoke enthusiastically about carrying on the fight as partisans in the rugged wilderness and the best hiding places of the Moroccan mountains, suddenly spoke of working together with Germany, and no longer knew England. England? Perfidious Albion, who conspired to draw us into war, and now only thought of herself and despicably abandoned us?

From all this, what would happen to the Legion? Would it be dissolved? Fear overcame the Albrechts, Waschkes, and Hinzes; they could lose their entitlement to a military pension after such long service. Again, we had brilliant proof how small, egoistic, and mean humans could be. The noncommissioned officers worried about their futures; we were the scapegoats on whom they vented their wrath.

The life of the company went on as usual; basic training of the recruits continued without any yielding to contrary orders. In the office, as always, we made pointless lists. Despite our worries, we often laughed about the self-confidence and also the collapse of surviving bureaucratic inertia. Every month we regularly attended to extracting the names of the Poles who served with us instead of with the Polish Army Association. Drawing up this list served to protect the affected Legionnaires against consequences for draft avoidance in the Polish Army. And even now the paper mill continued. Instructions upon instructions fluttered into our office as if nothing happened.

* * *

The sun blazed down from the sky. The earth absorbed all the heat and also reradiated it back. The arid ground showed fissures and cracks. Dried-up grass crumbled underfoot. Every bit of green had disappeared, and the wide landscape was rendered in tones of gray. Fine dust filled the air. No cooling breeze found its way through the mountainous wall surrounding our garrison. The stifling air mass was equally inflaming and suffocating. It seemed life had died out; only bloodthirsty gnats and flies swarmed about. At noon, we lay tired under mosquito netting.

My dear Robert's face had morphed into an impassive mask. His hometown was occupied. His loved ones no longer wrote. Where did they live, and were they still alive? The war was lost. Again and again, he yielded to the addiction to forget with wine. Often I dared not speak to him, with his glance so empty and cold. How could I console him? What else was there to say? We lived on, like automatons whose clockwork continued to run because no one turned it off.

Neither did I have any news from Martha; she must have certainly remained in Lyon. They said Lyon was part of the free zone. So I hoped for the early departure of the Germans from this area. Impatiently, I kept a lookout for the postal clerk, and like me, all my companions longingly waited.

* * *

An edict came: amid the misfortune of the nation, the army had to set a disciplined example. The screw constricting our life turned ever tighter. Our bedrooms were infested with bugs. Each company sent two men to conduct a vermin extermination course in Meknes. We lost the war and went bug hunting. The barrack rooms were emptied, beds, desks, and racks moved into the courtyard and rubbed with oil. Then the rooms were shut, every crack made airtight, and gas pumped into the rooms. Two days later the annoying critters strolled like before along their usual trails and slipped into our beds.

Then we built a street crossing through the camp from the officers' casino to the battalion headquarters. We dragged, huffing and puffing, the heavy gravel up from the Oued River. We hacked, we dug, and finally we leveled the street. "Heave ho!" With all our strength, we braced ourselves against the barrels while other comrades pulled with ropes. We sweated like the Jews of old in Egyptian bondage. Passing soldiers of regular French regiments laughed at us. Why didn't we use tractors? But the Legion was frugal.

Spent and despondent, we sat eating at our tables in the evening: spent from the hard work under the scorching heat, disheartened and despondent in thought about our future. The hard swear words, which we heard day in day out, rang in our ears. We were imprisoned for the smallest violation. In France disarmament had started a long time ago—not here. The worry that we might not be released entered into our racked brains. Despite the armistice, would we stay in Africa until the conclusive peace? Our superiors preferred such an option: for what would become of them if we were all released? The ranks of the career Legionnaires had thinned out; so many had fallen in Norway or France. To build squads out of the war volunteers, numerous appointments were executed. What was there to do with all the trained troops? In accordance with the condition of the armistice agreement, the Legion would become a police force and used on all occasions to protect the colonies from attack, particularly on the part of England.

Of course we would have gladly fought, but we saw that the regular French regiments were returning to their families. We wanted to go home as well. We too had wives and children. We too burned bright with the yearning for our loved ones. Should we now again be treated as pariahs? Leaves were—and would remain—frozen. Were we to have neither leave nor disarmament? Could we ever see our kin again? Would we even fight against England?

One day we were called into our captain's office. It was about returning home. He asked us if we thought about going back to Germany, Austria, or Italy. Was this a trap? Had perhaps—even this rumor circulated—the Germans asked for our extradition? We all decided for France.

Nonetheless, it leaked out that a few isolated career Legionnaires—we were all asked without exception, not just the war volunteers—asked for repatriation to Germany. In a few days they were posted to an assembly camp near Meknes. Wild rumors circulated about their fate. Oh, the rumormongers had information about everything, and in our confused state, we listened to every nonsensical report. Now, of the Legionnaires who wished to return to Germany, it was said that the Germans regarded them as traitors. Cast out by the French and Germans, they had to do forced labor in the Sahara. That was only the wish conjured up by an over-imaginative fellow. The Legionnaires disposed toward Germany actually went to Germany. The forced labor in the Sahara was our own lot. But it is just as certain that today the men who then turned to the apparently victorious flags—assuming they are still alive—forever regret their decision. It should happen to everyone who worships the momentary result and considers crime as their right, as far as it may benefit them.

For the first time since Petain's laying down of weapons, a smile flashed across Robert's face. The magazine storekeepers Köbel and Schlechter decided for Germany. So France got rid of its false brothers. They should suffer their deserved penalties.

Many of my companions earnestly believed in the extradition. One morning two young fellows were missing at the morning roll call: Jews ages eighteen and twenty. They had deserted. Their friends testified that they intended to cross into Spanish Morocco. Spain? What was there? Even there existed a Foreign Legion. It was true: there were many more joining General Franco's regiments. But wasn't that still better than Germany?

Fortunately for the two of them, the police force was promptly engaged. We immediately sent out telegraphically personal descriptions. Several locals brought the pair back into camp. They were absent for only a few hours. The captain knew that this was only the case of a foolish prank and not an intention to flee the flag. Desertion in wartime and in war territory, to which Morocco belonged, was subject to court martial and penal company, if not more. Woe to the unfortunates who were sent to the penal battalion near Colomb Bechar in the southern Sahara. The climate could kill you; the discipline was tougher, and the labor as hard as in the Bagno.

The young lads escaped with an arrest penalty. They were fortunate in their misfortune.

Others were not treated with such leniency. For example, a Spaniard had whistled "The Internationale" in the courtyard of the barracks. Unheard of in the Legion. His penalty was raised from eight days to one month of the strictest detention. His file went up to the general. Every superior raised the penalty and passed the file higher up the chain of command with the comment: the penalty needs to be increased.

Prison sentences rained down on us. A comrade had used a knife to enlarge the opening of a belt that held his sidearm. The sergeant noticed it at inspection. Even this unfortunate one had his head shaved and was imprisoned. Damage to state-owned property! Oh, the practice of law, which understands how to package every human act into neat and tidy paragraphs. Never had the courtyard of our quarter offered such a sight as now, with so many prisoners without shoelaces and suspenders, who under guard scrubbed floors and split wood.

* * *

The uselessness of our presence also frayed the nerves of the officers. They could not get over the shock of the defeat. Despite all the decrees commanding discipline and dignity, never had so many cocktails been consumed. The categorical prohibition against the sale of alcohol in our canteen did not apply only to those in basic training. The battalion commander was transferred to the front several months before and had fought courageously. He had returned, with his wounds barely healed, a tired and sad man.

They now cared for us more enthusiastically. Suddenly, the higher-ups discovered that healthy teeth were a prerequisite for good digestion, and for the soldier—essential to life. We sat at our typewriters late into the night to hurriedly prepare the papers for the dental examinations. Everyone's teeth were carefully examined. But with that, the uproar passed—even the most urgent treatment needs never came to pass.

In the blazing heat, the number of fever cases increased. We received quinine. I resisted as often as I could. Yet sometimes the heavy pressure would not let up, my limbs failed me, and hammers banged my head. We had to have quinine. It was the only thing that brought relief.

The physician explained that, after a two-year stay in Europe, all ill effects of colonial life disappeared. I hoped he was right. Numerous of the fellows who served in Africa had permanent damage to their health. Units of war volunteers built streets in the southern Sahara in over fifty-degree (C) heat. It was astonishing that as Europeans they worked this way, even if only for short stretches. But after all, what was the worth of a war volunteer's health and life.

* * *

We celebrated the national holiday, July 14, in a subdued mood. They stormed the Bastille a long time ago. Now the Germans were in the process of building a new Bastille for the stubborn people.

A delegation of the battalion, in full ceremonial dress with white gloves, went ceremoniously to the cemetery. We looked over the many tasteless graves of the many Legionnaires killed in action in Morocco. Many died—hit by bullets, brought down by illness—true to their oath, in service for a realm and objective serving only as foot soldiers.

All people and denominations were represented in that cemetery. Peacefully they rested here next to each other: Christians, Jews, and Muslims. All of them fought and suffered for France. They were now honored as heroes and shining examples. We only suffered; we didn't fight, and no one was killed in action. We could have been heroes also, had we died on the battlefield. Heroism is the highest honor that can only be won through the last sacrifice of death on the battlefield. Living heroes are a contradiction; they have an embarrassing and disturbing effect in the pettiness of the everyday. No, we didn't die and we didn't become heroes. Instead we were troublesome: the superfluous stateless, who no country wants on their soil and everyone swears at. We had come to eat, to be released from the concentration camp—or so we were daily accused. What did we want anyway? What were we promised?

No, we hadn't been promised anything other than combat and slaughter. But were we worthy to fight for France? And were we not worthy to live for France? Who were the people who dared to recruit us? We were given the great mission to protect the fatherland. Or was it not a great mission? Or was it only the fate of slaves to sacrifice their lives in order that others may enjoy theirs? How many masks did our society wear? The resonating words were only words for the plebes among soldiers, the pariahs of the army, the Legionnaire.

We saw everything, we knew everything, and we understood everything. But we were powerless. Ours was mindless anger and despair.

* * *

And I went there, buried my face in my hands, and bitterness fulfilled me. We were aliens, enemy aliens, when the war started. Now we were troubling Jews and, besides that, aliens again. I embraced the earth with my arms as if to unite with it, to finally find a place of refuge and a homeland.

* * *

Weren't those who fell in action better off, who were buried here for their final resting place? We fired an honor salvo at their graves, for they were heroes. As we so greeted them, the red and green colors of the Legion fluttered in the wind. We remembered them; us—they tried to forget.

Yet the dead knew nothing of all this. The shots could not call them back to life. Only we lived, but we suffered. For now our fight began, the battle for the very life of the stateless in a defeated land.

15

DEMOBILIZATION AND JOURNEY HOME

Things stood badly for France. Crowds of unemployed streamed from the factories, which until now produced war supplies. The changeover to civilian needs was met with difficulties due to the shortage of raw materials. The Germans seized the reserves of the country. A great part of the French army became prisoners of war and was sent to Germany. A further million soldiers, per agreement, were released from service within a short schedule. Where to with all these people? The Germans initially had no intentions to use French workers because they planned to bring the war to a victorious end in the shortest time. Unemployment threatened. Would they relegate us stateless aliens into camps again?

The dismal picture of the concentration camps came into our field of view. Peace—but was it peace?—terrified us more than the war. The German troops finally left Lyon, and I had news from my family. They fortunately were safe and sound, but now they needed me, for their need was great. Martha wrote that acquaintances assigned to the Legion's march regiments were home again.

In North Africa, disarmament also started. Different age groups of reservists returned to France. Only for the Legion were no directives issued. Should the Legion become a police force at its current strength? Seeing the French return home discouraged us to the depths. Always more oppressive, always more degrading seemed our life. We longed to be away from Africa, to wear civilian clothes, to be human again.

Several circulars I saw in the office proved to me clearly the difficulties ahead. As a result, I procured a proof of residence and begged Martha to obtain a work contract. I recommended all my companions do the same. But many laughed at me, and saw me as a pessimist.

Some enlightened heads knew what was going on. They agreed with me. A Belgian journalist, a lieutenant in his homeland, was driven here by occupational curiosity. He suffered terribly under the humiliating conditions to which we were subjected. Gaston wished only one thing: to be away from there and purge all traces from his mind. Poor Gaston also wrote letters left and right to obtain his papers. He had a tough time because the editors of all the Parisian papers had scattered every which way into the free zone, and many of his acquaintances had fled abroad.

July passed; August came, and with it new regulations regarding the return home of the French still in Africa. In September, we figured the last of the reservists would be released. Frenchmen, much younger than we, had departed for France. We were in such despair that even the wine didn't lessen our afflictions. What degradation awaited us? The new regulations, pertaining to the age of the career Legionnaires, clearly indicated the intentions to decrease the Legion's numbers. There were grounds for the supposition to intern us in Africa because newspapers wrote about all sorts of plans to bring the colonial riches to greater blossoming: there was the Trans-Saharan Railroad, which was to connect the rich lands of central Niger with the countries of the Mediterranean; there were rich mining opportunities for valuable raw materials; in short there was an abundance of everything, much more than in France.

If the lords of Vichy had just a little human sensitivity, they would have treated us differently. Germany at that time had not demanded sending war volunteers to camps. But the Vichy powers were the foot soldiers for Germany, even in spirit, and we were troublesome Jews or undesired fighters from the red brigade. It was precisely our honest will to serve that now separated us from our loved ones. Those refugees who served without weapons remained in France and for the most part at home. On the other hand, those of us who wanted to be soldiers were punished. Life was not just.

* * *

On August 6 we held a celebration in remembrance of the battles of 1933 in which the company had participated. In ceremonial dress and to the accompaniment of music, we marched past our commander and through the festively decorated quarter. The green-and-red pennant waved proudly at the lead.

An entertaining evening ended the day. One fellow sang a short song, a poem he had composed himself about the disarmament. Somewhere soldiers were going back to their families. The officers listened to the unwelcome song in silence. But we paid no heed to them. When the singer finished, a storm of applause without equal erupted from our ranks. The song had a real message. Yes, we wanted to fight—we wanted to do it willingly even then—but we wanted justice, and we realized the uniform had become an oppressive burden. A discordant note came over the celebration. Hardly ever had there been so much drinking as on this evening. Our corporal, a gaunt, emaciated man, could stand up only with great difficulty. With a bottle of wine under the arm, we staggered together into the magazine. I could still think, so I had to drink on. Even if I was an outlaw, I had to strive to be an old Legionnaire's equal.

And then too came the moment I could no longer keep up. That was when the corporal, totally drunk, searching for sensual passion, offered his disgusting body to the men. Spare me the picture. Legion! I was horrified. I went out and cried bitterly.

Yes, it was time to think about the internment. For a liter of wine, the store clerk left me a pair of new shoes. However gruesome the future might be, I still wanted to live. While I was gathering the papers for a possible release, I also gathered the necessary articles for the internment camp. I knew its needs. That's how humanity is: giving in to unavoidable fate and clinging tenaciously to a miserable existence, holding out hope in even the deepest misery. And only life is surety for the future.

* * *

My friend Gaston was transferred to Meknes. As luck had it, a simple Jew from Poland then became my best companion. What would have happened to us if we couldn't support each other? Camaraderie had to replace everything. It was our home; it was our family that compassionately shared our worries. We fled into its bosom when sorrow overwhelmed us; we shared our needs and also our joys. Always pushed hither and yonder, again and again separated from old pals, the soldiers tie the bonds of torn friendships to the thread of a common destiny at another place, searching and finding anew the good and indispensable comrade.

Gottlieb was a noble and brave man, filled with youthful cheerfulness. In addition he was an exceptional soldier and one of the best marksmen in the battalion. We were delighted that a Jew belonged among the ranks of the most highly rated, for in truth in the weeks following the armistice, some officers began to look upon us Jews with suspicion. Often I sat with Gottlieb on the bench in front of the quarters' gate. We attempted to puzzle out the course of the war. The English fought on and gave no evidence in the slackening of their resistance. So the war was not at an end. Perhaps the fortunes would change. In adversity, one demands consolation. We beseeched God, with fervor and piety, to stand by the English and give them strength to persevere through the German Luftwaffe attacks. With that, a whole winter would be won and the next year, just maybe, America would declare war on Germany. Could we properly fathom the profound despair dominating us? Germany at the high point of its power—Hitler in Paris announced his impending entry into London. He controlled all of Europe, which knelt before him, was ready to work with and for him, and in the face of this colossal power, only England, unarmed as we all knew, was still proud and fighting. With fear and trembling, we listened daily to the news. We breathed easier when we saw that the Germans had not yet succeeded in the big coup.

Sometimes Osman, a Turk who had served upward of twenty years on his bent back, would sit with us. He carried a pair of medal ribbons in his buttonhole, and now, as a loyal aide-de-camp to the battalion commander, he quietly led his life. He had divined that Turkey would soon enter the war and halt Hitler's advances. That was how the dear fellow sought to console us. It was a sad time. We worried about the course of the war, about our loved ones, about ourselves, plagued everywhere and everywhere powerless.

* * *

August 15 came, unlike any other day. The army command honored us with a circular: two densely written pages set forth under what infinitely difficult conditions the war volunteers could be demobilized.

I rejoiced. All the papers and affidavits they requested, I had practically in my hands. Thanks to my loyal wife, they were already on their way and would arrive via airmail in a few days.

My dearest Martha, how gladly you ran the many errands in the hope of having me by your side soon. You and my child: you were everything to me: home and fatherland. So it was then and remains so today. The letter that I wrote that day was happy and joyous, for my joy carried over thousands of kilometers to you. And I saw your loving face, into which the war engraved some painful lines, and despite all the suffering, all was well and hope blossomed anew.

The night following the posting of the circular letter, I worked at my desk like a man possessed until dawn broke through the window. I gladly did it and didn't tire because the meter-long list that I drew up concerned our release. When the lieutenant came into the office that morning, I could hand him the list. Now finally, we just had to wait patiently for a little bit.

The next few weeks would have been easy had there not been so many comrades without hope. Only a few had planned ahead and could hope to produce their papers quickly. How could the majority of us with our simple life assume that men who offered their life for their country would be denied a return there? Wasn't it anything but a prohibition if return home was dependent on affidavits for residence, proof of employment and means? For us money meant freedom; would that change after the war? Whoever could show possession of five thousand francs went home; those who didn't went to a forced labor camp.

Many of my comrades lived in the newly proclaimed occupied zone and lost touch with their families. What could the comrades from Alsace do? The regulations of the Vichy government gave them the difficult choice of either declaring themselves for Germany, or more recently, to go into an internment camp and never see their relations again. So the men of Vichy organized a shuttle service for Germany. At every opportunity, they put the words "work, family, fatherland" into conspiratorial mouths. The seriousness of moral propositions rests on their universal applicability. You can't be kind and limit kindness to only a few people. You can't call yourself a defender of the fatherland and evict from it certain groups and people. You can't pretend to care for the family and tear foreign families apart. But that was what the men of Vichy did, and because they were liars, their lies were appreciated at first only by us, the stateless, but consequently also by the children betrayed by their own country. The disregard for the families of foreigners led directly to a sellout of French citizens to Germany. It's not necessary to say anything more about it here. Only so much can be said here: the Germans, tolerating all the sorrow the Fuehrer brought over Socialists and Jews, in the end, in consequence, experienced that sorrow themselves. For not only are the world and peace inseparable, and not only is the welfare of the world totally bound to the welfare of all people, also moral law is a whole—whoever forgets that, destiny will remind by dreadful means.

* * *

On September 4 I sat as usual at my desk when suddenly the orderly came running, all out of breath, waving a telegram in his hand. There it was in black and white, or rather in green: Five men of the company were being called to Meknes for demobilization. I was one of them. I laughed and I cried. And Robert, good old Robert, laughed with me and gave me friendly jabs. I gathered my equipment, which had been sitting untouched in a corner, and returned it. A soldier who can finally give up his field jacket and steel helmet—the world was mine! I could think only of going home. In the evening we went out and sat in the best hotel frequented by the officers. The prospect of freedom made us self-conscious; the soldierly fear of the officers disappeared.

At five o'clock the next morning, we left the barracks. Gottlieb escorted me. We touchingly embraced each other. I wished him from all my heart that he too would soon be released. He was such a kind, good companion that I saw in his honest face only happiness for my fortune; I did not detect even the smallest hint of envy. That day, as once in the camp, I felt connected with those good humans because I had experienced the camaraderie of the stateless and their readiness to sacrifice.

* * *

We had assumed someone was waiting for us in Meknes; why else had we been ordered there by telegram? But that was not the case. The Legionnaires serving in Meknes, who had submitted their papers long before we did, were all still there and waiting.

Nonetheless, the transit company of the regiment was no longer dominated by the same discipline. In the morning we firmly but reluctantly went to roll call, were firmly looked over by the sergeant major and assigned various duties, though the swear words he reserved for us rolled off our backs without effect. His favorite expression was "Is this still a company, or is it a whorehouse?" We just smiled.

I got to know Meknes better than during my previous stay in January—what a clean, white, shining new city. The broad terraces of its cafes, restaurants, bistros, and pubs offered invitations. The gentle evening breezes wafted. We would have thought we were in France had it not been for the palms and the wonderful, clear, dark blue sky.

With several fellows, I visited the *quartier reservé*, the great attraction of Meknes. The reserved quarter was a whole city of multifaceted entertainment places and shops. All the houses served one purpose: soldiers had to have girls, and in Meknes there were still twenty to thirty thousand. The quarter was totally enclosed by a strong, high wall.

Guards posted at its gates kept order. Often brawls broke out between soldiers of different origins and races. In a small lounge at the gate, a medical worker held office, to prevent bad consequences from the pleasures of lovemaking. Here no one came down with a venereal disease. And whoever indulged in forbidden love outside the quarter and got sick as a consequence would be punished. A kind of labor community existed between the hospitals and prisons.

A lot went through my head, so that I couldn't muster the joy that someone on vacation normally experiences in the mystifying life of the Orient. But no one who traveled there could escape its unique magic. All races were represented in the houses of ill repute: Negro women with ebony faces, Morocco's fiery Berber women, the austere Slavs of Eastern Europe; from the dilapidated Arabic women of an evil-smelling saloon to the well-kempt European lady of a luxury establishment. They sat at the doors and offered themselves to you, tempted you with their advances, even embraced you around your neck and tried to drag you to her boudoir. The fight for customers was the delicate problem of the quarter. I forcefully tore myself from a dark-skinned beauty soliciting me hotly and heavily, and then I entered into a coffee house. The atmosphere of that place compared well to a European bar.

Slowly I took leave of Africa. Soon I would no longer belong there. I would take off the smart Legion coat and wear civilian clothes. A last look at everything, and soon I would be in a different world.

* * *

The head of the discharge office in Meknes was once the sergeant major in the First Company. I perceived that as an advantageous circumstance, the more so because my friend Gaston, the Belgian journalist, was his secretary.

Gaston dampened my confidence. The Moroccan bureaucracy was not partial to Jews and would have preferred to lock everyone up in a camp. As to the earlier fighters of the International Brigade of Spain, their internment was a done deed.

"What does one understand by a secure means of making a living?" Gaston asked me. "Who vouches that I'll be able to live from my essays, that your shop will survive the general collapse of the economy? There is no compelling rule. Everything is basically unclear and depends on the arrogant interpretations by the military powers. And even if our papers are considered sufficient, it doesn't mean we'll ship out the next day. There are only a finite number of ships."

My hopes hit bottom. In addition Martha wrote I should hurry because, with the exception of the prisoners of war, the entire world was at home, and people were starting to think we were after all not soldiers like all the others. "People"—that was the world, which in those days was ours, of the petit bourgeoisie, to whom everything that didn't move in the well-trodden paths of the masses appeared suspicious. In this case the petit bourgeoisie were right. We weren't like the other soldiers, the problem children of the state; we were the outcasts of Europe, unworthy of living in the circles of the good citizens. We of course also wore the honor garb of our time, but it was just a disguise. The masked ball had for the time being come to an end, and out of the soldier's clothes emerged the despised foreigner.

Suddenly our discharge became serious, but in another sense, the way we wanted it. Urgent directives finally demanded to reduce the stand of the Legion. Perhaps the German armistice commission had been at work. All the regiment's war volunteers were brought to Meknes, where in a few days the disgraceful deed was carried out. Discharged from the service, they were all placed into labor camps and, under the most humiliating conditions, forced to slave away in sulfur mines in the desert. Not everyone endured this disgrace. Our dear comrade Peiser preferred to take his life. The gentle lad with the sensitive fingers who coaxed melancholy tunes from the half broken-down piano in our canteen decided to seek his homeland in the earth, which the hard world had denied him.

I was called into the discharge office that same day. Though no better than my companions—in that they wrote into their service booklets, "Discharged as Legionnaire, transferred to the Company of Foreign Workers"—I was permitted to return home. My companions looked at me enviously. Why did I go free and the others not? Why does one bullet hit its mark and another doesn't?

Hot and heavy exchanges filled the discharge office. I presented my papers, the work agreement. An overly clever sergeant studied the writing, carefully inspected the imprint stamp, and then said, "And what then when the company goes under in a few months? Then you'll be out on the street!" Hot and cold flashed across my back. That was how the rabbit ran. Looking for help I glanced at the sergeant major I knew and heard him speak, "Don't make any ugly pranks. The agreement is in order." I breathed easier.

Gaston showed me a last bit of friendship; he put me on the first transport. I will never forget his kindness. Beyond all the adversity of Legion life, beyond all the hardship and humiliation, shines bright the friendship of good companions and the knowledge: there are also good people.

* * *

The trip to Oran took forty-eight hours. Rolling toward Algeria, we lay in dazzling sunshine high on top of the railcar heavily laden with corn. Only at night did we slip into our small, tight compartment. Of the approximately two thousand war volunteers under the jurisdiction of the Meknes' Army Group, twelve men returned home—of which I was one. As night came, I gazed up at the magnificent sky from which millions of worlds sent bright greetings. The train sped forward, the wheels clattered, and it seemed to me they were singing the song of life. It said, "Forward, always forward. The past is over." New strength stirred within me. I was like a person waking up from a grave illness and slowly regaining consciousness. In the face of his creation, I thanked God and bade him to show me continued mercy.

We reached Oran. Unfortunately, we had missed a transport ship by just a few hours and had to stay overnight in the barracks.

Here again was the Legionnaire quarter, unaffected by events. The old spirit of the Legion still prevailed. As soon as we had stowed away our things, we were ordered to the same duties we performed in December of the previous year. Again we whitewashed the walls, and again we had to scrub away the lime spray from the stone floor. Instinctively I looked around for the previous foreman, the corporal with the strained face, the perfect image for an advertisement poster to sell scrubbing and cleaning material.

The next evening I wanted to visit the city. Humans think, but the sergeant major decides. Enraged, he ripped up my pass. "I would have well liked to bring my wife a small present from Africa," I dared tell him. The barbaric fellow laughed scornfully and broke off a branch from a tree in the courtyard. "Here—you have a beautiful souvenir for your wife." And satisfied with this witty joke, he sent me off directly to work. Perhaps he would have given me permission to leave if I had told him I wanted to sleep one more time with an African woman. I was steamed.

In Meknes we received two hundred francs as a discharge bonus. To exchange the Moroccan notes, the sergeant major charged a hefty fee, which was why he didn't like having us go into the city, so that he didn't lose out on these winnings. In Meknes after my wallet was made lighter by eighty francs—a tidy sum in those days—someone stole my wristwatch in Oran. Legion, Legion, you stayed the same to the very end.

* * *

Finally the moment arrived to board ship. We feared the moment because a rumor circulated that a German commission would check the passenger list. But no one was there, and we breathed easier.

Slowly the ship began to move. We all fell silent. Good-bye Africa. The same *Sidi-Brahim* that brought us here, that had carried thousands of Legionnaires, took us back again to France. Lost in thought, we admired the African coast, the white limestone cliffs, for a last time until they finally vanished from view.

* * *

France—out of a faraway gray, the fine contours of the French coast emerged like a precious jewel, carefully wrapped in a delicate fabric. A light morning fog floated over the waves like a flowing veil. We were on deck and peered out. The city came into view. Many of us had tears in our eyes. A cherished moment we had craved for so long. A touching silence swept over us. An odd shudder racked my body. How dear appeared every corner of the old, trusted piece of earth—our home, despite everything. We belonged in France, and all the treasures of foreign lands could not replace the ancestral soil. Suddenly I had the thought: I really didn't know if my return to this country would be welcomed, and with envy I looked at my French neighbors.

* * *

Late at night we reached Lyon. The city appeared deserted. Darkness met us. We said our good-byes. Farewells sounded our new beginnings. We squeezed each other's hand tightly. "Good luck, comrade."

I remained alone. I wandered home through the dark streets, thinking of all the companions from the camps and barracks: Sertorius, Bartel, Grünwald; Germans, Poles, Russians; Jews and Christians. How many had been thrust from our torn-apart continent? I saw the quarters and the guard posted in front; I saw the camps and the barbed wire and behind it the suffering humanity. "Give us a homeland," they all cried and stretched out their hands. "Give us a homeland, for we too are people. We came into this world—live and love and die like you. Give us our due in your realm and let us be brothers."

I was sad as I walked on; they were my companions, and I had no power and could not help them. I too was searching for a homeland.

But then I entered my home and embraced my wife, and she led me to the child's bed. He slept, fists clenched, his cheeks colored rosy from slumber. He breathed lightly and was oblivious. I looked around the rooms that belonged to me; here lived someone who was at one with my feelings, and I knew I was not alone. This was my home; this was my homeland. This was my place infused with love that even reinvigorated the stateless. And I pledged to do my part for all humans to have a homeland—all and everywhere.

END

Legionnaire

Top: Sidi-Bel-Abbès, December 15, 1939. Bottom: Khenifra, April 1940

LÉGION ETRANGÈRE

ALGÉRIE
ESPAGNE
CRIMÉE
ITALIE
MEXIQUE

EXTRÊME-
ORIENT
DAHOMEY
MADAGASCAR
SAHARA
MAROC

2ᵉ Régiment Etranger d'Infanterie

Certificat de Bonne Conduite
(Engagé volontaire pour la durée de la guerre)

Le Lieutenant-Colonel FLAN, Commandant le 2° Régiment Etranger

d'Infanterie certifie que le légionnaire de 2° classe

Camille   Adler, Mle 89233

Né le 22 mars 1905   à Trieste

Département _____ Autriche

a tenu une bonne conduite pendant tout le temps qu'il est resté sous

les drapeaux et qu'il a servi constamment avec honneur et fidélité.

Meknès, le   22 Août   1940

H Flan

NOTA. — Cette pièce en cas de perte ne peut être remplacée par un duplicatum.

Honorable Discharge, August 22, 1940

Interniert

Interned

Warum klopft mir das Herz so bang
so schmerzlich und voller Trauer?
Und trotz der Wärme des Zimmers
durchschläuft mich fröstelnd ein
kalter Schauer

Why does my heart beat with such
fright,
so painful and full of despair?
And despite the warmth of the
room
I shiver with cold horror
throughout.

Und doch alles was ein Mensch
heute so heiss begehrt
hab'obdach, Kleidung, Trank und Speis'
Was ist's was in mir gährt.

And yet all that a man
So hotly desires today
I have roof, clothing, drink, and
food
Something there is I can't allay

Die freiheit ist es, die mir fehlt.
die kann mir nichts ersetzen
In meiner Enge kann mich auch
Speise 'Trank nicht ergötzen

It's freedom I'm lacking
Nothing can take its place
In my confinement food nor drink
can delight me

Es ist das verfluchte Reglement
die polizeilichen fesseln.
Ich spüre sie um mich herum
und kann sie nie vergessen.

It's those damn rules
The police like shackles
I feel them all around me
They will always raise my hackles.

Oh, komm doch Friede
Deiner harrt die ganze
Menschheit voll Sehnen
Sie wartet auf Frieden und
Freiheit so lang
Sie wartet auf dich mit Tränen

Oh, peace arrive
All humanity waits pining
It waits for peace and freedom so
long.
It waits for you weeping.

Komm und beendige unsere Pein
Und lose unsere Bande
Auf dass wir als freie Menschen
ziehn
in die befreiten Lände.

Come and end our suffering
and loosen the bands.
So that we can move as free men
in the liberated lands.

Original Poem by Camillo Adler

Translated by M.A.

PART II

I Am a Refugee: Experiences

Original Manuscript dated April 1944

To the Reverend Schweitzer and the parish community of Nesslau.

Dear Honorable Reverend,

It is a great honor and a great pleasure to be able to dedicate these writings to you and your dear parish community.

Your community invited and accepted a Jewish family—man, woman, and two children. Every one of you contributed according to your strengths to make our stay in your peaceful and quiet community beautiful, comfortable, and dignified. You brought a great burden upon yourselves, and every day we see anew how gladly you do it.

It's said we live in a materialistic epoch, in which human emotions mean very little. Yes, often people are apt to view goodness and kindness as weaknesses that must be overcome in order to fit into the times. Where are the times when people were honored to be able to accommodate guests? And yet we were bestowed this honor. We are allowed, even today, to experience the practice of hospitality, which is practiced with an enthusiastic heart in the fulfillment of a moral commandment. It is an experience, in the best sense, to take such pleasure in your hospitality. It shows us that in today's time, man is not evil who feels the need to do good depends only on inspiring goodness and understanding in one's fellow man to awaken him to action.

But beyond that we strongly feel your deeds, because we are Jews, and you have gone beyond the barricades of religion and view as humans those that have suffered and are in need of help. That is it—this shining example of living Christian duty—that brotherhood and goodness, kindness and cooperation are never blocked by religion or race.

In this sense, we too, my family and I, have a big assignment in your rural circles. Christians often have different and strange ideas about Jews. Often, rural areas offer few opportunities to see Jews, and one is prone to imagine Jews not as people like all the others. Even in your community, there may be those that have never seen Jews.

And now there are some—man, woman, and children looking like other creations. They live like other families. There is nothing unusual about them.

No, there is nothing unusual about us—humans like any others, creations of one God conferring on us the same divine spark of life. That which is special about us can't be seen on our faces or heard in our voices.

Only our fate is special. We don't think that God brought this fate upon Jews, but that evil people, breaking God's commandments, brought it upon us. If people knew each other better, it would not be possible for them to defile and deny their humanity as is happening today. And when we can show in your small circle, through our presence, that we Jews are humans, no better and no worse as others, then I believe we have contributed a little bit to the great task to foster a greater understanding among people that they should not hate each other, but stand by each other. And perhaps others will read these lines, those to whom hate has been sown and not evangelic love.

To my loved ones and to me it means infinitely much to be together and in peace occupying this small house, the Schneckenbühl. Whoever reads these essays will recognize what a home signifies to refugees.

For the experience of our stay among you, for your kindest hospitality, we thank you with all our hearts.

Nesslau, December 24, 1943

PREFACE: SELF-CRITICISM AND JUSTIFICATION

What purpose shall these essays serve? They are experiences and observations. They are our own trials, the entanglement of a Jewish family in the events of those fateful years 1942–43. What befell us was the typical fate of an average Jewish family that immigrated to France and one day was forced to flee from this second homeland. It is an example of what tens of thousands of people around us felt and experienced. This transcription should lead to a clarification for us refugees and, beyond that, to our reconciliation with our fellow humans.

The Swiss people have magnanimously absorbed the refugees, but it knows little about the lives of their guests. These lives for the most part take place in camps. They know little about our thoughts.

It's not easy for a refugee to write such a composition. We experienced and saw much in Switzerland, much of it beautiful that we will keep forever in our memory, but also things we found hard to bear.

Our first duty is the gratitude for of our rescue. Is it an offense against this duty when I also portray the ugly? Do I have the right to express that there were things we found difficult to bear? Do I not have more so the duty to forget them?

We Jews are very sensitive people. We know we have faults, but we don't like to hear that they are held against us. We reserve to ourselves the criticism of Jewish essence, on Jews in general. When non-Jews speak disparagingly of Jews, we are prone to see them from the outset as our enemies. What is right for us, others must deem fair. I have honestly tried to adhere to these thoughts in the following account.

And yet I believe and feel it is good, yes, necessary for a refugee to portray with complete openness what was experienced and the impact of these experiences. Not just because it is our duty to be thankful for the nice things, but I also see it my duty to point out those things that made life hard. I'm aware of how much of that was unavoidable and pales in comparison to the infinite significance of our rescue. The life of a refugee, by necessity, brings with it suffering, worry, and sacrifice. Yet our fellow humans must know the thoughts and emotions of a refugee. It is instructive and perhaps will contribute to the recognition of how ugly it is to eject people from the human community and turn them into refugees.

What concerns gratitude—it will never be superseded by the portrayal of the good and the ugly realities and what they hold. Nothing in this world is absolute and fault free. But our duty is to recognize reality and truth. And finally the thinking person who has experienced much, including poverty and suffering, would not want to expunge these from life, for these too enrich our lives. Even ugliness is part of the fundamental experiences that mold us. I speak therefore with an easy conscience about everything we experienced, for it is a whole, and only this whole can bring clarity and open the way to mutual understanding.

Neither have I written these essays as political polemic. I am not that way. I have written down my experiences and observations that have occurred in life, as a man for whom the fate of humanity, in of itself, appears valuable, and not from a political vantage point. That it is so comes out clearly from the portrayals and observations. With that I believe I have not violated the duty imposed on refugees to refrain from political activity. As can be seen in the writing, I have taken quite seriously this imposed duty, and I believe the restraint on political activity will continue decisively after the war, in regards to criticism. We owe Switzerland so much that even after we have left Switzerland, we will always be tasked to be very tactful when discussing our experiences here. That is self-evident. I have questioned my conscience, this highest and most uncomfortable judge, and my conscience pronounces me free.

In Switzerland, I participated in all forms of refugee life. I know reception camps and labor camps, and now I enjoy the freedom that makes possible for me to review the experiences in quiet and from a certain distance and in particular to get to know the Swiss outside the camps. I have endeavored to absorb everything and to arrive at a total picture. I will be happy if I am capable of conveying this total picture to the reader.

Although I honestly tried in my thinking to respect Swiss thinking and be objective in my depictions, despite everything some things may carry the stamp of subjective observation. That is unavoidable since, after all, as refugee I have a bias. A Swiss person can never portray the refugee problem objectively, as that perspective too contains bias. But I don't think it's a mistake if the subjective attitude shimmers through the theme. As a refugee I can and should in the end write from the standpoint of the refugee. The endeavor to be objective in this connection will mean only that the writer has honestly tried to be fair. For the refugee, the treatment of the refugee problem is a delicate undertaking. But if the product is to have any value, what must be recognized in the work and absolutely demanded of the writer is honesty. And I hope that when reading this book, it will be recognized that I attempted to honestly and readily tell the truth.

My assignment reflects my personal perspective in that it deals with the experiences of people, who because of their Jewish fate, became refugees.

I have tried therefore, in the framework of my own experiences, to stick to and to elucidate the specific moment of the refugee wave of 1942–43 and to bring understanding to the non-Jewish environment about the thought-world of the refugees, dominated by their Judaism.

Further I have taken the following point of departure: refugee masses are created through social clashes. Who is so bold to believe that the great societal schism, in which we live and which is only one component of this war, will end? As long as we do not succeed in establishing an enduring societal balance, the danger of creating masses of refugees will continue to hang over us. In this regard, we remain in the dark about what the postwar period will bring. But we can see already that the refugee problem will not end with this war. After this war, as never before, there will be stateless people searching for a new homeland. The life of refugees is everyone's concern, for everyone can become a refugee.

But not for that reason alone do I write. Europe has been destroyed. We don't know in what form reconstruction will proceed; we can only guess. Problems such as collective and individual living, working freely or working confined in labor camps, the right to work and the duty to work—all these will become in great extent the problems of the postwar period. The societal instance of the Swiss solution is therefore worthy of a thorough investigation, because from the reaction of refugees to a system intended for them, as well as from the reaction of people in general, result far-reaching consequences to analogous solutions. In this sense, this book is a valuable contribution to analyzing the postwar problems, provided I have succeeded in clearly demonstrating the outline of the Swiss solution and the refugee's attitude in response.

In this sense, this writing should form a bridge from person to person and from the refugees to the Swiss.

16

ABANDONING SHIP: LYON, NOVEMBER 1942

I t was a desperate time. To know it, you had to have lived through the ordeal. An unimaginable atmosphere of fear and desperation gripped all Jews during this, the second occupation of the free zone by the German troops.

Even before then, several categories of Jews bore the shock of the deportations. It was gruesome to watch and to hear how men were ruthlessly torn from their wives as well as parents from their children, and hauled away. And every one of us stateless Jews feared and trembled for our lives, even those that the statutes were supposed to spare. Mistakes were easily made, and quickly the most awful things happened. Once arrested, who succeeded in escaping from the police? In Lyon, an enlisted man was taken into custody despite the rule that wartime volunteers were not subject to arrest. The order to release him came too late. The train to the occupied zone had left Lyon. Our hearts pounded when the doorbell rang; we opened the door only with prearranged signals. Many stayed days on end on rooftops or in cellars and, during critical nights, hid in trunks or in closets. During those days, an acquaintance of ours slept in the elevator shaft; another one had searched out a precarious bed in a crate. But after all, you couldn't stay perched in hiding forever; you had to go into the street to eat. Timid, like harassed beasts with fearful eyes, fear and worry drawn upon their faces, when forced by hunger, they crept about the damned streets always giving wide berth to the many gendarmes and police. It wasn't the old police, our trusted constables that dominated the street scene. A new Vichy police, whose black uniforms identified their mercilessness, fulfilled their abhorrent task to betray innocent people to the mortal enemy. The renewal of the rationing cards, without which you couldn't live, and the fear of their inspections became a painful problem. You had to have seen and heard it—the tired gestures and the gaze of these people, a persecuted humanity.

In those days, I saw the renowned tenor, Josef Schmidt[9], a man of short build; I saw him not as an artist, just a harassed Jew fighting for his life. He waited at the train station by the skyscrapers of Villeurbanne for a friend to take him out for a meal. He didn't speak of artistic plans, or of songs and concerts; he weighed the possibility of hiding in a locomotive or on the back of a truck to flee into Switzerland. He indeed succeeded in crossing the border and fulfilled his destiny to die in Switzerland.

And yet, several limitations moderated the severity of the deportations. In the free zone, regardless of their residence at the outbreak of the war, parents of children with French citizenship, parents whose children were under two years of age, and Jews who had immigrated prior to 1933 were protected from the first wave of deportations. At the instigation of influential military persons, all those that served in the army as wartime volunteers were also exempted. Nonetheless, several places did not enforce the statutes uniformly and created unintended victims of the deportations.

You could also count on the noncompliance of some officials, and particularly the French population, when these measures initiated a

---

9 From http://en.wikipedia.org/wiki/ Joseph_Schmidt - Josef Schmidt, tenor, born in Bukovina, Austria-Hungary March 4, 1904. Trapped in France, he made a dash for the Swiss border, and was interned in a Swiss refugee camp in Gyrenbad near Zurich in October 1942. He was already frail. Harsh camp life and lack of medical care brought about a fatal heart attack on November 16, 1942. He was only thirty-eight years old.

storm following demobilization. Clear-thinking Frenchmen were aware that after the Jews they were next in line. Even such Frenchmen who were in general not particularly friendly toward Jews revolted against the thought that France, at the behest of a foreign power, would seal the fate of people by sending them to their death. The deliverance of Jews contradicted the most holy tenets of French history. Only once did I hear, "Thank God, now France will be made free of this international riffraff." But against this, a pitiless voice, I saw many testimonials of the finest human solidarity and experienced much readiness to help. It takes a lot to shake people out of their customary routine. The French were awakened to the tragedy of the deportations, even those that did not previously want to believe in the sway of German pressure and interference. It became clear to everyone that National Socialism meant bestiality and brutality and that a sad ending was in store were Germany to emerge victorious.

Many civil servants reluctantly carried out their orders. Before each raid on Jews, you could surmise when they were expected to take place and plan accordingly. There were départements and cities in which the officials openly disapproved of the deportations. That was the case in Lyon, where Hérriot's[10] spirit was not yet extinguished and, with the great influence of the clergy, racism was decidedly rejected. The military governor of Lyon refused to let his soldiers be abused by such executioners' handiwork. He was removed from office. Cardinal Gerlier, archbishop of Lyon and primate of Gaul, told the council and the government his unabashed opinion and revulsion. It was he who refused to surrender to the deportation of children hidden in convents. Through his forceful and decisive stance, he saved these children about to be hauled away to an "unknown destination." In those sad days, the French clergy wrote a glorious chapter on humanity. Thousands of Jews begged cloisters and church institutions for refuge. And though the police didn't always enter the holiness of a Jewish house of worship, they certainly dared not tamper with the asylum rights of the church. With the protection of the most beautiful and biggest cathedral of Lyon, the poor pursued could quietly stretch and rest their tired limbs.

---

10 http://en.wikipedia.org/wiki/Édouard_Herriot, **Édouard Hérriot** (b. 5 July 1872 at Troyes, France – d. 26 March 1957 at Lyon, France) was a French Radical politician of the Third Republic who served three times as prime minister and for many years as president of the Chamber of Deputies. He is buried at the Cimetière de Loyasse in Lyon.

But the Germans had moved in, and we all knew what that meant: no more exceptions and a loose interpretation of the statutes. Where, where could we save ourselves? Spain was far away, and the Spanish government was not favorably disposed toward Jews. In their attempt to cross the Pyrenees, many unfortunate ones paid with their lives. Some were murdered or robbed by unscrupulous guides and left on their own. In their distress, lost and abandoned, they perished in the mountainous terrain. Others were surrendered by Spanish border guards to French gendarmes. How could I dare to attempt this step with my family—my wife, Martha, and our two small children, Paul and Michel, six years and sixteen months of age? Not to mention passports, mostly forged, unscrupulous dealers sold to frightened individuals for large sums of money. Neither could an incredible escape by aircraft to England be considered. People in need believed in any possibility. The question of money did not, however, allow us to even entertain some of these approaches. As an Austrian Jew, I could not count on keeping my job. From what would we live? Where and with what money would we hide with our children? There remained only escape into Switzerland. But all our acquaintances advised against it. My wife trembled at the unknown. At the beginning of October, my brother-in-law[11], a bachelor who lived in Grenoble, was at the Swiss border, where the Swiss border police turned him back. Only with great difficulty did he succeed in returning unscathed to Grenoble. He described to us how many people passed through Grenoble to be handed over to the Rivesaltes internment camp. They were in part turned back by the Swiss and in part arrested by the French gendarmes before reaching the border. In handcuffs they were then transferred to Rivesaltes for collection into the transports to the occupied zone. He warned us not to risk the adventure. And the Jewish aid committee gave us the same advice, not to fall into misfortune and tempt fate.

But my decision stood firm, preferring an end with fright than fright without end. I needed to sleep again without fearing that in the morning a gendarme would be suddenly asking for me. They counted on the fact, that in the morning, at four or five o'clock, the unlucky ones could be most likely captured in their beds. I was arrested a year before by one of these raids on Jews. Despite all my papers, which I had with

---

11 George Kraus, Martha's brother, survived the war with false papers, in the French Resistance.

184

me and were in perfect order, I had to spend the night in a fort near Lyon. We were men and women mixed and packed tightly together on a ghastly ride into the unknown, in the dark of the night, in a locked truck. In that night we quartered in narrow aisles, between bug- and lice-infested straw sacks, pacing back and forth in a tormented uncertainty, asking ourselves why, on what account, and for how long. The pain of this venture stayed with me; I knew what it meant to be a Jew without rights, the meaning of a French dungeon and a French camp. My blood curdled at the thought of a German camp, to be delivered, without recourse to defense, into the hands of the mortal enemy and wait trembling in tortured fear for death. I could no longer sleep, no longer eat, and no longer think. I was like a hypnotized mouse staring at a big snake, knowing there was no escape. No, I was not such a coward. When war was declared, I volunteered for service and enlisted in the Legion. But that was to fight. But in the German camp, animals would mercilessly torture us and then martyr us. A colleague once mockingly remarked, "Is your heart in your pants, Adler?" He was right, but it was easy for him to say. He was French and "Aryan." If I had not a family, I would have joined the ranks of the resistance movement that was just beginning to be organized. A journalist friend often repeated to me that it was not the time to flee, but the time to work and do battle against the Germans. He was single and without a family to worry about. He was in his own country. I was here only as a guest. And what would I do with my family? No, for me there was only flight, as difficult as that might be. I could no longer listen to our immigrant acquaintances, whose fate was drawn and who gossiped about the latest shocking news. My will to live revolted against the tiresome and worn environment of hopelessness and passivity and the discouragement of plans to escape the occupied territory engendered by immigrants from Germany. I wanted to—I desired to—live, be well and alive, and to see yet another and better time. The war had to end. We had to persevere at any cost.

In those difficult days, I gained much strength from a visit to the Swiss pastor, Roland de Pury,[12] who had helped many Jews. Pastor de

---

12 Roland de Pury together with his wife, Jacqueline de Pury, née de Montmollin, were elevated by the Yad Vashem memorial to the rank of "Righteous among the Nations" in 1976. Born in Geneva in 1907, the pastor Roland de Pury preached resistance to the Vichy government's anti-Semitic policy in his church in the Rue Lanterne in Lyons. With the help of his wife, Jacqueline, a native of Neuchâtel, he hid Jews in his flat and helped many escape to Switzerland. He was arrested by the Gestapo and held in the Fort de Montluc for five months.

Pury assured me that families with children under six years of age would not be turned back. Our oldest was just six years old. That was the first authentic news we received about Swiss admission rules. So we could rescue our children and us with them.

As my wife saw that my decision was unalterable, she surrendered to her fate. There was only the question of how. My wife insisted that we take a guide. She did not want to accidentally surrender the children. I gave in. I don't want to describe the mistaken trips and attempts without results to hire a trustworthy guide. But, foresight and planning helped us.

Oh, that awful November 11! The German troops moved into Lyon; their tanks rolled through the Rue de la République; the machine guns in the center of town threatened to choke any germination of resistance, and their boots trampled on the last vestiges of French independence. Silently, with heavy hearts and grim faces, the Lyonnaise saw the occupying troops pass and their never-ending columns directed south. That day, I stood at the window of my firm, where I was employed, and looked out at the Place Tolozan. There, on the bank of the Rhône, stood a contingent of the Garde Mobile. The horses shuffled their hooves on the ground, and the gardes spoke among themselves about the events and waited for orders. A gray fog darkened the sky. I viewed the theater piece and with bleak thoughts wondered who of our acquaintances had the possibility and the will to help us. Only one person came to mind. And just as I was thinking about him, the door opened and he entered. He led me to a corner and said to me, "Adler, aujourd'hui je vous vois en peine; si je puis vous etre utile à quelque chose, disposez de moi."[13] That was so nice, sincere, and so friendly, and he was clearly cooperative. The look of his black eyes, and his whole being, exuded so much dependability that in my sorrow my heart opened. Never will I forget his words. We probably owe our lives to this man.

I turned to this friend. He tried at first to get us authentic false papers. We went together to a workshop near the prefecture. It was nice, the trust he had in me. The workshop was like a thousand others, and nothing pointed to the fact that other things were being done besides the manufacture of leather goods and bags. But you could surmise that the owner and the "clients" had been officers and soldiers and that this office

---

13 "Adler, today I see you in pain. If I can help you with something, ask me."

was a cell of the Resistance. My friend spoke first alone with the owner while I waited outside. Then I went in and was cheerfully received. The patron explained to me that he would try to get real papers for my wife and me from the Lyon prefecture. With those, we would truly be secure. The next day, when I went to pick up my papers, he explained to me that on the first day of entry, the Germans immediately occupied the offices of the prefecture. For the time being, it would be impossible to procure authentic papers. He sincerely regretted the situation, as did I, but there was nothing to be done. In this situation my friend advised me not to lose any time and to cross the border as soon as possible, before the German border guards could be installed everywhere. I totally agreed with this assessment.

My friend traveled on our behalf to Annecy to line up a guide for us. He found one in an organization that assisted Poles and war volunteers in escape to Switzerland on humanitarian and patriotic grounds. A rendezvous at the railroad station of Seyssel was arranged for Tuesday, November 17.

Now it was for real, and we had to prepare everything quickly. We did not have to confide our plans to our little Michou, but we had to tell Paul something. We explained to him that we wanted to travel into the country, into the Savoie. We told him not to speak to anyone about it. Promptly, despite forbidding him, he confided to his teacher our supposed intentions. Without any suspicion, the teacher explained to Paul that in this case he needed to bring a written excuse from his parents. We had to laugh in our sorrow, though truly there was nothing to laugh about.

* * *

When a natural catastrophe annihilates a home that over the many years we learned to love and has become dear to us, to which are connected so many experiences and memories, in which every object speaks to us; when a bomb crushes it and eradicates every trace; then against these events, people stand powerless and must accept the complete reality. What use is complaining? What has gone cannot come again.

But to give up everything of one's own volition, what you slowly fashioned and built up in the course of the years, and to renounce your trusted home and leave it to strangers, and transform yourself into a beggar and a refugee—that is infinitely, infinitely difficult. Those who have never left their home or experienced what it means to be dependent on the mercy and compassion of strangers cannot measure or comprehend it. Our hearts were broken, but we were not allowed to think. Could I blame my wife for expressing her lack of fortitude to tear her little children from our customary home and trust to an unknown fate? Could I be angry with her for wanting to spend another month, perhaps the entire winter, at home? Oh, how much I wanted to obey her. But could I wait and let precious time slip by? How, in the middle of winter, would we ever cross the border with a baby? If we had false papers, would Paul not betray us? No, it required we remain tough and resolute.

We lived in a suburb of Lyon, in the skyscrapers of Villeurbanne. Many Jews lived in this quarter, and thus it was a favorite spot for executing raids on Jews. It was easy to blockade from all sides, after which you followed a list of the marked, went door to door, and snatched the Jews.

Who in this quarter didn't think about the sad weeks in which one Jewish family after another liquidated their belongings and their apartment? Awhile before, apartments could be had for every price for every income, from the luxurious, fully furnished of the rich to the small, meagerly furnished apartments of the poor immigrants. All refugees know about the liquidation of such households. It's like a burial—a burial of a civilized life. Christians were pressured to buy radios, silverware, sewing machines, typewriters, carpets, pictures, bicycles, and baby carriages. After all, you couldn't take them with you, and you needed money. Those with money hoped to buy a 100 percent guaranteed successful escape in trucks, in official vehicles, in sealed compartments of trains to Geneva, or in locomotives. With no money, you had to rely on your lucky star and your resourcefulness. What money was left was converted into Swiss currency at fifty, sixty, or even one hundred French francs per Swiss franc. And even those who counted on a healthy one hundred fifty to two hundred thousand francs, after all the markups and after paying off their guides, became beggars.

And we also arrived at this point. Like vultures, smelling carrion, everyday people came to us who somehow heard of our intentions to escape. The housing need was great. Empty residences didn't exist. We received the most enticing offers to sell the apartment inclusive of all furnishings. No, we didn't want to and remained steadfast. What use would the French francs be, which in Switzerland were as good as worthless? What did it amount to when for thirty thousand French francs we would barely receive four hundred Swiss francs—a drop on a hot stone? No, we wanted to think, even dream, that once this evil war came to its end, that somewhere a room and a few pieces of furniture were ours, and our children owned their own roof over their heads. We, for years stateless, yearned for a small house. We never thought that in 1944 we would still be on foreign soil.

We packed the valises, the children's things into one and my things and those of my wife into another. Everything was separated. Did we know when and if they could be forwarded to us? Would we stay together, or would we be separated? What was happening to refugees in Switzerland? We didn't know. The news flowed sparingly. Why didn't people from Switzerland write to us? What did we know about the regulations of the reception centers? The reports indicated that refugees were placed in camps. But a camp in Switzerland had to be good. We thought about how Switzerland was so clean, so beautiful, and so well organized, and what good deeds the Swiss performed for children. Well, it had to be good.

Yes, we packed and repacked. We considered what was more valuable, what was more important. We were attached to every object. We packed and sieved, and still we left almost everything behind. Our morale was heavily burdened.

When, in those days, I walked in the street and observed the people quietly going to work, visiting the coffee houses, taking in a movie, continuing with their customary life—even as difficult as life was—I still became filled with envy. On what account did I have to escape? What had we done to bring on this pursuit of us Jews? Had I really engaged in racketeering, piled up money? Had I enriched myself at the expense of the community? All were the claims of the daily propaganda against Jews. Didn't we know we were measured with a special standard and that it made no difference what we did? Could a people simply be declared outlaws? Was there a God that permitted these things? Weren't my children just as good as "Aryan" children? What blame had they shouldered? I could not grasp it. Here were people no different than we, but only by circumstance born into a different religion or race, calmly going on with their life. They didn't suspect that I, dressing just the same as they, looking like they did, had to leave my home with satchel and pack and could no longer participate in that life. I heard their conversations in the streetcar and in the workshops. Their conversation was about the occupation, worries of nourishment, and coal for the winter. None of these matters concerned me. Fate had locked us out of the human community. Inwardly, I was a willing refugee.

At meal times, our last meals before the "execution," we ate indiscriminately the best from our reserves. The remaining food, delicacies in this city of hunger, I left to my friend who helped us so much and to a place that fed those without papers and ration cards. Our larder was superbly stocked for this fourth winter of the war. I smile at the mere thought of it: ninety kilos of potatoes, several kilos of flour, fourteen tins of condensed milk, and several smaller items. Not much as total reserves go for a four-person household, but valuable goods in a big city with heavy suffering. People are sometimes so silly and narrow-minded even in tragic circumstances. In the fall, just at the start of the roundups, we ate all our reserves of jams and jellies. It wasn't hard, and we were happy about it. As the French say, "Autant de pris sur l'ennemi" (So much saved out of the fire.) A comfort only—but such is human nature. It's lucky that small things divert us, for otherwise we could never bear or get over any misfortune.

So the eve of our departure arrived. Without enthusiasm we downed a meal that in other circumstances would have appeared to us as luxurious. Three rucksacks were packed with only the utmost essentials.

For the last time, we spent a sleepless night in our accustomed beds. Thoughts stormed into us and did not let us rest. Our life passed before us. Twelve years we lived here and built this home piece by piece. Then came the children. Those scribbles on walls—that was Paul. That scratch on the furniture, the ragged and torn book cover—Paul again. The children were sick. We calmed them and rocked them to sleep. Within those four walls, they had been growing. Yet all that passed and shall be no more. For restless and fugitive would we be on earth.

Finally the clock struck four. We got up, dressed the children, and made ourselves travel ready. Silently and mechanically we took care of the necessary.

We ate breakfast for the last time in our trusted kitchen and lowered the window grates. Everyone took a rucksack, including Paul. A last glance embraced the rooms that offered us stateless a home and shelter. I took the baby in my arms. The door fell shut. The key turned in the lock, and its grating sound penetrated our hearts. The muffled clang broke apart like the last shovel of earth cast on the casket at the funeral of a dear and close friend.

Carefully, with faltering steps in semidarkness, we descended the stairs and went into the street.

17

THE ESCAPE

The railroad car was crammed full with people and baggage. Travel was difficult, as everyone wanted to travel to the country to get food supplies. Everyone knew someone, an aunt, a brother-in-law, or a colleague from the military service, in some or other town from where he or she hoped to return with a full suitcase to augment meager rations. The train schedules were curtailed, and the connections were bad.

We boarded the overcrowded train in the last seconds prior to departure. I was happy that in this crush my wife managed to snag a seat. She took Michou on her lap. The small child did not tolerate the shaky train travel. After a quarter hour, he expelled his entire breakfast milk over my wife's coat.

Few words were spoken in the compartment. Did one know to which party the neighboring passenger belonged? Did the Gestapo travel in the train? A careless word could have dire consequences. So we kept quiet, as we had every reason to protect ourselves from notice.

Now, I spoke French fluently and my wife also quite well, and our accents were not really noticeable. Besides we had Paul with us, the French poster child of the family, who spoke well and a lot of French and spread an atmosphere of security.

But we only had our real papers with us. Our identity cards were in order and valid until spring of 1945. But one gathered from them that we were foreigners, originally from Austria, and by inference Jews seeking refuge. We naturally did not have a safe conduct document that legitimizes a foreigner's travel. An inspection was particularly dangerous for us, and there was a lot of checking in trains traveling in the direction of Switzerland. My only crutch was my military passport, from which can be ascertained that I was a voluntary war enlistee, and my honorable discharge paper from the French Foreign Legion. Valuable papers, as the French in general couldn't comprehend that a man with a French military passport was not French. That, hopefully, was yet to come, but only after the war. In the meantime, we were foreign Jews in flight, without false papers in our possession, and we could only rely on our lucky star.

False papers cost a significant sum of money in the trade. A whole set—identity card, military passport, and food ration cards—only the complete series of papers stood up to the muster of an inspection, and were valued in Lyon at about twenty-five thousand francs. My attempt to obtain authentic and registered papers through regular channels came to nothing. Besides complete sets of papers, individual identity cards were available in retail, so to say, but these were mostly not registered in the relevant community. Nonetheless, even such an individual card cost several thousand francs. For that, we didn't want to spend any money.

Nervously, I smoked one cigarette after another. At least, I could permit myself that. With foresight, I had taken an advance on my cigarette rations for the next ten-day period. Only our Paul really enjoyed the trip, which, in his childish innocence, appeared like a beautiful autumn excursion. Oh, happy childhood! In different times, we had frequently traveled this route from Lyon via Geneva–Zurich to Vienna. How my wife had looked forward to seeing her parents again; how her eyes lit up at this thought. Now she sat there immersed in herself, and only grief spoke from her eyes.

We neared Seyssel, the last station before Bellegarde. Bellegarde lay in the previously occupied zone, then the demarcation line and required a special permit to cross. The Occupation officials issued these permits only on the most compelling grounds. Only one gentleman in the compartment, I suspected, was continuing on to Bellegarde, as I gathered from his identity papers with the Third Reich eagle and swastika that he showed a travel companion. We got off the train with everyone else.

Other than the good fortune of no inspections, on this day we had no luck. They didn't give us the name of the man who was to meet us, but we knew the type of dress he wore. We, with our children, one of them a baby, separated ourselves from the crowd of travelers, so our guide could more easily recognize us. You can imagine our shock as we saw that no one approached us. We waited about twenty minutes in the railroad station. We couldn't stay any longer without calling attention to ourselves. Our hearts were heavy. What to do? Where to start?

In our desperation I had the thought to ask about our guide at the next place of the Chantier de Jeunesse. I suspected, wrongly, that he belonged to this organization. Disheartened, with the children, we schlepped through the small city. Through the gray and rainy November sky, the town appeared gloomy and hopeless. With a roar, the Rhône's murky, greenish waters surged past. A cold wind blew; the small city was like a ghost town. We were in no way expecting this hindrance and were totally desperate. Our plan suddenly evaporated into nothing. We were like nomads, who an evil magician suddenly put into a desert. We were courteously received at the Chantier de Jeunesse, with understanding and even sympathy, but they knew nothing of our guide and couldn't help us. This youth who led his soldier's life had not encountered problems such as ours.

My wife stood with tears in her eyes. I, totally exhausted, forced myself with great effort. Gendarmes passed us, and in our fear, they seemed to be looking only at us. At any moment, we expected them to demand our papers. In reality, they hardly noticed us, but we feared them. It would suffice to be under suspicion. A check on our papers meant Rivesaltes and deportation. Paul became hungry and moody. He was tired. What kind of a strange trip was this?

We went into the next hotel. Keeping a clear head and remaining cool in our thinking was imperative. With me rested the responsibility for four humans. The future of the entire family rested on my actions. First I tried to telephone my confidant in Lyon, but with interference on the line I could not get a connection. I could not reach our guide, and, as I later discovered, I did not get the correct spelling of his residence. Good advice was tough to come by. My wife would have liked most to travel back to Lyon. We didn't feel comfortable in the hotel and didn't dare trust approaching the owner. It was best to disappear from the hotel quickly.

We gave up counting on our guide. Certainly he was not a swindler. He didn't care about our money, as other smugglers deemed their businesses as moneymaking enterprises. Pure motives drove our guide. It could be that while guiding another group and performing his service to humanity he was arrested and was in jail serving penance.

Under no circumstances did I want to return to Lyon. The separation was decisively final. The departure was difficult enough. Would a return have solved anything? We began the escape and had to follow it to its end. It was destined: forward and never back.

So we decided, in the end, to travel to Annecy. There I had knowledge of the address of a smuggler. My friend also negotiated with him and agreed to an eventual guidance of our family in the amount of twenty thousand francs—a bargain price that he negotiated with much effort. Twenty-five thousand per person, fifty to one hundred thousand per family—these were at the time the going rates, and whoever had money paid. The smuggler's risks were not to be discounted. Some even paid with their lives. When people gamble with their lives and freedom, they also wanted to earn something. How high must we esteem people who with empathy, love of mankind, and God's wages risked their lives.

I again counted the cash in my pockets: approximately twenty thousand francs. Laboriously we had scratched this sum together. Even our silverware contributed. The sewing machine escaped its fate only because in our rush we couldn't raise a buyer. How gladly we would have sacrificed the whole fortune just to buy our security. When gambling with life, only then does a person realize, in reality, how useless all possessions are. As long as one can live and work, everything can be won back. Everything can be replaced, except no power on earth can magically bring back vanished life. With great effort, I succeeded in raising a taxi owner. Unfortunately he explained to me that with the lack of fuel, he could only take us halfway. That was still something. After eating lunch, we left. Having arrived there, we went into a coffee house, and while my wife looked after the children, I went on the search for another car.

And truly, divine Providence watched over us. It was no accident. What followed was a true wonder for which we will forever owe God our gratitude. In despair, I rang the bell at a taxi garage. I anticipated the answer, "Sorry, no fuel." And from where could they get it? I should have offered a high price for the trip, but to be truthful, I didn't dare raise any suspicion. Naturally, this taxi driver didn't have any fuel either, but in the course of the conversation, it came out that he personally knew our guide for whom we waited in vain in Seyssel. He even had been with him at the train station, where also in vain he was on the lookout for a family with two small children. Our guide, Mr. Dubois—I now found out his name—had overlooked the November 9 change to the winter train schedule, and the train from Lyon arrived an hour earlier. He criss-crossed the town in every direction but could not find us, as my wife with the baby for fear of the gendarmes didn't budge from the hotel.

I was overjoyed. Suddenly everything became simple and self-evident. The area laughed at me. A new lust for life streamed through my body. The more I was in despair of our rescue before, the more wonderful I found this development of chance. I was a different person. Quickly I hurried back to the hotel to bring the news to my wife. With faltering words, I reported to her how all at once how everything turned to the good. My wife stared at me in disbelief. She was not ready for this fortunate turn of events.

And yet it was so. Hurriedly we notified Mr. Dubois of our presence. He lived only ten minutes from where we were. In a half hour he was there: a simple man, father of a family, who fought hard for their bread. A mountain guide, but now there were few guests who called on this peaceful service. And he was friendly, cooperative, and full of under-standing for our situation. What can you say? Our smuggler in Annecy was a rich man and wanted to earn more. Dubois was poor. But he was good. Does money debase a person? Does it take possession of a man's soul, displacing initial noble tendencies? We saw Mr. Dubois for the first time. Right away we entrusted ourselves to him. With straight talk, he explained everything in detail. He had been on the border and had prepared everything. But for today, it was already too late to cross the border, and we had to unfortunately spend the night in that place.

Dubois took us to a hotel where he was known, and that was good. Between soup and vegetables, our hostess brought us the registrations to fill out. We were filled with fear and fright. What should we write? Would our hostess not want to see our papers as prescribed by law? I threw a questioning glance to Mr. Dubois, who calmed me with his silent gesture. He pushed a piece of scrap paper toward me on which he had quickly scrawled, "Strasbourg, Schiltigheim." And so I filled out the registration: Jean Klein, born in Strasbourg, Catholic, French: and for my wife likewise. That was the first time in our life that we declared ourselves falsely. But what should we have done? Our salvation demanded it. Mr. Dubois's presence covered us, and the hostess did not bother further about identity cards.

For certain, the next morning we quickly made ourselves scarce in order to avoid any other eventual hotel requests. We were uneasy. We disappeared with our rucksacks to the back room of the coffee house from yesterday. The owner was a friendly, heavyset woman. She liked the children. It is remarkable how these delicate beings immediately arouse sympathy and establish contact. We explained to her our critical situation, and she guarded our security. We felt safe in the homey atmosphere of the well-heated room.

Mr. Dubois came at ten o'clock. I had begged him urgently to arrive as soon as possible. His presence worked like a tranquilizer. We were afraid; something could happen to him. But he came refreshed, in good spirits and ready to help, with a broad smile on his cheerful face. He gave us courage, and thanks to his accompaniment, we boarded a bus without trembling too much. At the entrance to the bus stood a stout, well-nourished gendarme, who surveyed the passengers with a critical eye. Many Jews tried to cross the border. The gendarmes had strict orders to check out all suspicious people and in fact every passenger when getting on and off. Thank God, they weren't so exacting in carrying out their assignments. They could care less if Jews went past them. Ambition in service was foreign to them.

Finally the car moved. We headed in the direction of the free (Geneva) zone. Once again a gendarme came by to peek curiously into the inside of the vehicle. My wife changed colors. My heart raced. But we weren't noticed, and the gendarme didn't enter.

As the Germans already occupied St. Julien, we got off one stop earlier. From this little place, the road led directly into Switzerland. A young farmhand was to continue with us to the border. We approached a lounge. Again gendarmes. At the adjoining table, a customs guard consumed his lunch. But now at the end of our trip, we became more hardened. God had accompanied us that far, certainly he would not abandon us. We moved freely and without inhibitions as if we were descended from old Galiens and not stateless Jews. Didn't we have Mr. Dubois with us? His uniform engendered trust. He ordered and spoke for us. And Paul behaved himself like any French child on a pleasure trip.

Only my wife, who had really earned it, didn't do justice to the menu. It had been a long time since such a meal was available in a restaurant unless it was in a back room at black market prices. In Lyon, paying two hundred francs and more per person for a meal, in order to eat decently, was not a rarity. But in that little lounge, a complete menu of the day—hors d'oeuvres, vegetables, meat, fruit, cheese, and wine—cost only eighteen French francs or twenty-five Swiss centimes (at the conversion rate of those days). Oh, lucky Savoie. In any event, Paul and I attacked heartily.

In the afternoon we went for a walk, and as dusk came we strolled through the street toward the border to reconnoiter the area. Everything was in order. This village lay worlds apart from the storm-filled cities. No German guards yet. They came that evening, the German soldiers, to this village two hours after we departed for our final journey. Truly, Providence protected us.

Unfortunately, little Michou brought a shrill discordant sound into our undertaking. The child was not used to the rigors of traveling and suffered from an intestinal disorder that not only affected his usually quiet and friendly being but also affected us all. We needed to move forward. Our nerves were tense to the point of breaking. We could not muster the patience to deal with him. He was so wretched to look at, a small little heap of misfortune; he lay there like a small tousled bird, and my wife suffered from all the torments of a mother that fears helplessly for her child. Refugee children! When I looked at Michou, I became conscious of our entire suffering. We were vagabonds of the street. I didn't have the strength to console my wife. What would happen to us in Switzerland?

Finally, the child calmed down. We breathed easier. At seven o'clock we ate supper. The dining room stood clearly in my eyes: the low ceiling, the simple chairs and tables, the small iron stove and the wide plain buffet in the background. We heard the radio; here you could listen to radio London. Free France spoke to us. Good-bye to France. When would we be able to set foot into this land again?

At the advice of Mr. Dubois, we gave Michou some wine to help him doze off and not have his crying betray us; we were underway. We told Paul that unfortunately there was no place to stay overnight and we had to go to another inn. As soon as the guests disappeared from the restaurant, we also got up and went out: in front, the farmhand, who knew the area like his vest pocket and had "done" the border several times; then came Mr. Dubois, with two rucksacks; my wife, with one rucksack and Paul by the hand; and I, with Michou in my arms, pulled up the rear.

The night was bright and friendly; we crossed fields and meadows and stepped over a small brook. Peace and quiet and a relaxed night fell over the countryside. The trees threw dark shadows onto the moonlit paths, and only the rustle of leaves, awoken by wind gusts, accompanied us. In circumstances other than flight, we could have imagined it a family excursion, a night hike, something romantic in our silence. We stopped frequently and listened as our guide reconnoitered the way. Nothing budged.

Once Paul began to rebel. But he didn't get past the first attempt. He was totally exhausted and declared loudly he wasn't going any farther. With that, he threw himself on the ground and wanted to cry. The poor thing didn't get far. Mr. Dubois prevailed on him with a forceful voice. It was less the words than the tone and look that made Paul understand that this was not an ordinary excursion and he had to obey. Quiet and submissive, he hiked on. We marched for about three hours and were quite tired when suddenly our guide stopped in front of a street.

This street formed the border. It lay on Swiss soil. On the left was the Swiss customs guardhouse, and on each side of the street a vineyard. We saw the lights and houses of Soral on the right, the first settlement on Swiss soil; and in the distance, on the right of us radiated the lights of Geneva. In front of and behind us, the area formed a harmonious whole. God hadn't drawn a border. No barbed wire desecrated nature. Nothing signified that here one country starts and another ends. The same sky, the same stars shone on one side and on the other side. No, no sides—no separation was visible.

We experienced the border for what it was: the handiwork of humans. Humanity is so petty, vain, and evil; it looks down on and belittles creation; incompetent, we forget that we should elevate ourselves to Nature's level. When God created us, he didn't confine us into narrow borders. He entrusted us with the whole earth. So it must be. Without borders there would be no territorial or power expansion, and maybe even no more wars. And what would happen to humanity if from time to time it could no longer dive into the invigorating chalybeate bath of war? It would probably grow weak and degenerate while an iron race matures, as we can observe from all children in occupied territories.

But at that moment, we no longer thought that a land lay in back of us, unhappy and subjugating, and in front, free and peaceful. We were quite tired and wondered that a border existed and the next step meant we had crossed it. We had never looked upon a border with the eyes of a refugee.

We stood as our friends said warm good-byes and wished us much luck. They watched us for a long time as we put on our rucksacks and stepped onto Swiss soil. Illegal! I have to laugh as I put down these words today. What does "illegal" mean? At that moment we were certainly not conscious of the fact that we entered illegally, that small Michou was now being carried illegally into Switzerland. We were simply pursued people, searching for help, rescue, and compassion. We certainly didn't think about our illegality.

We guided our steps through the vineyard toward Soral. We wanted to spend the night there and travel to Geneva the next morning. They told us in Lyon that only in Geneva could we be certain that we would not be turned back. We therefore intended to skirt the border station and only report to the police once we were in Geneva. Our friend Dubois even promised to wait for twenty-four hours in a nearby hostel to guide us back safe and sound in case the Swiss rejected us. What a noble man. Only with great difficulty did I succeed in compensating him for his bar and food tab expenditures. He wanted to convince us to use our pocket money to buy a huge ham in the border town and resell it elsewhere in Switzerland for a big profit. We didn't have the head for such enticing speculation.

We had walked about two hundred meters along the street to Soral and thought we would succeed in getting through. We made this assumption without counting on the careful Swiss border patrol.

After barely ten minutes, we heard suddenly, "Halt." A glaring beam of light fell on our little group from the signaling lantern of a border policeman.

Paul screamed from fright and began to cry loudly. We immediately stopped on the command. My heart pounded audibly, as the policeman came toward us. Now everything would be determined. He was a tall, slim young man. He looked fabulous in his splendid outfit. His friendly nature restored our courage. He calmed Paul and asked from where and where to we were going, and then told us, "It's good that you have small children, as adults without children are being turned back. You don't need to have any fear; you will be admitted. You won't be separated." And so trustingly, we obeyed him.

These first words of a Swiss on Swiss soil were firmly engraved in our brains. In reality, we anticipated that we would be admitted, particularly after the expressed assurance from Pastor de Pury. We knew that adults without children were being rejected. But what particularly impressed us was his remark that we would stay together. In this regard, we hardly had any precise notion of refugee life in Switzerland. Why did this man assure us, of his own volition, that we would not be separated? Besides his kindness, it pointed out that it wasn't guaranteed that all families stayed together. Well, we would see. We were too tired to ask too many questions, and the warm reception of the policeman did us good. We were in no condition to react after the great tensions and anxiety of the recent time gone by, particularly the previous two days. The nightmare of persecution had been evaded. Life was rescued. Everything would make itself known. The border policeman took us to his small, adorned house. Everything there was so clean, beautiful and peaceful, truly Swiss as you wanted to imagine it. Everything was solid, firm, and secure. What a difference between the atmosphere of his little house and that of occupied France. We were in another world and felt redeemed.

The policeman began his written report. I gave my word of honor to our guide to give no information about his person, for he still had to rescue others. I told him therefore that we arrived via Annecy. Paul interrupted that we got off the train in Seyssel, an embarrassing moment. There remained only to tell the policeman that I had given my word of honor to not give more specific details of our flight and begged him not to put me into a compromising predicament. He understood and completed his report, a true testament but containing no implicating details. I was thankful for his sensitivity.

He even wanted to prepare tea for us and woke up his wife, who despite the late hour didn't grumble about unexpected guests and likewise made us welcome. It was really uncomfortable to bother these people, brave and full of goodness. I asked only for a little tobacco. It was wonderful that here I could smoke as I liked. That morning, in my nervousness, I had smoked all my cigarettes. Smoking relaxed the inflamed nerves.

In the meantime, the border policeman had called the nearest gendarme post. "I have here a group of four refugees," he said, "father, mother, and two children." That rang so peculiarly in our ears. The policeman said the truth. We were four persons and, as we shall see later, so to say, four independent individuals. The flight put the family unity temporarily on hold. Somehow and in an unconscious way, we were bothered and irritated by this dissection.

Soon a truck came for us. Paul was so tired he had fallen fast asleep on the wooden floor of the house, and we carried him into the vehicle.

The truck drove off. We were taken in.

18

INTO THE DEPTHS: BÜREN

O n December 1, I was transferred to the reception camp in Büren on the Aare. My wife and the children stayed behind in Geneva and were to follow on the next transport.

I was happy to leave Geneva. It was so sad to see little Michou lying on his straw bedding. He had neither proper nourishment nor care, a pathetic, dirty little worm crawling around on all fours through the rooms. In addition to his intestinal disorder, he caught a hefty cough from the draft in Charmilles and Val-Fleury, the two Geneva processing centers. We took Michel to the doctor at Val-Fleury and explained to him that Michel was sick and expressed our concern. To his question "When did the cough start?" we replied truthfully, "Since our arrival in Switzerland." The doctor took this response as an insult. "Why did you come here if you feel so unhappy?" We had to allow that in Val-Fleury as in Charmilles with the many children and the constant to and fro a tense atmosphere prevailed. The doctor had so many patients and in these first weeks of streaming refugees, so much needed improvement that his nervousness was understandable. Our nerves shattered also at the least provocation. The transition from one's own home to a cramped camp is not easy. I was so angry to have been accused of ingratitude, when the condition of my child and gratitude toward Switzerland were two totally different things, and I told him that in no uncertain terms.

This and other examples that other refugees told us awakened in me the impression that the officials of Geneva were not welcoming. In Charmilles as I presented an official my papers and he saw my military passport, he remarked, "Nice that you served. Many of your faith have not fulfilled their duty in France." He told this to the wrong person. It happened that the majority of volunteers were languishing in concentration camps. They were certain of the gratitude of the fatherland and did not need to worry about the travesty of the other world. I told him right away that there were few prior soldiers under the Jews who sought refuge in Switzerland because war volunteers, in general, did not fear deportation. Just these poor souls, brave and decent men, had waited so long and until it was too late.

Everything was so painful and without comfort. We ate the bread of charity and felt it. Our sensitivity lay bare, and at the least provocation we painfully felt the infinite void between the guarded homeless and the free. We retreated into ourselves, while some of the camp inhabitants, thick-skinned fellow sufferers, eagerly concerned themselves with the smallest chores that brought them some measure of relief.

Only Paul did well. At the doctor's examination, they diagnosed a rash, and he was transferred to a hospital. There he stayed two weeks and received the best care. Even we profited a little from his stay there, as we could visit him twice and had the opportunity to see Geneva again. What an incredible and indescribable difference between this beautiful, clean, bright white city, with shops that carried everything, and France at that time, where anything could only be gotten with the greatest of effort and need. The fruit, you could buy in the open, while in France, only laboriously and underhandedly could we obtain a little fruit for the children. The mountains of sardine cans and canned goods displayed had disappeared in France long before. And the baked goods, we ogled like children with eyes like saucers. But all these wonderful things were not for us. We did not belong to the stream of people that moved about the streets of Geneva, free and in peace, quietly and without worries. The camp was our home. Wherever we went, a soldier at our side reminded us constantly that we were suspicious people and needed surveillance.

We did feel, however, that there were still people who wished us well, for example, the nurse in Paul's hospital who made my wife a present of a big bar of soap so she could wash Michel's diapers. The allocations in general were limited and in the case of soap, totally insufficient for the many baby washes. But we were hermetically sealed from this world of the Swiss.

We were told that Büren was a camp for families. I have no idea why I had this vision of Büren as a Christmas town. Geneva was only a transit station; that was clear. A camp for families had to be something good. We had such lofty expectations of Switzerland. I imagined a white winter landscape, framed by mountains, with chalet-like houses in the shadows of pine and fir trees. Little houses, in which, I assumed, every family would have its own room, and in the middle of the settlement would be a mess and meeting hall.

In Val-Fleury, a woman warned me about Büren. She had heard quite a few things about Büren. Her husband, as Polish military internee, spent almost two years there. Yet, I thought she exaggerated. None of us wanted to believe that families would be transferred to an awful camp. When we arrived in Büren, our eyes were opened.

* * *

Büren lies in a kind of hollow; the climate is damp and cold. The town is about twenty minutes from the camp on the opposite shore of the Aare River, while the wide expanse of the camp was formerly a marshland and is still surrounded by bogs.

A thick fog filled the landscape as we marched through the town. The cloudy waters of the Aare tumbled toward us as we slowly neared the camp. Suddenly, unclear outlines of structures appeared. Not a pretty sight—the thick fog together with the many barracks strewn over this expanse gave an impression of unending dreariness. In the distance against a hazy background was drawn the blurred structure of the guard tower. The ground was covered with puddles of excrement. In furs and coats, with faltering steps, formless figures passed by. The cold damp air cut through our clothing and made the new arrivals quiver. A barbed wire fence bordered this shadowy realm and seemed to say, "Halt," as if this vision would otherwise dissolve into the unreal. Where the barbed wire broke, soldiers stood guard with rifles. There were many guards, as the camp was divided into three segregated areas. In front were the offices and barracks for the guards, just as in prisons, with their bleak cells often occupied by refugees. On the right of the main street of the camp were the women and children's camp, which could be entered by the husbands and fathers only at fixed times. Woe if the lockdown hour was exceeded. The camp watch controlled and protected our morality. Only in the rear began the expanse of the actual men's camp. Entrances to all the sections were guarded, and you needed an armband or pass to be let through.

I had always imagined a stalag to be like this. As the ghostly shadows stealthily passed by, I only thought, "How do these people live? How can you survive such a camp?"

And I did survive, despite hunger, hardship, and sickness. When, today, I flashback to that long winter in Büren, what do I think of first? The food. Nothing else mattered. In Büren, the maintenance of the body was and remained the primary worry. Everything else didn't matter. Everything else served only one purpose, to protect oneself for better times.

We had hunger. The thin soups and beets in which a few potatoes hid in disgrace were the characteristic feature of the Büren cuisine. The refugees pounced on the lean plates like hungry wolves and fought for the leftovers. I came from freedom. It disgusted me to participate. When I saw educated people from once good circumstances, intellectuals greedily fighting for beets, I was ashamed for us. Once I remarked to my neighbor at the table how undignified it was of him to fight over a couple of spoons of watered vegetables. The poor thing, an older gentleman in his late-forties, was so offended I was indeed sorry to have wounded him so. He only said, "If you had spent three years in a French camp, you would understand that eating and dignity cannot be united. Hunger knows no dignity." He was right. I, too, soon forgot to show dignity at meals. The fight about rations went so far that barracks fought against new arrivals for fear that their portions distributed from the more or less same mess bucket would be reduced.

Though we left the task of slicing bread to only the most knowledgeable, the pieces were in addition raffled off so as to eliminate the slightest appearance of partiality. Soon we learned that raw beets and carrots stolen from a nearby vegetable field also stilled one's hunger. Even I pulled beets from the field. If we somehow got hold of some cabbage, we turned it into a fabulously delectable salad.

Those with money could buy sardines and other items. Certainly, in principle, under the threat of being turned back, refugees gave up their money. There were a few who cleverly and carefully hid money on their person, though not many as most refugees disposed of their resources as they entered Switzerland. Those that owned a depository were remunerated five Swiss francs weekly as pocket money. These were used up very quickly in Büren.

The potato saved the refugees of Büren. Long live this fruit of the earth that truly preserved our lives. Potatoes cost twenty-five to thirty Swiss centimes, a price that even the more poverty-stricken could manage. But many didn't have a depository and didn't have a consulate that cared about them. Who envied the Poles, who received fifteen Swiss francs per month from their consulate? Whoever was born or whose parents were from Poland, registered, even if during that period many Poles had their citizenship revoked. The stateless without connections received six Swiss francs from the welfare services. Certainly that was better than nothing, but it was hardly enough for roll-your-own cigarettes. Those without money to buy potatoes had two possibilities. They could try to get on KP duty. The staff of the entire KP barrack was busy eight hours per day peeling potatoes and cleaning vegetables; they of course could always pilfer a few potatoes. It wasn't easy to get accepted, and competition was fierce. Those who didn't succeed in getting into the KP barrack and didn't have any means to buy potatoes had to steal them.

Theft was practiced on a large scale. It was reported one day that fifteen thousand kilos of potatoes disappeared from the storage room. I naturally don't know if this report concerning the quantity is true. Even with twelve hundred refugees, fifteen tons of potatoes is a lot of potatoes, but it must have been a big quantity. The fact was potatoes were only moved from the storage room to the KP barrack under the supervision of soldiers.

To cook potatoes was forbidden. However, the small oven that was supposed to warm the barrack, but couldn't, was barely sufficient for roasting the potatoes. That notwithstanding, we cooked them anyway and made the pot disappear when Captain Rübli[14] (nickname for our camp commander) entered the barrack. There remained the question of wood. We received wood only to heat the barrack and not much of it. In no case was there enough with which to cook. Fifty to sixty men lived in our barrack, and they all wanted to cook potatoes. Cooking cooperatives formed. Every cooking cooperative quickly added a piece of wood so that their potatoes would quickly become tender. So we also had to fetch wood. One of the barrack men was a specialist in the removal of doors from latrines and uninhabited sheds. Under the cover of darkness, he went out to pillage and always triumphantly lugged back another door that we hacked up and hid under the slats of our beds. Those were part of our ironclad reserves. To this day, I still wonder how no one noticed these missing doors and why no one instigated an investigation. For all the members of the twelfth barrack driven by necessity, these doors became a lasting memory of all the pranks we played on the administration. It was almost mandatory, when collecting wood from the wood captain, to put aside unnoticed, one sack of wood and in an unguarded instant quickly make it disappear. Two of our Frenchmen were artists of touch and turning invisible.

My situation was critical. I had little money, so I had to endeavor to improve my care by other means. I tried first with work.

Besides the cleaning tasks and the kitchen duties, there were in Büren two other work details: wood preparation and working in the vegetable fields. It's only natural that the refugees under the given circumstances weren't overly eager to work.

One day, we had a big roll call. Two refugees had left the camp without permission to beg for bread in town. They were caught and sentenced to prison. After a few days, the camp commander pardoned them in front of the assembled camp. He used the opportunity for a big lecture. Whoever volunteered for wood detail and work in the vegetable field would eat separately in the canteen and receive higher rations. He also intimated that these workers might receive additional portions of bread. That was enticing. Even I volunteered. But soon it turned out the ration

---

14 *Rübli* is a Swiss diminutive for *Rüben* (beets).

increases were meager. Apart from the morning coffee, it proved to be mostly water soup and beets, which in any case my intestines rejected. There was no talk of additional bread. On the other hand, the work in this awful winter weather was anything but comfortable. So at the first opportunity, one day, in the middle of working I fell ill. I sought the doctor and asked to be stricken from the duty roster. At my approach, the corporal overseeing the wood details let loose in a rage. From now on, I could only eat in the barrack. Yet every assignment change took place the next day after lunch. My barrack could grab for me neither coffee nor bread for breakfast. The corporal looked upon the second bowl of coffee we drank in the canteen as such a measure of good will that he forbade me to consume my coffee in the canteen for fear I might drink a second cup without working. We were treated with such pettiness. Well, I got over that second cup. This corporal wasn't the only one in Büren who let us feel his master race superiority, for whom every little thing, every piece was an act of grace and demanded gratefulness in return. I don't remember anymore who in Büren told us, "You didn't come to Switzerland to feed your faces." While to the contrary, we suffered from hunger and need. The comrades of Büren will surely remember this expression. It made the rounds through the whole camp. One day, the story went, a soldier, who regularly sat in the canteen, was rebuked to "Not visit the Jew canteen anymore." One told another. It poisoned the atmosphere and embittered the morale of the refugees. When only a few unworthy elements are present, the critic of the refugee is so bent to dismiss all refugees with contempt, that you must, after such events and expressions that rapidly spread among the refugees, understand the mistrust that most refugees even today feel against the Swiss authority. The refugee knew kindly little about the Swiss people and too many barriers blocked such an approach.

Some camp residents often received packages from friends and relatives. However, the sending of rationed items was banned. These packages contained other items of great value: canned goods, fruit, snacks, cigarettes, and postage stamps. The censors never questioned a booklet of stamps valued at 4.50 Swiss francs or a post card booklet for one Swiss franc. And that was just like cash. Cigarettes and tobacco helped save money, and the weekly allowance could be reserved for food. Oh, how the lucky ones receiving packages were envied.

A Swiss newspaper once wrote that packages sent to refugees in the camps, containing rationed food goods, were banned so as not to encourage a black market among the refugees, and that they in any event received rations equal to those of the civilian population. There was something peculiar about these equal rations. That the government allocated the same rations to the refugees may not have been in dispute, but certainly, in Büren, they never reached us. To clarify the matter, it should be noted that some in the Büren administration were found guilty of embezzlement[15] and jailed. This was also proof that the previous convictions were true and that we truly did suffer from hunger. It should be emphasized that the hunger explained much, including the less attractive side of refugee behavior. We knew we were unwelcome guests and often said we would understand if the government had explained that they could not grant us the same rations as its citizens. We found it as total mockery, however, to always read that we received exactly the same as the others from which followed the right to censorship of the "care" packages.

What concerns the black market, which the above rule was supposed to suppress—ugh, how you can be concerned about the ethics and the morals of the refugees—led to its full blossoming. In defiance, engaging in black market activities will always and to all be prohibited wherever hunger prevails and where there are people who can spend more money than others. Thanks to a particular propaganda espousing a certain point of view, there stand recognizably Jews in the lure of the black market. But just how was it in Switzerland? There were certainly no Jews there, hidden or with false papers. That land is race pure and inhabited by the noble master race. And in Germany, was there no black market? After all, you did read in the papers about death sentences. And yet, not all the news reached abroad. But enough!

A considerable black market did develop in Büren, particularly in bread. Other things came into the camp in only limited quantities. There were people who had such a dependence on cigarettes that they sold their bread and from the proceeds purchased their cigarettes. Instead of bread, they ate potatoes. A ration of bread cost seventy-five Swiss centimes and more.

---

15 Captain Lindt (Rübli) owned a pig farm and removed food destined for the refugees to feed his pigs. Interview with Gaston Levy also known as René Levy. Fabienne Regard, and Neury Lurent, *Memoire d'une Suisse en guerre: la vie—malgré tout (1939–1945).* Yens sur Morges (Switzerland): Cabédita, 2002, p. 266

A lot could be purchased in Büren, not just bread. Also work. Fifty Swiss centimes paid for a work duty substitute whether concerned with wood chores or kitchen duties. The flagrant differences between the rich and the poor in this wretched camp were evident. Whoever had money didn't need to work and could eat one's fill. The poor worked and went hungry and nothing could be done. The suffering was too much. The poor were happy to earn something. Several washed clothes, although mostly women were retained for this work. Tailors and shoemakers fared the best, earning mending money from their richer comrades.

It's a self-evident truth. Suffering awakes in man the less noble instincts. You lost all shame. The will to live is so strong, that it leads us to overlook many ills. Our conscience is more charitable. We commit deeds we would not commit under normal circumstances. In our barrack we had a strong stout man who was forever hungry. He always squinted greedily at the sardine tins that a rich Alsatian at the next table left, and carefully scraped out any remainder. Was there something edible that repulsed us in Büren? I hardly think so. When I picked out and ate the potatoes off my plate and offered the remaining beets, I always found grateful takers. Normally, you don't eat from the plate of another, a stranger. But in Büren, we never thought about such trivialities. Once, two cases of unsellable, moldy fruitcake were offered in the canteen. Everyone could have as much as they wanted. Every one of us graciously took several pieces. We carefully scraped them and dried them on the oven and then ate these pieces with great relish.

Another comrade was content to serve a group of rich gentlemen, to cook potatoes and prepare salad for them. He could then eat with them.

These groveling creatures that were submissive to these rich people angered me. Weren't we all equally good or equally bad? In the end, wasn't our destiny the same? An inner need to reject this mundane inequality led me to associate with people who also had no means at their disposal. I made only one exception: a man who no doubt had money, but never made a commotion about it and never judged another by his money pouch.

What I had, I carefully divided. To be sure I wouldn't be caught short, I always made sure to have a reserve of tobacco and postage stamps. It gave me pleasure to be able to offer poorer colleagues a cigarette. I don't want to make myself sound better than I am. I did

it perhaps less from affection than from the need to succeed in pre-
serving a certain rank. To this I understood how to get on, or as the
French say, *debrouiller*. After all, it wasn't for naught that I was in the
Foreign Legion. I had experience in situations that depended on my
own resourcefulness. In such circumstances, you come to realize, after
all, that regulations that overly constrict life and are morally unfair
need not be recognized. I never stole from another and endeavored to
respect the principles of friendship, but in respect to that, we all formed
our own morality. Büren developed some bad traits in me; today I am
astounded how I could become obsessed with money. Avarice certainly
did not belong to my usual character traits. But so as not to drown, I
needed to howl with the wolves and adapt to the most unusual situation
that existed in Büren.

My best friend in the camp, whom I mentioned before, was a Viennese
industrialist. Four years after immigrating and spending several years in
camps, there was nothing left from his prior wealth except the memory
of better days. At the time of the deportations, he managed to escape
from a French camp, and it cost him his last piece of jewelry. He showed
me pictures of himself from better days. The appearance of a once well-
nourished, stout, and surely very comfortable gentleman was no longer
in evidence. He didn't own any suits. From the clothing storage room
of the welfare service, he managed to snag a few pieces of clothing
and notably a pair of shoes—not easy to find, we were too many—and
these disparate pieces hung on him like rags. But his furrowed face still
had a stamp of old Austrian *Gemütlichkeit*, and it was such a pleasure
to chat with him. He experienced too much to take the petty camp day
seriously. For this he knew camp life through and through and was an
artist in procuring things, particularly vegetables from which he could
make a wonderful salad. With dedication he dressed the salad with vin-
egar, salt, and pepper, and salad dressing that he obtained from richer
comrades. You couldn't refuse him anything. He was the best comrade,
and he always divided everything fairly. He had a few addresses from
his once previous travels in Switzerland. But the results were not stunning. Instead, a Swiss peasant with whom he lived in hiding for a while
in France recommended him to relatives, a peasant and a retired school-
teacher. These simple people sent him fruit and friendly letters that he
never received from his richer connections.

This industrialist had a young friend and the two of them rescued themselves, escaping to Switzerland together. I never knew his real name. We called him the "Negus," in part because of his dark complexion and because of his constantly mussed up hair. Negus was the ultimate camp original. After several years in the camps, camp life lay in his flesh and blood. He was a vagabond, but home was not the street, rather some camp. For him camp life was the norm. I really asked myself what this man would do when there were no more camps. He went around in a torn shirt, a sweater full of holes, shoes covered with excrement, an old ragged pair of pants from which an end of his underwear always curiously fluttered in the air. That he never shaved was understandable. He worked diligently for as long as he could tolerate the work. He had intellectual interests, read eagerly, and could discuss any book but outwardly presented an unpleasant image. Only with force did we get him to shave. He also was competent in procuring foodstuffs, and his correspondence had results.

Refugees were reproached for writing beggar letters from the camps. No wonder. I too wrote letters, first from Geneva to two customers of my firm, which received no replies. Also another letter written from Büren brought no results. I had to obtain packages, not for myself, but for my wife and children in Val-Fleury, who also suffered need. In this early time, it was no pleasure being a refugee. As happy as we were to have evaded the Germans, having saved our lives, we were hungry, and nothing could change that. I knew one refugee who escaped Büren to return to France. He had money and counted on getting false papers and to be free. I doubted that he did well, but at the time there were others who thought as he did.

Paul was always hungry. With his plate, the child ran after the servers and begged for more. My wife even gave him her own bread ration, and she hardly had the money to at least buy some apples. My wife told me how she once—she received a remittance from me for five francs—bought a box of pralines and with Paul consumed the whole lot on the spot. And my wife was not into treats. She would have preferred just a plain, bare piece of bread. Michou had been removed from the camp after several weeks. His cough ultimately developed into bronchitis, and he had to be hospitalized twice. After the second time, the doctor declared him unfit for living in the camp. He was placed in a nursery, in a home of the Salvation Army in Geneva. And although he had the protection and the care of the sisters, he was plagued for a long time by an asthmatic cough that was only finally cured in Nesslau almost a year later. Paul, on the other hand, stayed with my wife in Val-Fleury until the middle of February 1943. At that point in time, a children's home for refugees was opened, and he was one of the first to receive foster care there. This children's home, Les Mureilles, was a lucky stroke for Paul. I will return to this home later.

In the two and a half months that my wife spent with Paul, she sank low from cares and worries. The child was rotting away in this life on straw and constantly in the presence of adults. Only when both children were cared for could my wife breathe a sigh of relief. She could take care of herself and do chores. Washing dishes brought her increased rations that she didn't have to share.

Surely we brought some money into Switzerland. At the exchange rate of seventy French francs to the Swiss franc, our fortune amounted to about three hundred Swiss francs of which two hundred went to our room and board and the rest paid out as pocket money. How long would this money last? Already at the end of December, the allowances to my wife ceased, and she came into great hardship, as she was now dependent on welfare. In Geneva, that amounted to one franc per week per person. I was a little better off as I still had a tiny amount in a custodial account, but with shock I could foresee the time when we were all dependent on the support of welfare. From the fifty francs that I had left at the start of 1943, I naturally had to transfer money to my wife and Paul. Fourrier, the camp director, approved for me a special payment for my family. I needed to present to him the stub for inspection. It took four days for me to receive the stub through the camp mail, which like everything else went through censorship. On the fourth day, I was summoned to Fourrier. "Have you transferred the money?" he asked me. I was already quite irritated, the thought that I could be taken for a swindler or had tried under a ruse to entice out money, my own I might add, brought my blood to a boil. I exploded; we suffered much hardship and were also considered morally inferior. What was he thinking? What did he take me for? Oh wonders, it had an effect. He became really nice to me and even endorsed my right to welfare support, which actually only people without a deposit account could receive. But what did thirty or forty francs for an entire family amount to? I really feared the future. In this wretched camp, you really saw how forsaken a man without a penny to his name was. Besides, we were without rights and dependent on grace, as we often heard. When you even begged for the smallest thing, you landed on the lowest step. Would I become like the comrade who gathered the leftovers of the well-to-do comrades? Would it also come to pass that I had to complain at the help counter of the bar- rack to get postage stamps? Would I wash the filthy clothes of the other comrades while they played cards, only because they had more money? Would I beg the rich comrades for cigarettes, only to hear "I don't have any either"?

I tried already at the start in Geneva to get in touch with my relatives in England, and even received mail from there. But there was no money, because my relatives were not British, and despite their greatest efforts, they could not get a transmittal permit.

I granted myself nothing from this money but was saving it for a later time when the custodial account would become totally depleted. I also fell ill that January and ate very little: not just of the camp's nourishment, but also of the tins that I later received in parcels. What I didn't share with colleagues or send to my wife, I sold and put away one franc after another until one day I had nearly thirty francs in my hand.

A fortune! I hadn't possessed that much for quite a while. I was seized by fear, lest they take this money away from me in another inspection or I succumb to temptation and spend the money. I was searching for a capital investment. Commerce in valuables—watches, signet rings, and so forth—though limited, existed in the camp. Refugees who possessed small pieces of jewelry or other ornaments but no money could not resist the temptation to sell something to gain cash. People in desperation also sold shoes, sweaters, and other items. Those who wanted to dispose of cash often put their money into valuables when a good opportunity pre- sented itself. I soon managed to find a broker who engaged in all kinds of businesses. He laid in front of me several watches for my selection. I chose an old Omega. I was sure I had overpaid, but wasn't sorry about the purchase. It was a remembrance of this unusual time, that I too could do a little business and be a small-time capitalist—with thirty Francs! It was a psychosis from which I suffered. Didn't all of us there go a little crackers? Didn't an association that oppressively restricted us and treated us like vagabonds subjugate us?

Yet I wanted to report about my letters. My past cries of help remained without results. I was disgusted to lower myself with this futile effort and in this fashion, and the thought occurred to me to give up on the idea of finding someone to show concern for us. And yet, dear God did provide us with divine protection, never refusing to give comfort in the worst situations. Didn't God protect me in the Legion, in the French camps, and lead me back to my loved ones? I always drew comfort and faith from the thought of God's miraculous ways, the meaning of which often escapes us. Perhaps Providence helped me because, in reality, my heart never lost trust in the future and remained steadfast in God's guidance.

On a cold December day, one of our barrack comrades was released. I begged him to take a letter. It was my last attempt to seek help outside the camp. I hurriedly wrote the letter. The comrade promised to smuggle it out. It snowed and rained, and I helped carry his bags to the inspection point, from where I could observe if the letter safely left the camp. The letter went through. Persistently, I had explained to him how much depended on this letter for me. And I waited—waited until I thought that this letter had shared the same fate as its predecessors.

One day, in January, I was called to the post office and handed a parcel. Beaming with joy I returned to the barrack and unpacked it with care. I thought I was dreaming as I saw the many food tins and quality cigarettes. There was someone after all who wanted to help us. We had a friend. A letter was enclosed, so pleasant and friendly, so from the heart and open, that I could glance out of the vagabond world of our camp into another better world. The parcel was worth at least twenty francs. There was someone who spent that much money on us. I had been elevated to Croesus, the wealthy king of Lydia. I received several other parcels but none made such an impression on me as that first one from the hands of friendship. It was a sign that God did not forget. This deed presaged for our entire family a different and better period.

To be perfectly honest, for the New Year, those without resources received parcels from the Jewish Welfare Services. I received one too. I ate some of it, and from the rest I made another parcel, adding a piece of cheese and a slice of bread out of my own rations. I included a note for the censors that these were from my own rations for my wife. The parcel went through. It was the first parcel that I could send my wife—in fact, the first one that she received from someone in Switzerland. A pathetic little parcel, more gesture than deed, but what joy it gave my wife and Paul. "Papa sent us a parcel," Paul told everyone, radiating with joy, as my wife reported. And for me it was such a pleasure, such a satisfaction, to be able from the confines of the camp to be able to care for my loved ones. In a way, the gentleman who sent the aforementioned parcel adopted my family with great kindness. He and his family eased our situation in many ways. No, by these people I never felt demeaned. Everything was so simple, kind, and natural. I understood it was possible to lower oneself for one's own family and not lose your self-respect, and even to be proud of the results.

We had permission to write one letter and one postal card per week. We understood why the mail was checked. We were under the watch of the military. But two writings per week were not sufficient. We wrote to relatives, who were often in other camps. With all the rest of the correspondence, the limit was quickly exhausted—we wrote a lot. Despite the threat of penalties, we smuggled out mail. There were people who visited relations in the hospital, those who were set free, and comrades transferred to labor camps. In short, there was always someone who could hide a letter and bring it to the outside—despite inspections.

* * *

Did I have only ugly memories of Büren? No, certainly not—on the contrary. We became so accustomed to our wretchedness we didn't see anything unusual about it. It was the lot of the refugees, and nothing could be changed. We knew nothing about the many people in aid organizations making efforts to improve our lot, and back then we would not have believed it. It had to be so. When you spend several weeks like this, totally cut off from the outside world, when someone always openly brings you to the realization that you are an unwanted refugee without rights, when so little possibility to change your situation exists, you resign yourself to your fate. *On se fait une raison*, you rationalize. You had to make the best of the situation and to accept Büren and its atmosphere. We lived in the joyless present, in the hope of a better future. The healthy ones hoped to be transferred to a work camp, from which we heard reports that sounded like fairytales. The old and frail hoped for a home. In the meantime, this bizarre, unreal world identifiable by soldiers, awful food, barracks, and barbed wire fences veiled by fog was our world. Büren reminded me of a theater piece by Rheinhardt put on in the Josefstädter Theater.[16] It was called *Ueberfahrt*.[17] We too were dead, the dead of civil life, but we acted as if we were alive so that no one would notice our death. We too were on a crossing into another world, the postwar world. Dear God, how it kept us waiting. In the meantime, we were meant to go crazy, have other thoughts so as not to think of daily life.

A cornucopia of talent existed among the twelve hundred refugees of Büren. A good ensemble was soon formed. How we laughed at the joke-laden revue, *Everything in Camp*, with its sad but ironic hit, "We Have Everything in Camp." Yes, we had everything in camp; it wasn't difficult to make the connection from the camp atmosphere to that of *The Threepenny Opera* and develop the motif for ridicule, biting criticism, and satire. And oh, the New Year's Eve presentation of 1942 with Réne Lévy as Charley's Aunt, who with his long legs properly strutted through the evening and made us forget the frigid cold of the theater room. With such sparse resources, we made costumes; talented hands transformed paper into artful decorations and collages. It was a true wonder. The theater group had a special benefactor in the person of Lieutenant First Class Blum, who did much to enable the shows.

And those evenings in barrack 12, when Réne Lévy grabbed his accordion and entertained us late into the night. Everything—Russian songs, Viennese waltzes, tangos—one after another in random order until we were no longer conscious of being prisoners in a filthy barrack. Those Russian songs with their heavy mood expressed our feelings exactly. *Hei*, how we stamped out the tempo with our feet until the guards begged us for restraint.

---

16 Josefstädter Theater is located in the Vienna neighborhood where the Adler family had lived.

17 "Crossing"

And again the evenings when Yiddish songs were sung and all the men from Holland, Belgium, France, and elsewhere shed these foreign identities and remained simple, pursued Polish Jews. The heads swayed back and forth, the faces transformed, and the hands spoke and gave the tempo. Here, with enraptured eyes, they were all back again in their little *städtels* in Poland, by their *heimische stubele* with their *mamele*. In their spirits, they were packing their bags, leaving these uninviting alien places, and finally traveling home to their Jewish Palestine.

Strange, lost, magical world—these women, who in filth and misery, still had the ambition to present themselves coquettish and chic, to flirt and to love. They lived in a past reality. To the previously mentioned New Year's Eve party, local Swiss were also invited. They came with their wives, simple, unsophisticated women from the countryside who made donations to the refugees, as our plight was well-known in Büren. What did these women think about some of the refugee women, who were wrapped in their fur coats, made up, and in full splendor, parading around with a cigarette dangling from their mouths? There was nothing to say against the fur coat. The unheated room was unbearably cold, and we froze. A fur coat could not be treated with contempt. When you flee, you take your most valuable things, to which undoubtedly belongs a fur coat, in so far as you own one. But it was tactless then to so fix yourself up and act this way. How could these women confuse, of all places, Büren with the halls of a luxury hotel and these simple Swiss women with visitors to a palace? Could they not even think how in these surroundings the impression such an appearance must have provoked in the Swiss?

So I thought then as others of my colleagues did, regretting when refugees themselves contributed to a negative attitude toward us.

And yet, "L'evasion, c'est l'illusion." Beautifully brandished lips brought us passionate, suggestive messages from another time; a flirtatious eye movement abducted us far away from the dank barracks buried in filth. In their misery they still brought us warmth, humanity, and revelry in oblivion. They opened the door to the barrack, and the desolate room transformed its face, and the fog receded. If we didn't disintegrate into complete slobs, if we still made an effort about our outward appearance and cared about our cleanliness, whom do we thank if not the women? And that was true even for those whose wives were not there. All were compelled to realize that women might see them. For women, Büren was not a beautiful place to stay, and yet we regretted when in January the women gradually left.

I close my eyes and there stands resurrected the world of a refugee's winter. The comrades of those unforgettable days resurface. The gentle Greek, who only thought about his wife. Next to him, the young nineteen-year-old French Parisian, who lived many years in the Dutch West Indies. He suffered from bulimia, an illness requiring a robust and plentiful diet because the digestive system works too fast, just the kind of illness for Büren. He understood how to fill a mess tin from scraps of our watery vegetables. In a tin can—every refugee knew how to make a primitive storage container from empty food cans—he carefully put aside beets for later consumption in the sleeping quarters to quiet his hunger. The industrialist from Vienna, two young pleasant Frenchmen, our unforgettable Worochiloff, whom we so named, sometimes Timoschenko, because he was a big strong Jew from Russia. He was without exception for all and everything. He could do any task, and none was turned down, as long as he could earn something. Everything that was offered disappeared without a trace into his wide stomach, yet without satiating him.

That was my table. There were many such tables in the barrack and on every one a number of types with unique characteristics and capabilities. In front, at the honor table, Réne Lévy, the head of the barrack, sat with other distinguished guests of the immigration. Here also sat Mickey Mouse, a small German lawyer who always got up especially early to place the largest bowls on his table. Once I got up earlier than he did and placed the largest bowls on our table. The poor thing, he fumed with anger.

At another table sat rich Alsatian Jews who could take advantage of money, friends, or connections, which were all equivalent. Many turned to this table after lunch, to where the envied opened their sardine tins.

The intellectuals of the barrack reserved a table. Here an attempt was made to remain intellectually engaged and to stand above conditions. Yet they didn't regard their food with disdain. Poverty forced even these lofty thinkers into dark methods to obtain food. For them too, the cooking of potatoes for potato salad was a holy undertaking. One of our medical doctors stood firm on the need for this additional eating, and after his hard labor, he certainly had need for this modest supplement.

A large, long table united all the Polish Jews. They were too many to find room at one table.

In this smoky barrack, which could not be made clean so deeply penetrated was it with dirt, we wrote, we discussed, and we played. Here we even danced to accordion accompaniment and drank wine. Here we held celebrations that let us forget our dour lot in life—pathetic celebrations that cannot be measured by usual standards. Here, on New Year's Eve in the company of women, we festively dined on potato salad with sardines, wine and apples for dessert. Everyone saved for this evening, and the rich made a special contribution. From the proceedings of the common purchases, the poor received a gift: a blood or liver sausage. And then we danced and sang and at midnight emotionally embraced each other and wished each other a better future.

What could all the aid action organizations and all the concerted efforts of the several organizations report in such a camp? Everything was just a drop on a hot stone. The whole camp had to disappear; the mismanagement had to come to an end. And it happened, but only after a long, gloomy winter. More about that later.

The inhabitants of Büren knew well how we suffered from all the shortages. They helped us willingly. When a work detail went into town, I happily went along. I put on a large wind jacket with large pockets, as I was sure to receive a piece of bread from a friendly woman who lived in the vicinity of the train station. Sometimes, I even succeeded in disappearing unnoticed for fifteen minutes. Then I went into this clean, friendly, well-kept house. I breathed freedom and security. I was always a welcome guest and drank hot tea with real sugar and ate bread to my heart's content. It existed in this world. On one side, indescribable suffering; and on the other, civilized well-being. The most wonderful baked goods were stacked up in the pastry shop. Magical powers pulled to the display windows. But oh dear, we had no stamps, and besides terribly little money.

* * *

My health could not tolerate these circumstances forever. In the beginning of January, I fell ill. The camp doctor examined me and without question determined the cause of my suffering. My ulcer made it again difficult for me to work hard. But it was impossible to be placed into the infirmary. Besides I also suffered from scabies and could not contaminate the sick room. It was no wonder, with all the dirt and the straw that had not been changed since the camp opened in September. In Büren many children and women had lice. But scabies was the worst. You suffered terribly with the urge to scratch the itching, particularly at night. Comrades avoided you like a leper. They feared shaking your hand and didn't want to sleep next to me. I had several fellow sufferers in several barracks. It was not possible to isolate us; there was hardly any room to segregate us. We had to stay in our own barracks.

The treatment, which in a hospital through thorough rubdowns and with application of a salve takes twenty-four to forty-eight hours to cure, took over two weeks in this environment. Always, the prescription was shower, rubdown, and salve. In the middle of winter, in the cold dressing room next to the showers, which was insufficiently heated due to the few people who used it, this was torture.

So passed two weeks—two weeks in writhing pain in which I squatted, wrapped in my winter coat, on the bench next to the oven in the barrack and still shivered from the cold. Finally—finally!—the rash was gone. With a true gasp of relief, I returned the blankets for disinfection. I could stretch out in the bed of the sick room. How it seemed soft and snug; in reality it was a hard bed, after weeks spent on the damp, cold straw of the barrack. The barrack was so damp that clothing and laundry developed mold in our valises and cardboard boxes. At night, water dripped on the walls. But it was good. For the first few days, I stayed totally under the covers; the warmth surrounded me, released the body tension; I was entirely happy. The room was well heated. At night, you didn't have to run to the toilet as in the barrack, which frequently occurred thanks to the watery fare. The toilet was far away, and the trail to it was muddy and laden with excrement. Many of us didn't go there despite prohibitions and fines.

I weighed approximately fifty kilos. The doctor prescribed milk, fortified nourishment, and a special diet. I often received rice, farina, noodles, corn, and other nourishing things. Slowly, I recovered.

There were a lot of sick people in Büren. Was it any wonder then that so many older people, people who suffered for many years in

French camps and whose nerves were shattered from war, fear of death, and bombings, fell ill in this place? My friend from Vienna also stayed here. An old heart ailment plagued him and left him short of breath. We cheered each other up and gave each other courage.

Two nurses, Annie and Ruth, gave their best. With sacrifice they cared for and consoled the sick. Their bright smiles awoke a new zest for life in alienated faces. They rarely had any respite. With all the men, women, and small children, they had plenty of work. I saw the diminutive Ruth usually doing double-time and always smiling, friendly, and cooperative.

* * *

Yes, we also had small children and women in the camp. There was a special barrack for mothers with infants, which had been furnished with some measure of comfort. But the other women and children were housed in the ordinary barracks.

I have hardly spoken about the women in the camp. It was so painful to think about it and to remember. Not that I forget how much we owed the women of Büren. Their presence made it easier to bear the dreary winters. But it was so degrading.

For a time there were so many women and children in Büren that one of the barracks in the men's section was freed up for women. I did not like going there. The atmosphere that dominated there was even more depressing than in the men's quarters. The women slept on straw, over which they had spread sheets. When you opened the door, heavy body odor hit you right in the face. Several women lay wrapped in blankets for the greater part of the day at their place; some did laundry, while others ate, wrote, or entertained each other. Wash hung from the ropes suspended across the ceiling. What dignity could these women preserve when they couldn't even be secure at the toilet with their own full privacy?

Couldn't you forgive these women when they sometimes felt the need to play women and ladies to forget their lot? And didn't they have to stay connected to the external, with make-up on the lips and red lac-quered fingernails, in this camp that stuck on us and remained unforget-table and indelible.

I once observed two women in the canteen pressing up against Swiss soldiers. They were certain of receiving a piece of bread. Hopefully they were not women whose husbands also were in Büren, but even that was not impossible. Here, the young girls learned that the most desirable lover was the one who could get you something to eat, be it even the kitchen boy.

How I thanked God that my wife had not been transferred here. Shortly before her transport was supposed to leave, the camp com-mander explained to his superiors that he could not undertake further responsibility for more women and children. And so no more came.

The ones that were here, stayed. Only after the New Year, did the camp begin to empty out. More comrades were transferred to labor camps. For women and children, the weak and infirm, a new, good home-type camp was opened in Prêles.

I was supposed to go there also. I was doing so well in the infirmary that I didn't want to leave. Where would I receive such plentiful and proper nourishment? I turned to the head of the camp, who convinced the captain that I could stay.

It was to be only for a short time. The days at Büren were num-bered. On February 12 the rumor spread at supper: Büren was to be closed. Fifteen hundred German soldiers had defected across the bor-der, and a whole camp was needed for them; we would all be removed. The "jungle telephone," the camp rumor factory that secretly spread news faster than the radio, had broadcast this news to all the world. Oh, how we wanted to believe that the Germans were defecting in droves. At eleven o'clock the news that Büren was to be emptied was confirmed, and we were jubilant. In our ears it sounded like the war had ended. With zest we packed the whole night. Sleep had vanished. We forged plans for the future. Even the infirmary was closed. The difficult cases were transferred to the Canton Hospital in Biel—except for one. As he heard we were leaving, he said they didn't need to transfer him. He was tired of living. Why change again? Why wan-der again? Softly, his will to live had been extinguished. He died that night, and lays buried in Büren.

* * *

That was the end of Büren. Three hundred eighty Alsatians—not fifteen hundred Germans—took our places, moved in under other statutes. Higher authorities recognized the deplorable state of affairs. Remedial action was taken, and the guilty parties were jailed.

But we, fifteen hundred women and men, we survived Büren. We knew it in poverty, wretchedness, filth, hunger, and cold. Together we froze, suffered, cried, and laughed. We shortened gloomy evenings with song, put on theater in the frigid winter nights. We celebrated holidays when we had the least courage. Here we loved and kissed.

We learned to be comrades. We made lasting friends.

We learned to love life, even its ugly parts.

And when today we meet other refugees from Büren, we say, "Do you know?"

And we are happy to have survived and to be alive.

It didn't kill us. It made us stronger.

19

From Camp to Camp: Schönengrund–Champéry

A fter Büren, I experienced several other reception camps. Schönengrund, Champéry, Geneva, and Prêles were all stages on my way to the work camp. None left the kind of impression as Büren did. These other camps were the norm. Büren was a life experience. I have no regrets.

My description of Büren should in no way detract from my deeply felt thanks for our admittance into Switzerland. Not just because Büren was still better than deportation. I'm certainly not servile to the point of view that our gratitude to God, fate, and Switzerland has gone so far as to hold bad for good and that for refugees everything is good. No, to that extent, my tough fate has not degraded me. Refugees, even without rights, are still part of humanity. But Büren was a mistake, and mistakes can happen anywhere. In France we said, "Il n'a que celui qui ne travaille pas qui ne se trompe jamais."[18] The being of a free state can't always prevent disgraceful conditions, but necessarily promotes that they be recognized and abolished. And in Büren that was the end situation. The kind of disgrace at Büren was understandable and forgivable, growing out of the landscape and climate, and connected with the reality of an unforeseen and unforeseeable influx of refugees. These refugees were not soldiers, but a colorful mix of civilians of both sexes and every age.

For me, Büren was, besides an experience, also a test—a test of my destiny that has graciously ended. To hold Switzerland or all Swiss people responsible for the misdeeds of a few, who are in fact paying penance, would be folly. But the significance of the reception camps in shaping the mentality of the refugees cannot be ignored. And for us refugees, Büren forged a concept—even for those who were not there.

Can a camp really be good? Only freedom is good. The organization of a camp, by necessity, brings with it things we detest. Inevitably, people relinquish their personalities. They dissolve into the crowd. A camp doesn't have any space for individuality. Most of all the loss of freedom weighs most heavily on humans. The work camps and homes are, in their way, very well organized and fulfill their purpose totally. The refugees would like and could have many changes, but the dominant direction has been established simply through the organization of refugee life. All refugees have the desire for freedom, all feel constrained by the shackles that have been foisted on them, and all look toward the war's end when they will be elevated from a homeless refugee without rights to a full-valued human citizen.

Surely all refugees are happy and grateful to be in Switzerland when thinking about the destiny of their unfortunate counterparts who fell into German hands. But it cannot be assumed that the feeling of rescue will extinguish in a person an understanding of and the striving for freedom. Yes, we are happy to have escaped the Germans, but nonetheless, we love freedom, and the Swiss will come to understand that.

I was transferred with thirty comrades to the reception camp Schönengrund in the Appenzell. It was a light, clear, sunny winter day. The fog of Büren had dissipated, and the landscape smiled on us. As soon as we were underway, the dampness retreated. A comrade pulled

---

18 Those who don't work never make mistakes.

out a mud brush and carefully cleaned himself. We followed his example. It was a symbolic action. We stripped away the dirt of Büren and were human again. Several compartments were reserved for us. The guard traveled with us, and we were not permitted to mix with the other travelers. Wistfully, I observed the Zurich train station. The last time I traveled through, I was a well and welcomed tourist and not a guarded refugee that people stared at with great curiosity. "This way out, in a single line, no talking, and keep moving," the guard harshly commanded as we changed trains in Zurich. Those were the rules, yet the soldiers closed one eye and even shut both eyes tightly as quite a few relatives and friends, who had been secretly notified, materialized.

There was one touching reunion. You could not receive visitors in Büren. We were, after all, under military supervision. One of our women and her husband, a Polish military internee, had not seen each other for over two and a half years. He had received permission from his camp to visit his wife in Büren, but she did not receive permission to speak with him. As she saw him, she tore herself loose and hurried to him and only with difficulty could they be separated from their embrace.

Slowly, slowly the strict measures were loosened, and the people who could see each other again after a long time quickly exchanged little packages; this trip brought omens of a gentler future.

Schönengrund was situated in a most beautiful place and at my time certainly the best reception camp. The Appenzell is one of the loveliest regions of natural beauty that extends through Switzerland. The weather was mild. The sun shone on the snow-covered hillsides. Where the snow had faded, the fragrant earth revealed itself, and grasses stretched their stems toward the sun. With wide-open lungs, we inhaled the balmy air. After the fog and filth of Büren, here we were in a nature paradise. The radiant, victorious beauty of spring stimulated us. Here we could live and breathe. It was good to be here.

And this friendly landscape, we could not only look at it but also enjoy it thanks to the care of our gracious camp commandant. He himself participated in our hikes, and we didn't have to walk in groups with even the barest presence of a benevolent guard to remind us of our refugee's shackles. When I first participated in one of these hikes, in which the spouse of the commandant also joined, I stood almost in tears. This woman spoke to us as equals. For her, we were human beings.

The commandant in every respect brought us understanding and sought to ease our situation wherever he could. He was always ready to listen with open ears and was accessible to everyone. No camp manager stood apart between him and the workers; no, on the contrary, the camp manager himself made sure that we could approach the commandant directly with any of our concerns. The men whose wives were located in a nearby camp could visit their wives regularly. The commandant took in the son of a camp resident. The young boy came to visit his father. The refugee boy slept naturally on the straw next to his father in the general sleeping quarters. The son of the commandant also came to Schönengrund. So there should be no recognized difference between the boys, it didn't disturb the commandant to let him sleep next to his comrade in our bedroom that rather than have his boy sleep with him in his hotel. I need not emphasize how his sensitivity positively affected our well-being.

The conduct of our commandant also provided an example to the guard. How nice and kindly the guard head held the daily roll call and reproached us in a fatherly manner our daily transgressions.

The commandant also brought us in as coworkers for the far-reaching inner camp administration. An envoy of our own choosing possessed real authority. He was in a position to settle disputes without reporting these to the Swiss. We abided by his decisions. I recommended this beneficial system to other heads of camp.

The bedrooms were located in a factory and in a vacation home, while our dayrooms, meaning dining hall and reading room, were housed in the nearby inn, Gasthaus zur Krone. This layout required that we frequently cross the street, and this reality gave us the feeling of being unbound, a feeling reinforced by the sentry placement, away from the entrance to the inn. The inn was open to all passers-by and all residents of the village. The sentry was placed in the street about one hundred meters from the inn. As we didn't have a courtyard, we were permitted to walk in the street about one hundred meters to the right and to left of the inn. In addition, after lunch we could walk a distance up the side of the mountain rising behind the inn. At the end of our permitted promenade was a bench with a spectacular view onto the surrounding mountains, where you could so pleasantly chat and dream.

We all felt well, but for those transferred from Büren, Schönengrund was paradise, a paradise in which even the most hungry could be satiated.

I was thinking of the young man from Büren who suffered from bulimia. Here, even he had his fill. Visitors from labor camps assured us that, with the exception of certain differences owing to the multiple assignments in the labor camps, the care in their camp was not better than ours. Our soups and vegetables were prepared together with the nourishment for the guard squad. Also meat was the same for all except that the soldiers naturally had meat more frequently. But our meat portion was a full portion and didn't suffer from embezzlement shrinkage as in Büren. And besides, the room and board charges were approximately 20 percent less. It came to 2.69 or 2.89 compared with 3.50 in Büren. Here the same rations as for the civilian population actually arrived on our table. To these we could add, in exchange of coupons, a piece of cake or *hörnli*. Coupons were albeit difficult to get, but we could obtain them since we did receive visitors and saw people.

The welfare organization functioned here much better than in Büren. Most of us could supplement our wardrobe in an agreeable manner. All those in need received warm vests, sweaters, one skirt, stockings, socks, and so forth. You didn't need to beg for these things as in Büren. When we arrived in Büren, we received two changes of underwear. That was already quite generous and valuable. Without this supplement, many of us wouldn't even have been able to wash our underwear to change it. We refugees, to not call attention to ourselves, usually traveled with a small piece of luggage, rucksack, or briefcase in which a change of underwear and some provisions for the trip could be stowed. It could take months for your bags to follow, if indeed they still existed, weren't stolen or lost. But beyond this one-time issue, for which we were certainly thankful, it was difficult to have something else issued from the store clerk. We sometimes had the impression that the store clerks feared to give anything away. They felt their first line of duty was to maintain the store's inventory. That they did conscientiously.

In Schönengrund everything was different. It was not a massive camp. Everyone knew everyone else and became friends. Bureaucracy did not prevail here, nor any unnecessary paperwork as in Büren. The house leader and other functionaries sat with the refugees at the same table. There was no preferential treatment. In order for a camp to be a real community and not a mass operation, the number of people must be limited to no more than one hundred fifty. Anything in excess turns into a massive camp in which individuals have no value, and by necessity turns into a bureaucracy with all its disadvantages.

Also appropriate leisure activity was provided. There were group games, books, and newspapers. I was amazed at how many publications were available. And you could get them. They didn't disappear, who knew where, as in Büren. No, Schönengrund was surprisingly well organized. Everything was done to minimize our sensitivity to the shackles that internment in the camp must bring. Gymnastics took place every morning in the meadow. A young soldier taught us many exercises. Once we had a presentation of the army cinema and a colorful, very clever theater evening. And of course there were the hikes in loose groups.

It is unnecessary to mention that here no black market existed. There was no need for it. There were no businesses or nonsense business as in Büren. As a result the camaraderie was that much more extensive.

My mental state changed totally. In Büren, I feared the future and strove to pile up as much money as possible. Here, with an open hand, I spent everything I received. I did it gladly. I recovered noticeably and my appetite awoke, as I had not known it for a long time. I readily gave in to temptation in the form of cakes and café au lait, which were brought to us. What did we say in Vienna years ago? "Eating and drinking hold body and soul together." I felt the truth of this proverb in my own body. We all wanted to be healthy and strong at the end of this war. When a comrade with whom I worked in the house office consumed something, he smiled and tapped on his belly and remarked, "I gained six kilos in Switzerland. And where does that come from? Only from the food." How right he was.

Between working in the house office, the hikes, and the free time, the days flew by. I regularly played chess with a good comrade from Büren. Where would I have found the patience and concentration in Büren?

Schönengrund offered a wonderful opportunity to observe the collage of Jews the massive waves of refugees assembled. Here, too, the Polish Jews dominated. Yet the countries in which Jews lived for decades before the flight put their stamp on them and differentiated them. To these belonged the authentic Belgian, Dutch, French, German, Austrian Jews, and so forth. Each group had its own characteristic. There was no lack of differences. Equally as colorful as the mix of nationalities was also the social layering. All occupations were represented, and among the Jews, besides the businessmen, we counted workers, farmers, tradesmen, technicians, engineers, lawyers, journalists—in short, virtually all the occupations you can name.

Who can undertake to describe all these lives, when each could fill a book? Every refugee went through the school of persecution; everyone saw death in front of them, closed their eyes fearfully in the evening, and thought about an uncertain morning.

At the start of the war, approximately five hundred thousand Jews lived in France, Holland, and Belgium. Hundreds of thousands were deported and possibly one hundred twenty to one hundred fifty thousand Jews lived in hiding, with false papers, in fear and worry. Of the twenty-two thousand Jewish refugees housed in Switzerland, an estimated half (ten to twelve thousand) originated in those countries. The number that managed to escape to Spain, England, or overseas was not overly high. Perhaps only fifty thousand managed to secure safety—hardly 10 percent.

Who would dare answer the question: were they the best, those on whom God bestowed the grace of rescue? We often posed this question: why me, why not him? It's a question of fate, a question no one can answer, voicing such unending sadness. Unfathomable and dark are the ways of destiny. We can only make every effort to be good and show our worth for the great mercy of life and rescue.

Although there was no shortage of contrasts, in general, the relationship among the refugees was good. People who had suffered and experienced a great deal understood the necessity to tolerate each other. Surely disputes occurred, but considering the frayed nerves of refugees, it's a wonder how relatively rarely these took place. You can't forget that everyone pulled together and worked toward a common goal. Naturally within such a population, groups and even cliques will form. Countrymen stay together.

* * *

A big difference prevailed between Eastern and Western Jews. For the Polish Jew, the German Jews are *Jeckes*, similar to the Austrian's image of the German, particularly the Prussians, whom they designate *Pieffke*. The German Jew carries the distinguishing characteristics of the German nature. The Polish Jew has little understanding for this sort of thing. He looks a little down, with suspicion, on the German Jew, whom he considers neither Jewish nor German.

In a certain sense, the Polish Jews were right. The power of truth shapes our time.

How did the German and Austrian Jews benefit by their Germanic and Austrian identity? The Nazis stamped them as Jews; the German Jew, through the power of facts, was a Jew whether he wanted to admit to his Jewish destiny or not. The further he separated himself from his Jewish identity, the more difficult it was to bear this fate. It could come only as a small consolation that the National Socialists were wrong, and that even a Jew could be a good German or Austrian. The Polish Jew had the psychological advantage of inner unity. He knew he was not a Pole, and it made no difference to him. He was only a Jew, wherever he chose to live, and Yiddish accompanied him over the whole world. Whoever wanted to communicate with those from other camps in Schönengrund had to learn some Yiddish. The son of the owner of the zur Krone, a boy of twelve or thirteen years of age, earned a great storm of applause for his role in a one-act play as a *bocher*, Jewish youth. Between September 1942 and March 1943, he heard Yiddish spoken and learned it from the internees. How we had to laugh when after a powerful Swiss song, and without urging, he burst into a melancholy Yiddish melody.

Certainly, even Polish Jews have been torn from their roots, people who grew up in a milieu outside of Poland. They didn't attend the Cheder, the Yiddish school that would have given them Jewish culture and tradition, nor did they connect with Western culture. So they stood between two cultures, often bereft of either culture or tradition. I observed such people in France and met them in several camps. In their essence and in their language, they were Polish Jews. There were some among them to whom Judaism was foreign, that even on Yom Kippur, the Day of Atonement, they didn't fast and even worked in the labor camps, though there was no compelling reason to do so. They didn't feel that this was a matter of respect for their own identity, to keep this High Holy Day. Neither were they nationalistic Jews—they are just totally uprooted. What moral boundaries could such people have? They were to be pitied more than the German *Jeckes*.

A contrast also exists between German and Austrian Jews. The Austrian Jew, as many Austrians, possesses a lighter and freer spirit than the more stiff and buttoned-up German. Fundamentally, in their hearts, German Jews and Austrian Jews had the same attitudes toward each other as Aryans had between them.

There is no more overwhelming evidence to debunk race theories than in a refugee camp in which you can observe so many Jews. The differences in the countries of origin are in the character and are recognizable in individuals. It can be clearly observed that the influences of the environment on the development of an individual surpass the inherited preconditions in significance. And outwardly, all types, from the darker Mediterranean type to the lighter Nordic type, are all proportionally represented. The only determination one can make in regard to the outer appearance of Jews: they are a special mix of races, a people that traces its bloodline to all races. Can it be any different for such an ancient people?

The enemies of Judaism seek to rationalize the so-called Jewish characteristics and features. It is important to be disassociated from this reproach. Beyond the debunked race theory, we Jews owe ourselves a defense.

I know very well that we have one and that sometimes it becomes unpleasantly noticeable. Where is the fault? The Jews have not had a homeland in over two thousand years. I don't want to talk about the time prior to the emancipation, when they were treated as aliens and were suppressed. But even since the enactment of laws mandating equality, Jews were never really regarded as fellow citizens. Even in the era of full official equality, certain differences were made even if just in social regards. Who among us, even under the fully "assimilated" Jews, didn't have these experiences sooner or later? We never felt ourselves really at home, never equal to the others, and these feelings gave rise to certain resentments, many times unconsciously, but they existed and found expression in our interactions. It would be interesting research for psychologists to determine if some of these Jewish characteristics are nothing else but suppressed inferiority complexes. Sometimes these are actions without regard to the community or fellow human because the concerned person says or unconsciously finds that whatever one does, one will still be regarded as a Jew. This community that doesn't wish to be Jewish, and in the whole isn't endeared to the Jew's well-being, doesn't deserve any particular consideration. Even a democratic country such as England was not exempted from this disregard and disrespect. We only have to think about the excellent play by Galsworthy, *Loyalty*, wherein the poet attempts to rationalize this problem.

And hand over the heart, would the Christian reader turn inward and ask, how far, to what measure, he himself is ready to recognize goodwill toward Jews, toward individual Jews as full participants in his community, and as members of his people. The average person, even if not an anti-Semite, perceives in Jews something foreign and special. It is often really peculiar and alienating, and shows how much we are subjected to influences and instincts, which we don't rationally put aside.

Let's take the case of the baptized Jew. Why is it that, for the most part, life has been made easier for the baptized Jew? They are given concessions; although in most cases, is the baptized Jew or those that act this way truly a believing Christian? Although many Jews convert to gain only material advantages, inwardly they reject their baptism, and still they experience reproach. Can we acknowledge therefore that this Jew took the last step to be closer to the guest community and with great effort sought to become like the others? If it were so, it would also be proof that the influence of the Christian idea of community is far stronger ingrained than one wishes to admit and that the majority of Christians, and even the detached Christian, possess some feel for Christian community. And the certain contempt that the world holds inwardly for the baptized, that runs beyond the attestation of respect for Judaism, a respect, maybe fear of this secretive and unusual community, which through indestructible eons shows such peculiarly rigid staying power.

In any event it's not to be questioned, that just in the relationship between Jew and non-Jew, the unknown plays a big part. The enacted laws granting equality to Jews, their proclamation to citizenship is insufficient to drive out the misunderstandings between the two if at the same time you don't make the effort to educate both. For one, that Jews are people like all others and that Jews themselves have the responsibility to act irreproachably as people, which they owe their own conscience, to insist on it spotlessly, without regard to what others might think or their attitude toward them. The last is really difficult, maybe more than people can handle. It must be essential that Jews receive the feeling that where they live they are truly at home.

Anti-Semitism can be effectively combated and annihilated only when the notion of equality and equal rights becomes a fundamental principal of our society, when we make our goal the wholeness of humanity. In this sense our fight against anti-Semitism is in part a fight for humankind in general.

How far distant we are from that! Have we in fact ever succeeded in establishing the material fundamentals for the equal rights of people? And isn't the material security the essential prerequisite for intellectual development.

Oh, if only we could succeed in achieving a result on a smaller framework, to come to a concept for a smaller framework for a people's community and beyond to a concept of a Europeanism, to recognize that our small Europe is in reality a single unit, that belongs together and must prosper as one, or perish.

In the many camps, and earlier in the Foreign Legion, but particularly in Switzerland, I was always together with a whole variety of nationalities. It was not an easy assignment for a camp manager to bring unity to this colorful multitude. Of course only responsibly conscientious people undertake such tasks that may lead to the most promising of future assignments. Many camp managers just let the institution run without thinking of the human significance of their assignment to the camp, in which a dozen nations and nationalities are together. Is not— should not a Swiss, whose own country is so multifaceted, be skilled to mediate this mix and to bring these people closer together?

The essential goal for the future is the reconciliation and restoration of harmony of the people. Was there success in bridging the many contrasts in just the small framework of the refugee camp? Not always. Besides a few, the splendid examples showing mutual accommodation, for the most part "side by side" replaced "all together." Only in regard to one matter were all united—in their rejection of Germany and German characteristics. Yes, in a peculiar way, I didn't have much sympathy for the terrible fate the bombings brought to the circle of German Aryan émigrés and certainly no sadness for the political diminishment that

Germany would suffer as a result of this war. These émigrés cut themselves loose from the country that played such sinister games. When you are tossed around for many years, when you must resettle in one country after another, the word *homeland* loses its original context.

When I was young, I believed I had a homeland; I believed I could not live without a homeland; it pained me as I recognized that though I lived here in Europe I was nowhere a full-valued person or a person endowed with equal rights. Today I have experienced too much to be willing to stake my luck and my future on the concept of a homeland. Where have I read it? A home can replace a world, but the world cannot replace a home. My family is my beloved home. I could care less if others like me. If only they leave us in peace, if only they let us lead our lives in freedom, that will be sufficient for me. And no—no matter how beautiful a passport in my pocket, the identity of a shabby refugee will lead me to the errant assumption that I am French, Austrian, or something else. Maybe it was good that I freed myself from the tight shackles of a limited homeland and remain just a human being, a human being who had to recognize the futility of many old ideas in the tough school of life—and as I, so too my companions. Many Aryans among us didn't think otherwise. They too wanted only peace and quiet. They just wanted a small spot on which to resurrect their lives. Perhaps it was the most valuable experience of the emigration for all of us—that we recognized refugees, who stood above the society of humans.

* * *

In mid-March, I was suddenly and abruptly torn from Schönengrund and transferred to the reception camp Champéry. I was sorry to leave, but I did intend to be united with my wife.

I was permitted to travel to Champéry without a guard accompaniment. With a wonderful feeling of independence, I boarded the Autobus in Schönengrund to Waldstatt. With no soldier at my side, I felt like a schoolboy playing hooky. In Zurich I spent three unforgettable days. After months of lockup in camp, even one as good as Schönengrund, a saunter through a big city after a long absence is a priceless pleasure. In Zurich, I found a friend from Vienna whom I had not seen in many years. He was able to put me up, so I didn't have to worry about the expenses for a hotel.

These three days in Zurich were not foreseen in my travel plans. I have to go back a little to explain this vacation.

At the time, in January when I was sick in the infirmary in Büren, I heard that men unfit for labor could be interned in a so-called free place. Hearing this, and concluding that my suffering could make possible my way to freedom, was something. Didn't I suffer for years from a chronic crisis that repeated twice yearly? This freedom was particularly enticing to me as I knew that my wife, with respect to little Michou, could be released from her camp without any problems. Mothers with small children could, under the statutes, live outside the camp, provided their support was secured. I sat down and wrote to the Jewish Refugee Welfare Organization a long letter in which I described our situation and bade them to unite all of us in a free place.

In Schönengrund I received a request for my resume. The camp doctor received a questionnaire about my health.

We all knew that an eventual release to freedom was dependent on the camp doctor. When I received the request to send in my resume, I knew that at the same time a recommendation from the camp doctor was also requested.

A Swiss doctor was responsible for every refugee camp. The doctor attended to the camp only on a part-time basis as he also had his regular practice. There were plenty of doctors among the refugees. So a refugee doctor practiced in every camp as a Samaritan doctor, whose competency was checked by the Swiss doctor. It rarely happened that the Swiss doctor would make a different diagnosis from the refugee doctor. The proposals and the decisions of the refugee doctor were binding and, by the rules, sanctioned by the Swiss doctor. For the refugee, the refugee doctor was totally authoritative and only through him could access be gained to the Swiss doctor. The refugee doctor was in a delicate position. He himself was a refugee and had an interest in the approval of the Swiss authorities. On the other hand, his heart drove him to do as much as possible for the refugees, his partners in destiny. That every refugee yearns for freedom is a self-evident truth. Everyone who sees even the slimmest possibility of transfer to a home or freedom from the camp comes to the camp Samaritan. Yet he couldn't declare all of them unfit for camp life. He might have wanted to; he could, but could not. He had to act honestly; he couldn't send everyone into the hospital; he couldn't recommend expensive cures and had to stay within his monetary budget. We saw his difficult position and his great responsibility. A refugee doctor once declared to me, "I constantly feel I am between two fires: the sympathy to my comrades for whom I would do everything in my power, free all of them if it were possible; and the Swiss authorities whom I can't deceive: I must be truthful in my findings, and I may not impose on them high expenses. I do everything for which I can accept responsibility according to my knowledge, and yet I have not done right by all my comrades."

This refugee doctor was an exemplary human being, who wasn't given to obfuscation and didn't delude himself with standing above his comrades who worked with pick and shovel. He embodied the ideals of a refugee doctor: honest, straightforward, like a companion, and cooperative. But not all were like that. They were humans, with all the human attributes. There were those that were guided by sympathy and antipathy, those that feared the Swiss authorities and dared not make or propose far-reaching diagnoses, and those who thought they were better than their colleagues.

I needed to include this long introduction, so this book should not engender any sympathy or antipathy for me personally, but give an honest portrayal of my path, the path of a refugee. No doubt, things were significantly better in Schönengrund: I gained several kilos, and I certainly felt better than in Büren. Nonetheless, I still suffered from severe ailments and vomiting from time to time, and had much pain at night. The doctor knew all this, but I could not know if he believed everything I told him. He examined me thoroughly and apparently concluded that I did not suffer from an intestinal ulcer. In the end, there was only one way to establish an indisputable diagnosis—with x-rays. My condition appeared to him such that the cost was not justified. He absolutely wanted to cure me by other means. I should give up smoking. I knew very well that smoking was damaging, but I just couldn't do without. When I heard this surely well-intentioned advice, I was reminded about the anecdote on how to reach a hundred years of age: A patient visits a doctor to seek advice on how to reach old age. He responds to the doctor's advice, saying that he doesn't smoke, never drinks, and never touches women. "So why do you want to reach one hundred?" asks the doctor in response. I didn't drink and excess lovemaking doesn't even enter into the picture as a refugee has no opportunity to touch women. No freedom, nothing. Smoking was my only vice. I believed that as long as one didn't engage in excesses, everyone could have a weakness. Angels have no weakness, which is why they live in heaven and not on earth. But humans who live on earth have weaknesses, and that is good. I personally fear people who don't have any visible weaknesses. I fear they could be secretly depraved. In other words, smoking is my weakness; it's an old habit, and I'm convinced it's not damaging as long as it's not done to excess. And I believed, rightfully so, that the care outside the confines of the camp had greater significance than the great abstinence from the hotly desired nicotine. As I heard from the Jewish Refugee Welfare Organization, my doctor gave an unfavorable opinion in my case and there could be no discussion of a free place. I had been recommended to an outstanding internist and went to see him.

This man was so nice and kind to me, a refugee without resources. He explained when I had a few days of vacation that he wanted to take x-rays. He gave me accordingly a letter certifying the need for x-rays. On the grounds of this letter, Colonel Kuhn, head of the Territorial Command in Zurich, authorized a vacation. I was certain of my situation. I had the same symptoms a year ago when I was x-rayed in France and diagnosed with a duodenal ulcer. In fact the Zurich x-ray findings came to the same conclusion.

I didn't complain to the doctor in Schönengrund. I believed he acted in good faith, and after all he didn't have an x-ray at his disposal. The delay in my release, resulting from that denial, had enriched me with interesting adventures. Here in Nesslau, everything has fallen beautifully into place, so we wouldn't want it any other way.

In the meantime, despite the findings of the x-rays, my way to freedom went up in smoke, and I was transferred from one camp to the next so that I could undertake nothing. As I finally stayed a longer time in Prêles, my condition improved to the point that the doctor there classified me as fit for work in a labor camp.

This was the delicate position of the refugee doctor, but the refugee also had the difficult task of being convincing when medical attention was required. In freedom, everything is different. When someone visits a doctor and spends money for healthcare, the doctor knows that the patient has a real complaint. Otherwise, no one would really spend the money. Where medical attention is given gratis, it's easy for the doctor to tend to attach less belief in the patient's complaints.

Reduced health for a refugee was a double disadvantage. The young, the strong, were naturally better suited to the rigors of the reception camps. They were also the first to leave the reception camps to be transferred to a labor camp. The sickly had often to wait months for a transfer to a home due to the shortage of available space, if finally they were not transferred to a labor camp for lighter duty. So these young people preceded the elderly and weak in finding the pleasure of the manifold advantages associated with a definitive camp or home. And the elderly thirsted for freedom too, without which even the best accommodations are just a golden cage. It was of course more difficult to find suitable accommodations in a hotel than to erect barracks for a labor camp. But it's a sad reality that even among refugees, as everywhere, disadvantage falls on the elderly, sickly, and indigent in comparison to the young and the well-off. One finds the same misfortune from which our society suffers in the world of the refugees, but owing to their special situation, they are more susceptible to such ill effects than those leading normal lives.

* * *

Champéry was one of those golden cages—a luxury hotel in which refugees even had their own private baths. That such rooms were for the use of refugees came as a revelation. And still I was unsatisfied and disappointed in Champéry. I was, in regards to freedom, spoiled by Schönengrund. The bare view of the majestic landscape was no substitute for my accustomed outings. I only saw it from the window or balcony. There was no courtyard. Unguarded walks were only available on the wide hotel steps. A sentinel with rifle stood at the entrance by the revolving door. This sight was enough to turn me off to the stay in Champéry. During nice weather, a walk was planned every second day, yet I would rather have missed these walks flanked by one soldier in front and by another in the rear. The marches in columns were, to my inner core, most unpleasant: a human herd driven like cattle out to the grazing fields. No, I am and will remain a civilian.

I was therefore happy that my wife was not transferred here and asked for my transfer to Geneva, where I presumed my wife to be. I didn't understand why I was transferred to Champéry when my wife wasn't there. It impelled me the more to Geneva, where also our children were accommodated. Vacations from reception camps were rare. My request was wondrously granted immediately, as the camp commandant could also not understand why I was placed in Champéry. But just before my arrival in Geneva, my wife, after five months there, had just left for Prêles. We crossed each other. Something was not totally in order somewhere in a central coordination point for refugees. We crisscrossed all of Switzerland but could not meet up. In Geneva, of course, I immediately requested my transfer to Prêles. The authorization took about three weeks, and in the meantime I stayed in Val-Fleury.

I had a frightful experience on the trip from Champéry to Geneva. The soldier that accompanied me told me that he had orders to transfer me to the police guard in the train station of Geneva. I didn't know that Geneva had special registration regulations for refugees, and even if I had known, I would never have thought that this also applied for a simple change of camp when I was, in any case, under the guard of the military. What could the police want from me? I hadn't committed any crimes. *Geneva, extradition* swirled through my head. Weren't once two refugees from Büren sent back without us knowing the charges? I was overjoyed, as I saw it was just a formality.

A refugee is always afraid of the authorities. He is without rights. Which refugee doesn't have some small thing in his closet? Which refugee has never stepped over one of the many strict camp regulations? Which refugee has never said something that might be held against him and isn't in the danger of a denunciation? Throughout the whole trip, a mental registry of transgressions went through my head, and with a true deep sigh of relief, I marched behind my soldiers down the steps at the train station. Uff!

20

THE CIRCLE CLOSES: GENEVA–PRÊLES

After a long absence, I was again in Geneva, the starting point for my wandering through Switzerland: not as the novice that I was the previous November, for whom everything about camp business was alien and unaccustomed, but as an old experienced camp hand. I had to smile about the impatience of the new arrivals, who could not understand why release from the camps took so long. They thought they would immediately be sent to a labor camp. They cried when their wives went in a different direction than they themselves. I had become hardened.

I had a roommate, a dignified older Frenchman, who participated in the Resistance and was pursued by the Gestapo. He fled into Switzerland and had been in the country for three weeks. He couldn't understand why, despite posting bail and warranty, he was still here. He found the restrictions of the camp operation unbearable. He told me that after the war ended, he would categorically view Switzerland only from an aircraft. I met him again several months later, during a vacation in Geneva, cheerful and in good health. There was no talk about aircraft. Yet in Val-Fleury, his impatience and lack of understanding were typical behaviors for a novice who suddenly had to forfeit his freedom. The emotions change nothing; life has been saved. These people in turmoil, shattered from their change in destiny, needed more understanding from those in charge. They needed an insight into their psyche, which a military commander couldn't summon up. Stark were the differences between the two worlds in the first reception camp: the military power and the entangled civil life and the sensitivities of the refugee. From these develop misunderstandings, harsh reprimands, and the accusations of ingratitude.

Abroad, the Swiss enjoy the reputation of competence, know-how, and production of quality products. The Swiss watch embodies in total the impression abroad of Swiss workmanship. Prior to the war, many refugees traveled in Switzerland. As tourists, they became familiar with Switzerland, traveling with their excellent trains and staying in their exemplary hotels. They went to Switzerland for rest, not to study its internal problems. They formed a simple idealistic image of Switzerland, of a well-arranged country organized through and through, which thanks to the active and capable Swiss propaganda spread throughout the world. Then, the loss of personal freedom and legal status didn't enter their consciousness. They had more pressing worries than to think about such things. They had to save their unprotected lives.

However, the more firmly these idealized images were rooted in the refugee, the more severe appeared to them the raw reality of the reception camps. The reception camps were erected in all haste and had all the character of the provisionary—a stopgap measure of which one is tempted to say "Il n'y a que le provisoir qui dure."[19] They couldn't be compared to the carefully produced export products. The military commandant of a reception camp was not an assiduous service director of a tourist resort accustomed to international guests.

Certainly the refugees knew they didn't come to a spa and weren't entitled to services and comfort, neither could they request them. But it can't be denied; the all-too-high expectations of Switzerland made the first reception camps appear even more severe than they were in reality.

One evening, our house head explained to the refugees that they were without rights and to expect or request nothing in the way of entitlements. In the sense of the house head's explanation, we were legally

---

19 Only the temporary lasts.

entitled to nothing: everything the Swiss did for us, they did of their own free will and as an act of mercy on their part.

And it was all correct. There was no refugee right of asylum that entitled us to any kind of hospitality. With regards to rights, the refugee was totally suspended in air. How bitter it was then for the refugees to recognize that they were of second standing. The newly arrived could not fathom that they had been stripped of their personality and their lot was to be a number until the day the war ended. Since 1939, how often had I been a number? The Foreign Legion, 89233; Geneva, 2999; Büren, 871; 9499 is yet to come—it's the labor camp. When would we be human again? Would it ever happen? After this war, would we fall into permanent oblivion in uniform masses?

Yes, my old Geneva camp number was 2999. We had come to number 5500. Twenty-five hundred additional people arrived in the rooms of Val-Fleury. And still there was no end in sight to the flood. The difficulties of flight had grown, but still the will to live drove the pursued toward the only sanctuary open in Europe.

I was pained to see the many women, children, and infants arriving in Val-Fleury. Among the new arrivals, they dominated by far. Did a Jew even have the right to bring children into a wicked world? Would life for these children at some point be different, for these poor worms; would life be more compassionate than it was for their parents?

The Jew hangs on to life. He affirms it like few others. These children, born during the most horrible times of the persecution, prove it conclusively. Were it not for this positive outlook on life, the Jews would have been exterminated a long time ago. For the Jews, the children are the ancient and most certain continuation of their own person. What do we know of the hereafter? Doesn't the literal word of the Bible apply to us: "From dust thou art and to dust thou shall return!"

* * *

I went to room number 12, in which we were provided lodging. Four families slept in this room, the size of a living room, with space for all their worldly possessions. On one side slept my family, four persons, and a married couple; on the opposite side, a family with a three-year-old boy, and a pregnant women with her husband. Here, I said good-bye to my wife for five days. Four and a half months passed before I saw her again.

I thought I was dreaming as I entered the dining hall at noontime. I saw a couple that had been with us there in November. I was speechless. These people were still there, waiting. They instructed the children of Val-Fleury. Was it possible that they had spent the entire four months in one house and garden? Without children of their own, they really had no reason or excuse to leave the house. Did they still know about life on the outside? Did they remember that a whole world existed on the other side of the sentry post? In the meantime, what hadn't I seen and experienced! For them, time had stood still. Removed from reality, their faces were stamped with depression and melancholy. It was as if some-one had turned down their life flame to very low, and it burned only like a pilot light.

Since November 1942, great strides had been accomplished in Val-Fleury. Each of the women sewed together two blankets and made a straw sack. No longer did the straw cling to your clothes and get dragged everywhere. There weren't as many people, and the rooms were more spacious. Some of the inhabitants made their rooms really cozy. Creative specialists put their carpentry skills to work and fashioned tables and benches from crates and planks. Covered and decorated with flowers, these improvised furnishings looked elegant.

Things went well for me in Val-Fleury. My wife had been there such a long time and left such good memories that her husband was cheer-fully welcomed everywhere by the many tarrying and busy refugees. I enjoyed all the advantages that Val-Fleury could offer.

Most happily of all, Geneva enabled me the opportunity to see my children again. I could now swim through the strict regulations of the camp like a fish in water. I inundated the head of camp with my proper and formal requests to visit my children and transfer to Prêles. Five times in three weeks, I managed to extract visiting rights to see my children.

And I could stroll through the streets of Geneva even accompanied by a soldier. Geneva—the city that binds Swiss solidity with the niceties of a somewhat animated French atmosphere to a happy and harmonious unity—I knew and loved Geneva from earlier and better days. I went on walks with my wife on the shores of the lake. We watched the seagulls living on its waters. A dream-like steamship-crossing in light and sunshine brought us from Geneva to Thonon in France and back again into Switzerland. No one asked us for passports or papers.

Our children were well, although Michou still had a small cough. He still suffered from the aftereffects of the bronchitis he had caught in his susceptible condition right at the start. Michou didn't recognize his papa anymore. The many children around him and the friendly sisters—those were now his family. Without responding, he let me take him into my arms and be caressed. But I was foreign, and he could care less. No wonder at his age. Yet for me, it was a stab through the heart. The children of the refugees don't belong to their parents. It is for the children that the parents want to live, but they are not together and can only see each other now and again. After the war, how many children would not recognize their parents? How many would not even be found again? Insane world. It doesn't help to think.

The more so I could take joy in Paul. With his residence in Les Murailles, he won the big prize. I was there several times and knew it well. It soared as a model example of a good home, and I am so happy to be able to say such good things about it.

The home was located in a villa-like house in the middle of a big garden. The care was simple but more than adequate and healthy. The children were neat and clean. Every evening before going to bed, the children showered with cold water, singing joyous songs. They attended various schools: the young ones, the village school; and the older ones, the appropriate schools in Geneva. They received religious instruction. They learned to keep the Jewish holidays and look forward to the festivals, which were celebrated in high esteem. Every child had a two meter square garden plot to care for individually. It was a pleasure to see how willingly and with what great enthusiasm the children took care of these plots. Boys ages six to sixteen years were cared for in this home. In the stimulating environment of Lake Geneva, they grew hale and hearty in body and soul. The entrusting and rearing of a collection of thirty-five boys is not an easy assignment and places great expectations on the home's personnel and leadership. The director always did her best. All the parents with children at Les Murailles were happy and satisfied.

When I arrived, Paul was still in school, and I had the opportunity to observe everything and converse with the director. I received the most calming impressions about Paul's situation from this friendly woman, who I'm sure also knew how to be strict and authoritarian.

And then he arrived, the little devil. A bashful glance in his rascal face, he ran and hopped to his papa. He had fat, red cheeks. His appearance showed no traces of sleeping on straw or the poor nutrition at Val-Fleury. But he well remembered everything and related to me a thousand details of living with Mama. That went like the torrent of a waterfall. And from the home, from the wolf troop of the boy scouts, and as a proud and youngest member of the squirrels—he again had found his equilibrium and was happy and satisfied.

On one of these visits, I had the great joy to visit our Geneva friend and thank him personally for his cooperation and involvement on our behalf. I wrote at one point that only the poor really understand misery. No, when I think about this fine person, I honestly must admit that there are also rich people who honestly need to do good.

The soldiers accompanying me on so many of these outings were no bother at all. They sat on a bench in the garden or in the corner of a room and gave an appearance of unconcern. They were good, decent, kind people, simple peasants or laborers with full sympathy for our situation. The guard duty company was headquartered in Bern. Many did not know Geneva. The accompaniment of refugees gave them a welcome outing. One Sunday, I was in a hurry to return to camp on time. With a broad grin, the soldier said, "The camp is not running away." We made a big detour and drank a good coffee on one of the inviting terraces, a small infraction for which we readily accepted guilt.

Geneva would have been even nicer if our camp commandant had demonstrated a little understanding and moderation in our interactions. The captain was a big, handsome distinguished officer, distinguished from head to toe, certainly from a patrician family from the Wallis part of Switzerland. What a chasm between this worldly person and the unkempt, nervous, gesticulating people whom he oversaw. He couldn't identify with any particular sympathy for the refugees, mostly he understood better the French pilots, several of whom found asylum in Val-Fleury. My time there was the epoch of the pilots. They covered many of the camp functions. Jews, on the other hand, who previously held various office positions, were transferred to other camps in central Switzerland. Prior to the pilots was the period of the sailors in Geneva. Generally, a homogenous group sets the trends. Most of us found the atmosphere that prevailed at that time in Val-Fleury most oppressive. It was an atmosphere saturated with romance novels and denunciations. A young man in our midst, the captain's intermediary, faithfully reported to him everything we did and said. We lived in constant fear of investigations and scandalous affairs. I was glad when my transfer was approved and I could leave Geneva with my skin intact.

On April 12, the day of my departure, I had breakfast in the kitchen with the kitchen staff. My eyes opened wide when I saw what was served. There was unlimited bread, butter, coffee, and milk discreetly placed on the table. Yes, that existed also. The kitchen staff ate exceptionally well, and likewise the refugees who were part of the house leadership. One day the rations were particularly limited, and we complained bitterly. The kitchen staff sent up the mashed potatoes intended for the house leadership. We licked clean the plates and spoons. The purée was full of milk and butter, quite different from our vegetables. My God, as an old camp hand, I knew all about this. These conditions were very similar to those we experienced last November during our first stay. It remained to be determined whether the cooking in general had improved and if the more sumptuous meal preparations were shared by all or just the kitchen staff and their cronies —friends, brides, their girlfriends, and relatives— to the intolerable detriment of the ordinary refugee. The refugees were no angels either. In Büren—the story goes—the captain came into the kitchen one morning to taste the coffee. He tasted it and found it first rate. But the coffee he tasted had been poured from the pot intended for the kitchen staff. In Geneva, we held to the principle of reward based on performance. Whoever was on a duty detail received something extra: the peeling crew got a large piece of bread spread with butter, and the others received an apple. The permanent employees, wood crew and so forth, also received a *Znüni* and *Zvieri*[20] Those costs of course came out

---

20 *Znüni* and *Zvieri*, Swiss expression for 9:00 a.m. and 4:00 p.m. break and snack. The nine o'clock snack is sometimes quite substantial.

of the general budget and, when taken with the above comments, made some things clear.

* * *

Prêles, a good and beautiful camp, perched high up on the slopes of the Bernese Jura. A cog railway climbed up from Ligerz on the Bieler Lake to Prêles. During the trip, the scenery unfolded slowly to reveal a broad, dream-like, beautiful view over the lake and the surrounding mountains. Standing on the small platform, you floated into the rendering of multicolored framed heights. In the evening, the lights of the opposite shore, lanterns blending brighter into the aromatic night, and the babbling waters of the Aare, flowing under the lighted dam into the lake and losing its whiteness in the lake mirror, surrounded us with the magic of this isolated mountain world. The hotel was outside the settlement, between fields and woods, amid the fresh, shady mountain forests of the Jura. Here we inhaled peace and beauty, and were beckoned to walks and excursions. In the woods a tree stump or soft moss invited us to idle away the time or to dream. The woods were our province. Here we could go freely. The guard stood down by the street.

My wandering from camp to camp had brought me to almost every region, and opened to me Switzerland's natural world, which became dear to me. What irony! Through the constant change in the internment, thousands of refugees became intimate with the natural beauty of Switzerland. After the agitation and vexing life of the war years preceding the flight, we were so ready for peace, for this beauty not afflicted by war. Too bad that not all people of battling Europe had the opportunity to see and enjoy these magnificent streets, the neatly kept cities, the delicate little houses, and the green alpine meadows. They would recognize the meaning of peace and the criminality of war.

We did well in Prêles. Being together was a long-missed vacation. The time flew by, and there was plenty for us to do. So many people were sickly and weak that without fail the more energetic were drawn to the several duty rosters.

At the beginning of my stay in Prêles, a fat, little man ruled the kitchen roost. With his round, well-nourished face, two little eyes, and stump nose, he wanted to appear in his white apron as the embodiment of a well-run kitchen. But his kind looks deceived; they just camouflaged his craving to control the refugees. The little girls that helped in the kitchen trembled in fear of him. It came so far that they refused to take on the kitchen duties. It must have taken a lot if these pleasant, gentle beings could no longer tolerate him. He customarily came into the dining hall at lunchtime, winked at us, and held a penalty sermon, in which the refrain always returned: "And whoever isn't satisfied, to the border..." So he spiced our food, which was mostly poor rather than well prepared. No wonder that "the Hebraic clientele," as he expressed it, was difficult to satisfy. His reign didn't last too long, thank God, for we refused to eat as long as he tarried about in the dining hall, until the captain relieved him of his duties and transferred him to another company. He was a typical example of a subordinate organism possessed with a power complex, ready to humiliate and embitter the life of a refugee.

After his departure, the food was much better prepared. The new cook really applied himself. I, too, had kitchen duties every two weeks. It was very interesting to learn about this part of the camp operation from personal experience. By the captain's orders, the rations to which we were entitled were posted in the kitchen. I can't remember the details, but we certainly received the same rations as the civilian population. Naturally, potatoes, carrots, and fresh vegetables were the mainstay of our meals. We cooked ample amounts. Often vegetables came back into the kitchen. We put these leftovers into the next day's soup, so that our soup was thick enough even for the most hungry of the clientele.

The kitchen duties were particularly interesting in Prêles, as we cooked for the guard at the same time. We always had a little bit of the Swiss food. The captain advocated the position that in the kitchen we could eat as much as we wanted—only, it was strictly forbidden to take out food. And that was proper and important, for in other camps the friendship management was unfortunate.

Besides the kitchen duties, I was a member of the arbitration commission, which gave me plenty of work. Who in the camps didn't know these sometimes senseless mutual accusations? There were always people—mostly a small minority—that are suspicious of all their comrades who serve in some capacity. Loss of rights engenders mistrust. Shattered nerves, everywhere misery in the air, without regularly staying busy—one easily surrendered to dark thoughts; some people saw only evil where at most neglect was to be admonished. So it was in Prêles when we examined the books of the canteen and the aid accounts. Despite a thorough investigation, we could not find any evidence for an "enrichment" of the functionaries, only a certain sloppiness in the bookkeeping. Certainly there are people who, with material hardship, attempt subterfuge, but how slight are the advantages that some manage to gain. They are so small and wretched as is the whole situation of the refugee.

It was different with the advantages that many refugees were able to secure for themselves, not at the expense of their comrades, but from the strength of their positions as functionaries. The advantages were not charges to the general cost but came from the connections created in the practice of these functions. There were such cases. You can understand the outrage that such events provoked as they aroused in us the feeling of unequal treatment.

Our house leader's youth and lack of experience was the chief evil in Prêles; he didn't possess sufficient authority, though he had the full trust and confidence of the camp commandant. As a result, we suffered from massive collective punishment. When he didn't know what to do, he turned to the camp commandant, and then penalties rained down on us. Collective punishment unfortunately continues to be a favorite method to maintain discipline. Yet there is nothing more unjust than collective punishment, which totally contradicts the cornerstone of modern penal law. No penalty without guilt. After a fight in which three or four refugees participated, the exits, or rather the walks to the routes, were temporarily closed. Another time they found several boiled potatoes in the garbage pail on the second floor of the camp hotel. Whoever disposed of them there would remain a mystery. As a result the exit from the second floor was closed, and the post office was closed for several days. Post office closure was severe for the refugee, who fearfully awaited news, longed for every letter, letters that were the only connection with the outside world. In the internment home in Brissago, revocation of postal rights was a favorite punishment used against the poor women, who perhaps allowed themselves to talk at the table to the great displeasure of the camp leader.

What was hoped to be gained by collective punishment? That among the innocent victims there would be an informer, as if people didn't have enough bad attributes without it being necessary to breed and further acts of denunciation. A deed that wasn't perceived to be particularly insulting and did not endanger the well-being of the community would never outweigh the feeling of solidarity, and a hard collective punishment would not lead to the revelation of the culprit. Collective punishment in general is considered an act of sheer revenge and a crass injustice.

As if the confines of the reception camp didn't anyhow awaken in us to a sufficient degree small and suffocating instincts, when the more fortunate or advantaged was lucky to bring a piece of cheese, condensed milk, a sausage or similar kind, it was eaten in secret and in quiet. When consumed at the table, how the rumors flew, whispers hummed, with no end to envy, greed, begrudging looks to plate and to bread, criticism and vile talk.

* * *

So passes the time for the refugee in the reception camp. Soon there are difficult days, and he grumbles and denounces his state; soon there are sunny hours, and he takes joy in his life and his rescue.

I recall various women in Prêles who, separated from their children, emotionally atrophied. Their husbands had been deported. Where did these women find the courage to go on? Their narrow shoulders were bent and pressed down from burden and responsibility, and even their laughter had a drab tone. Poor Jewish family—these women were for us a reproach to be aware of our fortune, that we were all alive. Always busy and diligent, they sought consolation and forgetting in their work.

* * *

257

And suddenly it was May. I went on walks with my wife. It was the best relaxation from trivial camp conditions and disagreements. As long as we were together and our children were well cared for, of what concern was everything else? We were as happy as one could be in a camp. Only, we yearned for our children, and particularly my wife for little Michou. We looked for lilies of the valley, thought about France, the first of May in Lyon with its obligatory nosegays, hugs, and best wishes. It is such a sensible custom: life's spring rebirth reminds us to think about our fellow humans and to wish them health and happiness.

This was to be one of our last walks. On May 3, my wife was transferred to the internment home of Brissago in the Ticino. We parted with heavy hearts. We had just applied for a vacation to Geneva and hoped to travel there together and built air castles, when these aspirations were shattered. In such moments, how painfully we realized that we were not masters of our own person: the refugee's concept of family had become a different one, belonging more to the past than to the austere reality. But the feeling of dependency upon and the loss of conscientiousness on the part of those in charge hit hardest.

As soon as my wife had departed, our vacation was approved. I wanted to cry over this coincidence. We had luck in misfortune. The usually strict camp leader, after only fourteen days, approved my wife's anticipated vacation. I had to postpone my own, although the military authorities gave approval to my vacation in principle but got hung up when an outbreak of disease in Geneva caused several days of quarantine. For this first vacation, we had to fight to the last moment! My wife had to fight for her own vacation. And there I was—not knowing when the Geneva quarantine would be lifted. There was also the hard question of how to cover the travel expenses. How often I spoke with our social welfare worker until he was ready and authorized the travel to Geneva and the costs of the stay. Only recently had the regulations regarding vacations in reception camps been issued. The questions of how much the social welfare could afford and contribute were not resolved. We could not raise this money ourselves and had to write, write, and write some more—and beg. Until finally, we had come so far, and we could board a train: the battles and patience that signified. Today, everything runs in well-regulated channels: the possible benefits provided by the social welfare have been carefully documented, and only with hindsight can we appreciate the advance in organizational and material achievements.

Finally it had come so far, and I was allowed to travel. My wife arrived in Geneva a little later as the trip took close to twelve hours. The two days went by as in a dream. Back and forth, hurrying between the two homes and the committees left virtually no moments for us. The greater the effort to maintain a schedule, the faster the time flew by. In the twinkling of an eye, Monday afternoon arrived and we had to take leave. Only as I sat in the train, overly tired and with my eyes closed, I came to consciousness. The complete sadness and hopelessness of our situation stared me in the face. How much longer? Would this war never end? What were the small advances at the fronts in relation to our burning longing and impatience? After two days of freedom, how difficult it would be to report back to camp, to partition the day according to the signal whistle.

I was fortunate in that the work in the camp diverted me from gloomy thoughts. Besides the work details, I had a rather large circle of clientele waiting to be served. There were so many refugees who spoke only Yiddish and needed a friend to write letters and take care of petitions. There were so many petitions to write: for vacations, transfers, contributions from social welfare, and many more. I had no time to think or get bored.

New labor camps were established to free the refugees from the reception camps. I too was part of one of those next transports. On June 1, we traveled to the work camp of Mezzovico in Tecino. I was happy to be in the neighborhood of my wife. Because of this opportunity, I jotted down some notes to convey to my comrades, but on the evening prior to our departure, an incident really soured the mood, and we were in no state of mind to speak or to hear. We actually trembled from anger. A refugee filed a detailed complaint to the Neuchatel police about the theft of a bank note of five thousand French francs sewn into his trousers. What madness, this complaint. He should have surrendered his money like everyone else. Considering this man's predisposed nervous condition and his suffering from paranoia, was the complaint based on fact or just an act of revenge? It never became clear. Our bags were thoroughly searched, ransacked by the embarrassed soldiers. You could see on their faces how they regretted the whole business. We even much more so.

All our things were in total disarray. I was so upset that I was incapable of putting my clothes back in order. As they were, I threw them back into the suitcase. The poor soldier, who was only doing his duty, apologized. Refugee life! "Revue de detail." When would we be free?

For the refugee, the leaving of the reception camp was a first key milestone, truly a day worth remembering. I had wanted to say the following to my comrades:

My dear comrades,

It is not my custom to make speeches and put you to sleep. But our departure is a milestone in our stay in Switzerland. Tomorrow we leave the reception camp, actually the reception camps in which we have found ourselves over the many past months. We are journeying to a labor camp.

For us, it represents a certain freedom: money we will earn ourselves, not by charity or by begging. We get back a little piece of human dignity, without which we can't live forever. I look on that as the greatest fortune. I certainly don't want to say anything against the soldiers and the military leadership of our camp. They were good and humanistic. They fulfilled their duty and minimized the burden of the limitations that the law imposed on us. For that, we thank them kindly.

It should not be held against our guard team when we look forward to living some place where no soldier, with his rifle, stands guard in front of the house door. We look forward to writing to our loved ones as often as we want and what we want. And finally, we look forward to journey to a beautiful sunny place, one of the most beautiful locales in Switzerland.

Of course, on such a day we look back and are a little introspective. What brought us all to Switzerland?

The will to live, the will to rescue our lives—which were no longer secure in the lands from which we came.

Switzerland, which has always taken in refugees and emigrants, also opened its borders to us. We should not forget how thankful we must be to be able to lay down in bed—even if it is a straw sack—in the evening. Let's think about our comrades in Poland and their terrible destiny.

Where there is life, there is hope. We may hope to soon experience better times. Our rescue also puts upon us certain duties: the duty to give thanks to our guest country, the duty to extend friendship to our comrades. All of us, whether we like it or not, are in this lot together. Let us be good and upstanding comrades. The strength of a community lies in the solidarity of its members. Let us promise to stand together, to help each other and support each other. We want to be good to each other, for then our burden will be lighter, and we will prove ourselves noble to the grace God will grant us.

21

NEW DIRECTIONS: THE LABOR CAMP

T he first impression my comrades and I from Prêles had was not good. We saw the typical barracks that are standard in every labor camp. While they were well built and practical, after living in a beautiful hotel in Prêles, in the first instant they appeared lackluster and pathetic. In Prêles I shared a room with two other comrades, which we furnished agreeably and comfortably. There were only straw sacks, but we arranged them cleanly and neatly. We put in a washstand and a small table with chairs that we brought in from the hallway. We were especially proud of a mirror we hung on the wall. The room was so livable and intimate that we painfully felt its loss. After lights out we often covered the window with a blanket so that the guard didn't see the light, and we stayed up until midnight. That was all over now.

At the work place, we saw the comrades dressed in blue work clothes, mostly with bare upper bodies and with pick and spade digging up the earth and pushing heavy carts on the tracks. This scene was foreign, and we were not accustomed to it. The work, with the barracks for a background, seemed more like prison labor. We feared the camp, the labor, and believed we would not be able to acclimate ourselves to life here. The first few days of adaptation were very arduous, then it went better, and with time even this life seemed quite natural. It seemed peculiar as we picked up our work clothes and admired each other, as if it were something unusual to be wearing such an outfit. Of course we never were manual laborers.

I recall a discussion with a comrade from Prêles, who spent a total of eight months in the reception camp. He explained why he would have preferred to stay in the reception camp. He became so accustomed to staying in that the outings and vacation meant nothing to him. Of course the conviviality of the stay in Prêles was pleasantly supplemented with good meals. After several weeks, though, this comrade became one of the most enthusiastic walkers and never passed up a vacation. Any thoughts of returning to a reception camp were put far from his mind.

* * *

Before we were assigned work, we again had a medical examination. The weaker ones were assigned inside duty, and the stronger ones were assigned to the work place. The laborers received health and accident insurance. They pressed a leaflet from the health insurance into our hands. This leaflet was oddly composed. First are noted all punishable and unsavory acts for which the insurance may bring you to account and penalize you, then came the benefits of the insurance: certainly not the usual way, as if the laborer were a person particularly more prone to despicable acts.

I came to the workplace and was first assigned a group that had the task to level uneven terrain. We chopped down an approximately one-meter-high ridge, shoveled the dirt into a transport cart, and poured the load into a ditch two hundred meters away until both sides were of equal height. I had to exert myself to maintain the same tempo as my more thoroughly conditioned comrades. Our supervisor appeared to be possessed with a false and inappropriate ambition to fill an especially high number of carts. It was June. The sun of Tecino burned hot. The back hurt and the arms ached. The first days after work, I sank dead tired onto a bench, hardly able to move or go out. Yet I stuck to my ambition to conquer such work. Only someone who has engaged in physical labor for many years can understand what it meant for me to be equally productive as others. I was happy to get into shape and thought it could only do my body good to show physical accomplishment. I was happy to be outside and worked without hesitation as soon as I could do the work. I soon discovered the swimming area in the Veggio, the stream behind the wash barrack, where a dip after work refreshed and strengthened the body. None of us wanted to miss this invigorating opportunity.

After some time, I was transferred from this group to group six. This group worked farther away and cleared flat terrain. We cut down brush, felled trees, and dug out untold number of tree roots. Skillfully, the undersides of the roots were cleared and then a tree jack used to pull them out of the ground. For large or particularly broad tree stumps, we dug out the earth all around, out to the root extremities, and then blasted the tree stump free with dynamite. We were left alone for most of the day and could partition the work as we wanted.

* * *

In the labor camp, we rapidly became accustomed to one thing: freedom. Even if it was not total, after the limitations of the reception camps, it seemed to be boundless. We could not avail ourselves often enough to search out all the little towns of the region and like true free people visit the various establishments. We took advantage of the first day off for an excursion to Ascona; the next Sunday we went to Lugano. We had an indescribable need to retake life. We owned the world.

And how we gorged ourselves on cakes from coupons and money we put together. The bakeries and pastry shops tugged at us with magical force. We had been so long without sweets that we experienced a boundless need for them. But we also knew how to be satisfied with bread, as long as it was in quantity. In Büren we ate bread for dessert, the way you consume a cake. After breakfast, we stowed the precious piece in a place on the wall. And then the struggle against yourself started, against the rising temptation to stretch out your hand, take a hefty bite, or eat the whole thing. Should I or shouldn't I? And finally with a "oh what the heck" grabbed the bread and liquidated the entire day's ration in less than a minute. And even in all reception camps bread was something especially rare and precious. How could it be procured in large quantities? And here there was bread; the bakeries were filled with this delicacy; you only needed to walk in and buy it with a few stamps. We had access to all the stores. We received more bread here than in the reception camps, about three hundred grams with our supplement, and even that was not enough at the beginning. Many were able to obtain bread stamps from friends and acquaintances, and we stuffed ourselves to full capacity. I sometimes ate six hundred grams of bread—I was insatiable. My friend, a strong eater, could make a whole kilo of bread disappear into his stomach. Yes, we learned what a precious, good, and wonderful thing is bread. Only slowly, after some time, did this burning hunger subside. But *noshing* was something the refugee would be susceptible to for a long time even after the war's end.

* * *

Our camp leader then was a likeable young man, who gave us a lot of his time. He attempted to bring us closer to Swiss authors and poets, especially the lesser known, and often read to us from their works. One day he recited from memory a poem by one of his friends. I was amazed at the depth and sensitivity these rough-hewn people could bring forth. Unfortunately, there developed an unbridgeable difference between him and the technical camp head. Whereas the camp leader placed value on the development of a strong community among the refugees, and didn't attach much importance to our labor accomplishments, the technical leader considered the fulfillment of our assignments the most outstanding purpose of the labor camp. Unbearable friction arose, which came to a head when both left our camp. The technical head, tired from battling, returned to private industry, and the other left to run another camp. And even if his successor was equally motivated to do his best, we energetically regretted the change because he had been so imbued with this genuine endeavor to educate, as no other was capable to create a community out of the multicolored assemblage.

After four weeks, I had settled in totally. I tolerated the work well, and I thought that the stay in fresh air and the substantial, robust nourishment had eliminated my ailment.

My joy, unfortunately, was short-lived. At the beginning of July, I suddenly felt pain in my abdomen. At first, I didn't think the matter significant. A few days later, the pain became more intense. Soon I could hardly stand outside and needed to see the doctor.

The relapse disturbed me greatly. Not the crisis alone, but my vacation was imminent. Were I ill, I could not go on vacation and be together with my wife and children. I lay in the infirmary for four days, and then I had to get up. I neither could nor did I want to forfeit my vacation.

I looked so forward to this first vacation out of the labor camp, and yet despite the reunion with the children, it was torture. I could only go with great effort. The distress of the travel took even more out of me. I had to spend virtually the entire time in Geneva in bed. My wife mostly picked up the children and brought them to us in the hotel. On Sunday we were invited to the family of our Geneva friend, with whom Paul spent his vacation. They had prepared a wonderful menu and served it al fresco in a garden in bloom. What a difference between our mess buckets and the specially selected porcelain serving bowls. Today, I still look back with regret that I was not capable of partaking of the enticing feast.

It sounds paradoxical, but I was overjoyed as the vacation ended and, after the difficult trip, I again saw the barracks of Mezzovico. Yet I could not immediately return to the infirmary. It would have led to a poor outcome if upon returning from vacation I immediately reported sick.

Nonetheless the doctor insisted that I be assigned to peel potatoes, work that could be performed sitting down. It was terribly boring to peel potatoes for eight hours a day. Even conversations with your comrades didn't change that. And in the long run, peeling potatoes was also tiring work, even if easier than the work at the construction site. After several days, the camp head reviewed the work assignments. There were too many of us covering the inside services. The camp head expressed the view that he could no longer carry as healthy in the day report two others and myself in need of rest and recuperation. We were to either go to the worksite or report to sick bay.

I could not go to the construction site. I was bent over in pain even while sitting peeling potatoes. Time and again, even in the middle of work, I had to lie down for hours. I told the doctor that under no circumstances would I go outside, and he took me into the sick room.

My illness played a decisive role in my future and that of my family in Switzerland. So marvelous are God's ways, even bad is good, and often we aren't capable of recognizing them. That crisis unlocked the way to the burning craving for freedom—but more about that later.

Our camp Samaritan was very knowledgeable. He insisted that I have new x-rays taken. Again, an ulcer was diagnosed. I didn't need to go out to the worksite, was treated, and was to be transferred later to a home. At the recommendation of our doctor, I was for the time being placed into the camp office to help out. The coincidence was advantageous for me as an officemate then also enjoyed a rather lengthy recuperative vacation.

For the most part, I was very satisfied with this work. It was similar to office work I had performed for so long in civilian life. It was also really interesting to learn the never ending, complicated, administrative operation of the labor camp. The camps and homes under control of the Central Directorate of Homes and Camps[21] provided lodging for approximately ten thousand people. The central directorate was one of the biggest Swiss enterprises, carrying out public service.

But it was more than that. Because they provided shelter, food, and clothing for the internees, their laborers and employees—the Swiss held only management positions—the central directorate worried about how the internees spent their free time, certainly when they could go on vacation and when they could see their families again. They were a travel agency, one of the most significant in Switzerland, from which travel directives were issued for all of Switzerland. In general, the internees were guaranteed a three-day vacation every six weeks. For this they received a free travel voucher to visit spouses, parents, or children (not for the visitation of siblings or more distant relatives such as in-laws,

---

21 In April of 1940, Switzerland created this special agency to administer the new system of labor camps and internment homes operating within the framework of the Federal Department of Justice and Police (EJPD). *Switzerland and Refugees in the Nazi Era*, Independent Commission of Experts—Second World War, Bern 1999, page 59

uncles, etc.). The free trip was guaranteed, regardless of distance. Internees who didn't visit family were given free fare for travel within a fifty-kilometer radius from the camp and had to use their own resources if they wished to travel farther.

The central directorate also provided a savings bank for the laborer. The salary of a laborer came to 1.50 Swiss francs per day, of which one half was paid every ten days and the other half was credited to the savings account. It served to cover the expenses of the vacation destination. The accumulated worth of all the laborers' accounts could amount to almost three hundred thousand francs—quite a sum.

Most of all, it was the central directorate and the police authority that looked after—and when indicated, penalized—the refugees under its care. Everything was available in the central store of the central directorate: from tables, beds, blankets, linens, and pillows to cooking ware, dishes, and drinking glasses; from infant's clothing to shoes for camp participants; writing materials, tools, special foods, and more. The ordering catalogue of the central directorate was, naturally, standardized, and so extensive that it could have competed with the catalogue of any large department store. Every item carried a number: black shoe paste, brown shoe paste, ink, rubber erasers, brooms, dishrags, and sick buckets. Everything was catalogued and numbered—even the people. Internees all had a number and a folder that provided data on everything: in which camp they had been, and how they performed their work there; when they were sick, and where they were treated; when and where they went on vacation, and which travel vouchers were issued; how much was in their savings account; what clothing and underwear they purchased, and when they were issued. Even the distribution of detergent was noted.

The world of the internee—it was a small world unto itself. The world of the camps and homes, knotted together with invisible threads, parted from the big world with limitations, which like walls surrounded and imprisoned the refugee's life. A world in which everything was planned, in which the individual carried a number, in which everyone was the same, and in which there was no place for individual destiny— would that be the world of tomorrow?

The personnel record report was one of the most important office tasks; the long list of all the camp participants' records were updated.

Each day, for every person a symbol was added. Clever combinations of available typewriter characters formed the symbols:

/	Meals taken in camp
0	Meals taken outside camp with meal coupons (MC)
=	Labor
:	Day off
∧	Rain
%	Sick
/̲	Accident

These could be combined:

≠	Work in camp
:/	Day off in camp
0=	Detached to work outside camp with MC
0:	Day off, MC provided
0+	Prison
0̲	Hospital
∧/	Day off due to rain with meals in camp

When I first saw all these symbols, I thought I was dealing with hieroglyphics, but then I quickly learned to deal with them. Added to these were the diverse monthly reports, lists, bookkeeping ledgers, pay-out lists, correspondence, and so on.

Everything had to be typed in painful exactness and neatness. Reports could not have any erasures. We sometimes worked late into the night because an unnoticed typo crept onto the penultimate page of a bank statement. Just when you thought to be done and you breathed a sigh of relief, the tense attention to detail waned, and you fell into the wrong column, instead of a 3 there was a 5, and you cursed for you had to start over. Our office head, having achieved the rank of first group leader, the highest position an internee could aspire to, didn't want to risk any confrontation with the central directorate. Everything went quite well, but we received admonitions from Zurich even though we made a concerted effort to complete everything precisely per instructions. No private office could be more exacting than we were.

Mr. Otto Zaug,[22] director of all Swiss labor camps—not just those of internees but also those of the Swiss—liked to make unannounced inspection visits. Even there, he materialized one day and without any regard inspected every report. Everything was correct and we were satisfied, but we audibly gave a sigh of relief as the door closed behind him.

* * *

In such a thoroughly organized and orderly world, clashes will occur between individuals and regulations.

In our world, vacations were the greatest cause. Vacations of spouses, when both were under control of the central directorate, had to be approved together. In the end, one had to be postponed or the other advanced. This led to much correspondence and many telephone calls and often very stormy disagreements with the affected parties, who never consented to a postponement. It took time to straighten everything out.

One example of many: the two big Jewish Holidays, New Years and Yom Kippur, in 1943 fell at the end of September and the beginning of October. In regard to these holy days, the central directorate issued a special regulation. I imagine that the Jewish council intervened with the central directorate to offer refugees the opportunity to observe these holidays outside the camps. In practice, this is how the events unfolded.

A ruling was released, whereby those Jewish refugees whose vacation fell in September could postpone their vacation to the New Year's holiday or advance their October vacation to Yom Kippur.

My vacation came due at the end of August, my wife's vacation two weeks later. We joyfully looked forward beyond all measures to again visiting the children; my wife was consumed with yearning for Michel; the weather was sunny and bright, and my health had improved. Short

---

22 Director and founder of the Central Directorate of Homes and Camps. Independent Commission of Experts—Second World War, *Switzerland and Refugees in the Nazi Era*, page 154

and sweet, we promised each other to catch up on everything we missed the previous July stemming from my illness. We wanted to travel on September 10 or 11, eight weeks after our last visit. Of course, vacations were in fact authorized every six weeks, but the state of finances implored us to always slightly extend the time between vacations.

In the middle of our plans and hopes came the regulation regarding the holy days. My vacation was an August vacation to which the regulation did not apply but did affect my wife's vacation. Theoretically she had the opportunity to take vacation prior to the holidays, but she would then be obligated to work on those days. Practically, this was not possible. The non-Jews in Brissago were simply put on the lists to work on these holidays. The casual observer may think, "What's the big deal of a three-week postponement? Aren't there more urgent matters in this world?" The refugee who criticizes these regulations seems petty.

But it was just the opposite. Such small things showed how far the intrusive care of the refugee went, how we were tied in all and every respect to regulations that let us know that we were free nowhere. Over our heads, the decision was made that we should spend the holidays with the children in Geneva. Why? Was it a sanctified day for a family, whose home during the vacation was an uninviting alien hotel room, and who had to go back and forth between our children's homes and, as in my case, make visits to the hospital? A poor refugee rejoiced to be invited by a Swiss family and there enjoy the holidays in the atmosphere of a real home. But a larger family like ours had no home for the holidays. Doubly oppressive was the hotel on such occasions; doubly was the feeling of homelessness. Who would invite a family of four? And would we have to beg for an invitation and become a burden as other people? Couldn't we spend the holidays with our comrades in camp in our temporary home?

Naturally, rules were rules. Everything was implemented by a white horse—the bureaucratic white horse. I described my situation to our camp leader. He called Brissago for me and bade them to grant my wife her vacation. But the Brissago leader explained that for reasons of principle she couldn't go along with it, as there were five or six other women in the same position. For reasons of maintaining discipline, no exception could be made. These five or six women were, I take it, also mothers who took no particular pleasure in moving into a hotel just for the holy days.

All my efforts were useless and fell through on account of the rigid rules. And many of my comrades had the same experience. The well-intentioned aim developed into a repulsive coercion. General rules couldn't consider individual cases, and often turned into utter callousness. What would Christians say if they were forced to take Christmas vacation and spend the holy day of Christmas Eve in a hotel room? Or alternatively, asked that they work on Christmas Day because they couldn't go on vacation at that time. Such pettiness frightens me of collective living. To be one's own master of nothing, to submit in everything to a foreign will, even at such joyous occasions as vacation and festive days, is to feel the shackles of restraint. Should established plans, necessary requirements, consider individual life events, it would surely discredit the whole planning process and evoke resistance to all measures, even the necessary ones. There is a realm where people want to be free and must be free, where it concerns itself with personal matters, and in that realm they will defend themselves to the utmost.

Collectivism. You had to have been a refugee to understand the significance of collectivism. Collectivism of goods would be nice. However, too much self-sacrifice is required, and instead of collectivizing material goods, it is the individual that is collectivized, and called progress—a requirement of the time.

Yes, I and many of the others became outraged and rebelled. We rose up against the management of our own character; we yelled and we cried—but only inside. Life forced us to wear a stiff mask; the thoughts were free, but the gestures were not. And why then when it was all useless.

* * *

Few penalties were assessed. Usually any infraction was redressed with a warning.

Thank God, in the labor camp, all misdemeanors were dismissed that in the reception camps could make life so difficult. Smuggling letters, obtaining rationed foodstuffs and smuggling them back into camp, leaving the camp—all these didn't amount to delinquencies. But in the reception camps, who had not been guilty of these delinquencies. The goal was to not get caught. In Büren, our pockets were examined frequently after returning from authorized outings.

In certain cases, as in absence violations, being away at night, naturally the infraction resulted in stiffer penalties. Anything pronounced "uncomradely behavior" resulted in orders for transfer to another camp.

There were only two cases of transfers to a detention camp: one case for refusal to work and the other for gross lack of discipline. Arrest and pay revocation could only be imposed by the central directorate of the labor camps in Zurich.

Detention camp was a very severe measure. We had several comrades who had spent time in detention camps. The cause in most cases: they arrived in Switzerland prior to the arrival of the general wave of refugees, and for fear of being turned back, lived illegally, often for months. Discipline in the detention camp was very strict. The supervision of work was painfully exacting, and the demands much greater. The inmate of the detention camp least tolerated the limitations, that is to say, the withdrawal of vacations and outings from the camp.

The overthrow of Mussolini in Italy also had consequences. Several refugees from the Tecino camps were sent to detention camps. They moved out in the hope of joining up with the Allied forces in Italy. But mostly after a few days, these adventures ended in the hands of the Swiss border patrol.

This overthrow evoked so much hope and disappointment! It happened on a Monday, early at roll call, when the news was brought into the camp. Spades flew into the air. People screamed and turned into lunatics. Soon, soon—thought many—the war will end.

At lunch, in the cheerful mood, I noticed a comrade, sad and faced outward from the table, who did not join the general jubilation. To my question, he replied, "I think I must soon look for my relations. And I am afraid…afraid that I will not find them again."

But the war was not to end that soon. Life went on.

22

TIME: ITS STRUCTURE AND PROBLEMS (THE LABOR CAMP, PART 2)

"Gentlemen, rise and shine. It's time." The polite, but energetic and forceful cry not-so-gently jogged the worker out of his best sleep at five thirty or six o'clock in the morning, depending on the time of year. In the Mezzovico camp, we had the special privilege to have as night watchmen a Kapellmeister and superb accordionist. The full tone, the warm music of the accordion, and the intimate method ameliorated our reluctance to get up and reduced the number of those sleeping late. The group leader's effort to return the workers back to duty, more or less pulling the late sleepers' feet and pushing back their blankets, was less pronounced here than elsewhere.

Then we quickly washed up and straightened out the blankets. A half hour after getting up, the steaming coffee awaited as well as bread with cheese or jam. A big bowl and a second helping warmed the body and spirit. The whistle beckoned roll call. Armed with pick and spade, the worker proceeded to the work site.

Most camps were engaged in land reclamation. Others built streets in the mountains or cleared sections of forests. Still other camps were engaged in vegetable cultivation on the flats of the reclaimed land. Hundreds of kilos of tomatoes, green beans, and white cabbage were harvested from the camps of Locarno and Gordola. And not just by us alone.

The work fields were big; the day was long. Far into the distance stretched neglected plains, sparsely covered with grass, sandy soil, and a few shrubs, which rewarded the great exertion of the hardworking Tecino peasant with only a meager yield. The meadows stretched for kilometers between the Veggio and the train tracks, and wedged into the steep cliff walls. The yearly spring runoff washed away precious topsoil and left behind sand and stones. We provided ground leveling, built canals to tame the water, and secured an even distribution of the water for irrigation.

The laborer looked at this expanse, which seemed unending, with a heavy sigh. How meager the completed work looked in comparison. "Never again will we be breadless here," one thought quietly. "The war hasn't ended; why hurry?" But the technical leader, supported by the group leaders, saw to it that the laborer didn't succumb too much to a certain penchant to rest.

It was nice to work in the springtime or late summer in the woods or the fields. But when the July sun beat down on bare, well-tanned backs with full vengeance, and even the grass, scorched from the clobbering heat, drooped down to the earth as if to extract strength and coolness, then the laborer's tools seemed doubly heavy, and the pick wanted to negligently slide from the exhausted arm. When in the fall and winter, cold, gloomy weather wrapped everything in gray reluctance and the laborer had to work continuously so as not to freeze, then the work became an oppressing burden. Tired and frayed, the laborer returned home.

The morning was the best, but after the tea break at about nine thirty, fatigue slowly became noticeable. Gradually the tempo slackened. Fewer carts rolled over the tracks. The noontime whistle signified the end of the shift and was welcomed with delight.

In the meantime, the house staff had cleaned the barracks and washed the tables. The dining hall tables were set. Famished, the laborers took their places at the table. What would the fare be today? Soup, two vegetables or one vegetable, with meat and salad, and always the ubiquitous potatoes. In Mezzovico, we consumed one hundred kilos per day. There was enough for everyone. The meals were budgeted at two francs per person per day. Woe to the cook when his creations turned into failures or the quantities were insufficient. At once, the hungry comrades voiced their complaints. The camp management ate with the work force from the same comestibles and in the same dining hall. This democracy had a positive effect and pleasantly surprised the newly arrived refugee from the reception camp, unaccustomed to such treatment. It was also an inducement to the chef to do his best.

Prior to the meal, the postmaster had placed everyone's mail on the table. The internee impatiently opened the letters from his family members or comrades from Switzerland or abroad. Sometimes, the fervently yearned for letter still hadn't arrived, despite weeks of waiting, or bad news from a dear relative arrived, and the refugee, with a sorrowful gesture, pushed his plate away.

The radio brought the latest news from the war scene. The strategists—every table had at least one deranged general who failed in his career—began to explain the situation to their comrades and move the troops over the maps. They knew exactly why the second front had not been opened and when it would be. They predicted the war's end in spring or fall, only they didn't know the year.

Most internees took a small siesta after the meal. Work started again at a quarter of two or two o'clock and lasted until a quarter past five. Then the worker could thoroughly cleanse himself, and was free after supper. Only the house staff and kitchen staff continued to put everything in order.

The camp Samaritan didn't remain idle. Small wounds needed to be dressed; headache and digestive tablets were distributed. More serious patients were placed under observation. Often the doctor was on call at night: even in the labor camp, many were not in the best of health owing to the long war often spent in unfavorable conditions. The susceptibility to illness was great and certainly above the norm.

During work, he saw the accident victims. An inept swing of the pick, an unaccustomed tool, or the inadvertent release of the crank of the tree stump jack could lead to serious injuries. Or one of the transport carts would tip over and contuse a laborer's ribcage.

Tragic accidents were, thank God, seldom. The fatal accident of our comrade Sterling was a singular event. At the time, it roused the refugee deeply. While cutting down a tree, Sterling was killed by the falling tree. Rescued from deportation through flight, transferred to a labor camp from a crowded reception camp, and here fate caught up. He left behind a young widow, who was expecting a child at the time of the accident.

The women in the homes were also kept busy. The internment home in Brissago—one example among many—accommodated approximately two hundred women and girls. They did the laundry for about seven to eight hundred residents of the Tecino camps. That meant: wash, mend, iron, and darn socks. And there was so much to mend and sew. The refugee wanted to maintain clothes, which became more threadbare, more worn out. And from where would they take the resources to acquire replacements? Sometimes even the great talent of these women failed. A note let the poor refugee know, "Can no longer be repaired."

And so week after week, month after month went by. Always more workers completed the two hundred seventy days, certifying the worker as qualified and entitling one to a supplement of thirty centimes per day.

* * *

One of the most important problems of the internment camps was the satisfactory fulfillment of leisure time. In a broad sense, the morale of the refugee depended on it. It contributed to the creation of a communal spirit. Besides the work, the common evenings cemented the workforce together. Every camp had a social committee, whose task it was to organize varied evening programs, entertainment, courses, lectures, and sports.

We had varied successful events in Mezzovico. Song, music, serious and lighthearted scenes, satirizing the camp residents and their weaknesses provided a much-desired change from the daily routine and chased away the gloomy mood.

The central directorate of the labor camps supported a theater group established by internees that was very welcome in every camp and home. Who among the refugees didn't know Kolpe, who gave us gifts of so many fulfilling, spirited, and deeply touching poems, which expressed everything we felt and everything that moved us? And who in Mezzovico didn't think of Kupermine and Wandel, who with their violins turned our poor barrack into a concert hall? This music resonated with our spirits, and on its wings our thoughts soared into the realm of dreams and fantasy. Who could forget René Lévy, always funny, cheerful and bubbling with jokes, as if he still sat on a terrace in Montparnasse?

* * *

But Saturdays were the best—when you took off your blue work outfit, when the weekly shoe and locker inspections finished—and you once again turned into what in your heart you always were: a civilian.
For our camp, Mezzovico, located in the fortified military zone, the coup in Italy had the unfortunate consequence to close the exits to the nearby areas. Although there were no sentries at the exits of the camp, we still had to follow the regulations.

But before then, how nice and without much effort and expense, we eluded the hustle and bustle of the masses in the camp. We took pleasure sitting alone or with a good friend in a shady spot, enjoying the solitude of nature in the light Italian landscape. Or to rest in the shadow of chestnut trees on the stone benches of an outdoor tavern and chat with comrades while watching a game of boules. And then hike back over fragrant meadows in the fresh night air under star-spangled skies. What wonderful hikes we undertook in the beckoning Tecino landscape in dreamy, isolated hidden valleys seldom explored by the tourist. In the apparently time-forgotten villages, standing sharply apart from other Swiss villages, with their deteriorating picturesque stuccoed houses from the seventeenth and eighteenth centuries on whose walls crumbling pictures of the Madonna in joyous colors attested to the piety of the occupant, these simple people received the foreigner with an open friendliness and understanding.

But there remained the broader reaches of Lugano and Lucarno. For the young men, Lugano meant casino and dancing with beautiful young Tecino ladies; but for all of us, Lugano signified cappuccino and cake.

I once read in a Swiss newspaper—I can't recall which one—that refugees in the Tecino cafes behaved as if they owned the place. How could you deny anyone this modest pleasure? All week the refugee toiled in the camp. On the weekend they could leave. Could a free man even comprehend what that meant? Where should refugees go in their free time? Could they only search out the most hidden room; shouldn't they be permitted, not begrudged, to be seen in the light of day? What dangerous act or infraction of the law did they commit? They sat on terraces, had a coffee, admired and enjoyed the landscape and the life of the city to which they were attracted after the week in the camp. How these same people, a few years later, were welcomed as tourists—no talk of owning the place then. They wouldn't stand out! They would be served courteously and with zeal. But then they were just tolerated refugees. Could a human adopt such a narrow-hearted position? Could one and would one not understand that for us too life beckoned, that refugee women liked to dress up as was the general fashion in France, that you didn't always want to be the refugee in a shabby outfit squeezing meekly into a corner? It was not easy to find the right balance or boundaries. But when refugees stepped out of their frame of reference, there were often those ready to judge us with a stricter measure than they judged others.

* * *

The lucky ones whose wives were in the internment home in Brissago—I too belonged to this advantaged minority—never missed the opportunity, if finances permitted, to arrange a rendezvous with their wives. After a week in the camp, always aware of our close proximity, we appreciated doubly those sweet hours in the Lido of Locarno and Ascona, the walks along the lake shore, the palms and magnificent flowers—all that this southern beauty offered. Could people tell we were camp residents? Sometimes Martha and I felt like newlyweds, the same as the other couples who in the evening tightly embraced and returned to their camps. Only the thought of our children conveyed our incompleteness. We didn't want to look at our watches for fear the precious time would pass faster, and even faster our departure would approach. And evening did arrive, earlier than we wanted. Then they came running from all sides, those who spent the whole day in hidden corners. We parted with a last kiss in front of the autobus, we the weekend couples. These encounters were an excursion into wedlock, late-summer love, an escape from a place in which everything was so precisely and scantily measured: time, money, and affection. And our longing accompanied us on the way home. Our comrades' averse and sarcastic comments called us back to reality.

* * *

A vacation every six weeks: for days and weeks prior, the next vacation was discussed: to arrange the where and how, to make proper use of the free days, and to do everything and exploit all possibilities. Oh the poor camp telephone—when the men and wives talked and the tormented office orderlies tried to shorten these uncomfortable conversations. There was no end to the connections, successful and unsuccessful. The two hundred women, for whom a man's heart beat openly or just secretly— what was this mysterious camp, always speaking with Brissago? When asking for a connection, the operator responded in a weary voice with her stereotypical answer: "Besetzt, occupato, occupé." We tried it in all languages and intonations.

Finally the big moment would arrive. Both were ready. With borrowed hat, shoes, and valise, the tie from a friend artfully tied, the coat of a comrade on the arm and in the hand the gloves of another, there they stood, gussied up and shaved with freshly curled hair, trousers with ironed creases, looking like ladies and gentlemen. One couldn't leave work early enough. The group leader forgave the vacationer. He knew how it was. Quickly we visited the camp office.

Vacation coupon: woe to workers who didn't get their vacation coupons validated at the vacation spot; they were threatened with vacation denial the next time. The precious meal tickets, the beloved savings account, seventy-five centimes per workday paid out—poor savings account, you could never deliver what was asked of you—and with a fast flip of the wrist into the thin wallet, and it was off to the train. Thanks to the free travel voucher from the central directorate, like a big shot you slumped onto the bench. Whew, independent, free for three days and owing to the lengthy distance from Tecino, you were your own person for four days.

The worker enjoyed the trip and yet was impatient thinking about the spouse, the parents, the children, who somewhere were expecting and counting the hours. You got out, and then came the fervently anticipated reunion. If people could empathize with what such a vacation included with respect to wishes, hope, expectations, the joy of reunion, love and sensitivity, then they would never speak of the "pleasure trips" of refugees, who must travel oh-so-far to exchange their home for three days every six weeks for an impersonal hotel room or an inn full of strangers.

The time had to be exploited, to see each other, to love each other, to talk, for the next six long weeks you had to live on those memories. The time went by unmercifully. Had you hugged and kissed, caressed your child enough; had you really ingrained a picture into your memory as your child stood in front of you full of life? Had we sufficiently considered or envied the lucky ones that had a place to live and were at home there? Had one drawn sufficiently from this peaceful life to feel the dagger through the heart as the barracks reappeared on the horizon?

That was the vacation of the refugee—a rush and hunt after happiness and joy.

* * *

The refugee family, the family of a Jew—you must visualize the position of the family in the life of a Jew to realize the emotional response to the refugee family's plight.

For them, always, family life was profoundly important and heart-felt. After their expulsion and emigration from Palestine, they found in Europe only a wretched homestead. Second class people, persecuted and overlooked, their family became so much dearer and important the more insecure their position. The word of God was for the Jew the spiritual homeland, the family the only place where one could be a human. Whatever might have been the relationship between Jew and non-Jew, the Jew in the fight for daily bread was often forced to put dignity aside, to bow, to beg, and to crawl; the outer impression that portrayed the Jew's conduct—glances, gestures—receded the moment one crossed over the threshold into one's home. Here at home, one was cut off from the place in which one lived, from the foreign, from the people who looked on with suspicion, where the Jew's children like other children could enjoy their childhood; would they not find out soon enough what was the life of a Jew? Here was the loving spouse, the sensitive providing father and mother, here was a human among humans and only a bitter covering of the mouth, a shrug of the shoulder, a surreptitious sob, revealed the harsh treatment of one's environment.

The emancipation reduced the pressure that befell the Jew and led to a certain loosening of family ties. But as a whole, the traditions persisted and the Judaism of the East, this source of Jewish life, continued to renew the assimilated Judaism of the West. Even into recent times, no noticeable change could be discerned in these existing conditions.

It's part of human nature to realize the value of goods only when these assets are threatened with extinction. While we work, we lose sight of the real value of what belongs to us. How many people have discovered the most valuable in their lives through this war, albeit these discoveries were often made too late? To these valuable assets, whose ownership we accept as a matter of course and usually do not assess their true value, belong the family and the home that provides shelter.

In this war millions of people made this discovery. For many this was a new experience. For Jews, it was a repetition of fate experienced over thousands of years. For them, the family always fulfilled a sacred function.

So much more tragic, the blows to the fortune of Jews suffered in this war. Not just the Jewish community lamented the loss, the greatest loss relative to their numbers, but the survivors, in their innermost, were most deeply affected.

You must appreciate the catastrophe that befell the Jews, from a standard of special significance that the family in an essential manner brought into their lives, to measure the gruesomeness of the physical and emotional impact of the mutilation.

All those that succeeded in fleeing into Switzerland bemoaned the loss of dear family members: seldom the distant relatives, but parents, siblings, or even spouses, who were deported from the German occupied areas or lived in Germany, Austria, or Poland and fell victim to the rage of annihilation. Many women only found the courage to flee after their husbands were deported. In many cases only the man sought to hide, in the mistaken belief that the extermination drive of the persecutors would stop before affecting women. How many children were torn from their parents and orphaned?

Misfortune binds stronger than fortune. The tragedy of the survivors, the knowledge and anxious concern about the missing, brought the survivors closer together and enlarged the need for the consoling closeness of their companions. The family became that much more precious the more they lost and the more they suffered together.

So what were the consequences of camp life? The isolation of the genders, in hindsight, had the effect of heightened excitability. It was a manifestation of a natural psychological reflex. We once organized an interesting and entertaining afternoon in Mezzovico, to which we invited the women and young ladies from Brissago. By coincidence I overheard a refugee woman exclaim, "Oh, so many men are here; it gets you all excited." A naïve but proper expression, a confession. In freedom, where men and women continually have contact with each other, a representative of the other sex appears only in special circumstances as a bearer of sexual relations. The isolation of the sexes underlined the contradiction and only furthered the sex drive.

But it was not just that. The coolness and the lack of attachment to someone in collective living, performing work without conviction, raised generally the need for love, affection, and sympathy. Under the guise of a rasping intonation, faintly shone the need for warmth, for beings close and intimate, for escape and forgetting. The more conscious a refugee became of leading a life lost in the masses, the more that refugee demanded people who only belonged to him or her, whose embrace extinguished everything, helping to forget all debasement, whose whispers engendered the feeling of still being a human, a human being that has value, on whom others lean and need.

The need for love and affection thrust itself into the harsh reality in numerous ways. There were the men whose wives were deported or remained in France. There were the women, torn from their husbands, whom they may never see again. The honor bestowed on the absentee, the fear of committing adultery—a sin that in the misfortune of the refugee appeared more difficult to weigh and led to the failure in the establishment of most and occasional relationships to the opposite sex these unhappy souls attempted. The motivational factors, as honorable as they may have been, also led to disturbances in which the mental equilibrium of the distressed was even more impaired. The damage, affecting woman from such an imposed fortune and accepted abstention, could even lead to hysteria. Every leader of a home for women could attest to that.

The absence of satisfaction, the inner despair, often sought a desired, clear-headed objective for its external escape. As always and everywhere sexual relationships were discussed, even in the camps and homes. And when these discussions were not always conducted with sufficient restraint, then it was traceable to not just the absence of the opposite sex, but also to an unconscious need to react. In addition so many different people were together, including people of not always the highest standards. In these matters, you couldn't expect grown men to conduct themselves as in a temple. And when you consider that in the promiscuity of the camp so many men had to shed their sexual fears, a certain outer coarseness appeared sad. In more sensitive natures, and in particular in young people, it could trigger, through a spiritual reflex, repression that in later in life could intensify complexes and make the establishment of relationships with the opposite sex constantly more difficult. Torn from their natural development, the sphere of family life obviously weighed heavily on a young man or young girl.

I don't know if the atmosphere of a labor camp, with separation of the sexes, was more advantageous for the development of young people than the atmosphere of a reception camp where men and women were together. But one thing is sure, that for refugee youth as for any youth, the absence of a home with parents signified the greatest loss.

The placement of the young, even into special youth camps, could only be a stopgap solution resulting from the aspiration to do the best under the given circumstances. But those aged seventeen to twenty needed a special leadership and guardianship as the operation of a camp could never provide. And in addition, refugee youth could for years have not experienced structured family life. These people could variously have come of age in an unsympathetic and unbridled environment. They matured early, without being mature and knowledgeable about life, without having learned about life. They belonged in their own educational institution or family, so that in the last chapter of their development their life would achieve some measure of structure.

I often had the opportunity to get together, in the Tecino, with the residents of a youth camp. There were some fine and smart fellows among them, self-assured and refined, with understanding, companionate, whose inner striving caused them to widely forgive and forget the necessary manner of existing shortages. But besides, there were fellows who in a sought after roughness with a misunderstood realism sought their way. A youth, for whom beauty, warmth, and kindheartedness failed them, who could only see evil, would often consciously disavow all ideals. A thrusting harshness, an atrocious soberness led them to a perspective of material triviality and destitution. Do I need to add that the first ones were those, who until the most recent time, lived in the bosom of a family whom they carefully nourished, and of the others, disinherited their lives, children of "our" time?

The upbringing and housing of children separated from their parents was another difficult problem. The question of whether it was better to place a child into a residency home or into a foster family was not easy to answer. With placement into a family, it was sometimes difficult to match the environment of the family and the refugee child. Placement into a luxurious environment could in this respect be a disadvantage, as after the war the child would have difficulties adjusting to the simpler relationships in the home of his parents. Placement in agrarian settings would not always be welcomed by totally city-dwelling parents. Such parents may be inclined to view the agrarian simplicity in food and clothing as a kind of deprivation. All that became a non-issue with placement into children's homes. After all, you lived there in a kind of communalism, and whatever your view may be, in our era it is a necessity to accustom children to living together. We don't know what the future has in store for us. It is to be feared—the more life develops, the less space there will be for the individualist. In the interest of the child, it is important to strike a balance between individualism and collective living. Naturally, the ideal setting would be a family with children to integrate the child into a community and to have the benefit of learning a well-ordered family life.

The refugee parents, as all parents, wished for their children the nicest and the best. In their special circumstance, they were even more attached to their children than others. For them, the children signified a life's work. For whom should they reconstruct a new life if not for them?

I had a comrade who had nine close family members in Poland. He dared not hope to find them again. He often said to me that after the war he would no longer take any pleasure in working. He would miss the satisfaction of caring for his mother, his greatest pride and his greatest joy. This man focused his thoughts only on his spouse and most of all on his small child. And he had never seen this little girl, his daughter, born only after his flight in France.

So it was by many refugees and particularly by mothers. Only the thoughts of their children let them hold their heads high and connected them to life. Many mothers could not be satisfied easily. Could you blame these mothers when they put their entire heart into their children, the only thing left to them from better days? Such women always felt disadvantaged and set back. Among these victims, I knew of one mother with two children. Angered and embittered by the events, this woman could never be satisfied with how her children were looked after. Since her husband had been torn from her, nothing in this world would satisfy her. In such unusual relationships, by the psychological breakdown of some parents, the children could often, unfortunately, have an advantage, as their upbringing would not be in the hands of their parents. The children who lived in hiding in France, those that experienced the flight and stayed in the reception camps were deprived of their childhood. The even rhythm of a different environment was better for such children, and they were more likely to receive a needed harmony than if left to the blind adoration of their mothers—mothers, who themselves were in need of spiritual treatment and were altogether too much inclined to overlook the failings of their loved ones. Certainly, even strangers, home directors, educators, foster parents could also be overly lenient and shy away from treating these heavily tested beings too harshly or too roughly, because in their sympathy, their awareness of the tragic cases of the refugee children was overly strong. Behavior you might not condone in your own child, you might pass over in that of an adopted child whose past has been so touched by fate. I do, however, think that in this respect the expressed rationale of the Swiss will lead to the proper middle ground, but you cannot simply skip this sensitive aspect of the upbringing of refugee children.

Naturally, with the delicate question of raising children, you can't just follow a template. Every case is different. The Children's Relief Organization was faced with a daunting and delicate task. The treatment between parents and children was not amenable to differentiation and led to regulations that for many parents were unnecessary and burdensome. But how could exceptions be made without breaking down the principles of child relief?

The Children's Relief Organization permitted parents to visit their children once every three months. Not because of financial reasons, but on the grounds of childrearing, the parents could not see their children too often. They wished to avoid interrupting the continuity of the daily life of the children. It goes without saying that with such seldom and joyous occasions the parents would see their child through rose-colored glasses and would spoil the children wherever and however they could.

I need to add: in practice the rules worked against the poor. When the parents had vacation, no one could deny them a visit with their children every six weeks; but the Children's Relief Organization contributed to the expenses only every six months and thus forced the more poverty-stricken to compliance with the rules.

Considerations were not just for the continuity of the daily rhythm of the children's well-being, but also the atmosphere of the institution could not be disturbed. In order to have parents stay out of the upbringing of their child, the Children's Relief Organization provided off-sight vacation homes in which parents and children could enjoy their vacations together. The Children's Relief Organization did not hesitate to cover the added costs and clearly demonstrated that they were serious about the undesired stay of parents at the child's residence.

The exclusion of the parents was not an ideal situation. It underlined in a crass way how little the refugee family belonged to itself. It left the parents without parental control—they were severely sensitive to subordinating the upbringing of their children—and developed in many a distrust of collective welfare.

In this connection, if I may cite a case that showed how difficult it sometimes became in practice for parents to prevail in their one and given right—supervision and right to object.

My wife and I made the acquaintance of two women whose husbands had been deported. Both had children that had been boarded at a home. This home—a really seldom case—left a lot to be desired. It suffered from a personnel shortage that inevitably led to the neglect of the children. Even the nourishment was inadequate. I had the occasion to speak to several refugees with children in these homes, and they confirmed these facts. As these women saw their children, their most cherished, after a long separation, in their unbalanced spiritual state they suffered from a mental breakdown. As neither spoke German, they begged me, beseeched me to write a letter to the Children's Relief Organization to improve the children's situation. At first I turned down the request and only after much prodding and many questions to convince myself of the conditions and to ascertain that this was not a case of criticism founded on blind adoration, I wrote for them and in their name a well-balanced letter to the Children's Relief Organization in Zurich. I requested an inspection. The Children's Relief Organization forwarded the letter to the home; from the children's home, it was forwarded to the home where the two women were interned. They wanted to know who had composed this letter. Neither of the women would say. The poor women were subject to all sorts of chicanery, and although conditions improved in the children's home, the protests to which they were entitled brought them nothing good.

The refugee children knew and understood that their parents were themselves only internees and not able to care for them. With younger children, in place of the normal authoritarian relationship, a friendship-based relationship developed between the refugees and their children, compensating for many ills. It was touching to see by what means children made the effort to prove their love and care for their parents.

Besides the parents, the children also showed their concern for younger siblings. With childlike tenderness, the unaided letters of our oldest never failed to mention his little brother, whom he wanted to visit in place of his parents and look after him as well as the younger siblings of his comrades in other locations in the same city. They knew what the significance of family meant; they felt in solidarity with all members of their family, and for their younger siblings, they were ready to take on the roles of father or mother. And after the war, for many awaited the toughest task—to resume the battle of life at the side of a now single mother.

* * *

One of the most beautiful and most solemn memories I took from the labor camp was our Yom Kippur holiday.

Yom Kippur is the most significant holy day for Jews. It is the Day of Atonement, the day we acknowledge and regret our sins and beseech God's forgiveness. Even the Jew who has lost many ties to Judaism honors, at a minimum, this holy day. On this day, one acknowledges one's Judaism.

How much more did this holy day signify for us refugees? There were those among us who had become strangers to Judaism. Only persecutions brought to consciousness their Jewish destiny. On this day we prayed for our dead, thought about our loved ones whose fate we didn't know and for whom we were afraid.

So we made every effort to approach this day, particularly in the camps, thoughtfully and with dignity. Our camp leader showed much compassion and help. So too the Jewish community of Lugano, as was their natural duty, did everything possible.

The holy day fell on a Saturday. We transformed the reading lounge into a prayer room. The middle table was covered with a blanket and turned into a prayer table. The carpenter built a dais for the prayer leader. The Torah scroll arrived in one of the central directorate's crates, which was configured as an ark of the covenant. It was the best place we could offer it. A rope closed it from the outside world.

Our prayer room was meager and wretched—a prayer room for refugees. But, certainly, the prayers were said with ardor and conviction. The biggest temple could claim no greater devotion than our little prayer room in Mezzovico. And God is everywhere, and ready to hear us anywhere. The magnificence of the great temples is but trash in his eyes when not filled with reverence.

The eve of Yom Kippur approached. We ate a splendid meal. The body had to be strengthened for the coming fast day, to serve the Eternal with unflagging power. Then we entered the prayer room. The service started. A camp comrade was the prayer leader. He prayed with all his strength and spirit. With a totally God-fulfilled heart, he sang the "Kol Nidre."

Here we prayed, one next to the other. This one from France, another from Holland, that one a simple Polish Jew, another an intellectual West European—all were murmuring the same prayers. All languages are extinguished before the holy language of the Bible. We experienced the unifying bond of prayer. The solemnity of the holy day descended into the small room.

The next morning, the community was again assembled. There was only strength through prayer; until evening we could not take any bodily nourishment. No secular thoughts may come between man and God.

We read from the Torah: fortune to those who are honored with a call to the Torah and to read to the assembled community that week's portion of the Torah. I was ashamed that I was not knowledgeable enough to go before the Torah. I feared standing bare. But in my heart, I also belong to God. I was delighted to have been called to open the ark and show the Torah to the assembled. I was delighted to have been invited to roll up the Torah. I was delighted to have been allowed to be a servant of the Torah.

With what devotion did these heavily tested humans stretch out their hands to kiss the seam of the Torah as it was carried past them. For us the Torah provided strength and blessing. For its sake, we have been suffering for thousands of years. Wrapped in a cover of velvet, in one spot the ripped seam hangs down. Its dress was so taken, as were our bodies and souls—this Torah scroll of the refugees.

We thought about the dead and our fate.

The prayers went on. The time advanced. Unforeseen, the evening was at hand. The closing prayer—the holy day had ended. Tired, we quickly stepped into the fresh air for strength.

We had prayed much to God. Would he hear us?

23

LIBERATION

A fter months in the camps, did we still think about freedom? Did we think that here in Switzerland our own home might become available? Alas, we thought about freedom in the same way you think about owning something expensive, something unattainable—an unrealizable reality. We were interned refugees in the camps and had accepted that we belonged to the refugee community, a community condemned not to live our own lives. It was difficult enough to give it up, but slowly, gradually habit overpowered us, for it made no sense to hang on to dreams that couldn't be fulfilled.

One day in August, I received a letter from the Jewish Relief Organization from Zurich. The Evangelical Free Place Action offered us a small house in Nesslau in the Toggenburg of St. Gallen, in which the four of us could live together. The local Evangelical ministry would support our stay. For the time being, the department of police in Bern authorized me a three-month leave and totally agreed with the release of my wife from work service. Did we want to accept?

How did all this happen? We racked our brains, but for the time being could not solve the puzzle. I no longer thought about my petition from so long ago. Eight months had gone by since then. After I had my x-rays done back in July, the police section in the camp inquired about my fitness to work, but I never attached any significance to the matter. We pursued only one thing, that my wife and Michel be placed into a home for mothers with small children. Already in June, we directed such a petition to the central directorate of the labor camps. I personally gave it to our camp director. But through a later intervention from acquaintances, the central directorate replied that they were not familiar with such a petition. In which wastebasket was it filed?

And then we were offered freedom. Something we had given up for the war's duration. It's so true that many of our dreams and wishes are fulfilled, but hardly ever when we wish or expect them. So often, luck falls into the lap of the weary wanderer through life's journey only after he has become old and learned to do without, so that he no longer takes pleasure in it. We had to decide to appreciate and enjoy the offer. It was our big chance, which, without our striving, fell all by itself into our laps. For this, as for so many other things, we had our Geneva friends to thank. Prompted by my July vacation, he took my condition to heart and intervened on our behalf in Zurich at L'Organisation Suisse d'Aide aux Réfugiés (OSAR). My file there again appeared. OSAR discovered that I had had a relapse and the possibility arose to free us. Now they could again do their business. Yet we knew nothing about it; who reopened our petition and took responsibility for its follow-through we would only find out much later.

But for the moment, we had no idea that for us it was *the* opportunity, the lucky draw. I met my wife in Ascona, and we discussed this offer for a long time. It was not easy for us to reach a decision. I had come to terms with camp life and, in any case, had been recommended for a home where I would find better care. There I would probably again work in the office and earn my own support. Should we live by the grace of strangers?

How powerfully freedom beckoned. But what we were offered— would that be freedom? Would we trade dependency on a known entity for one even more suppressive? Could we maintain our own household? We agreed: we could not accept unless we could maintain an independent household. And how would the people treat us? Could we maintain ourselves in Nesslau? And if we did manage our own household, would we receive enough to get by adequately? We knew cases of people who were set free and could not live on the support they were given, and they finally asked to be transferred back to a home or camp. In other cases, those at free places did not get along with their hosts and also went back to camp. Colleagues explained to me that we would not be comfortable for the duration in such a small place, with people of such different natures, and in such isolation. We didn't belong in the countryside. But then we thought about Michou. The longer the separation went on, the less my wife could tolerate it. How many tears did she cry last September when our vacation was postponed three weeks? And this child was growing up without knowing its parents, without asking for them—strangers and unknown people. He showed no interest in our company and smiled when we brought him back into the home. A visit with Paul consoled and strengthened us; a visit with Michel laid bare our wounds we could not heal.

Did we think then that the residents of Nesslau would be happy to receive guests and do something good for refugees? No, we did not. I could not draw any precise image of Nesslau—it was foreign to us. I thought only of our dependency, which we might find even more oppressive because we were direct recipients of gracious support.

And so I wrote and asked for details. And I received such a warm and kind letter from Reverend Schweitzer that our hearts opened, and I thought we should well give it a chance. Should it not work out, the way back to the camp was always open. My wife, once united with Michou, could then be allowed to stay with him. We wanted to leave Paul, for the time being, in Geneva. He was in such a good place and attended a French school and through the flight had already missed a year of school. It would have been a mistake, ill-considered and perhaps rash, to remove him from his accustomed surroundings.

That was approximately the middle of August. September passed in waiting and hope. We went to Geneva for vacation at the end of September, during Rosh Hashanah. Friday, October 1, we were just at the children's home of the Salvation Army, La Maternelle, visiting Michou, when the matron informed us that the central directorate—or perhaps the internment home of Brissago—had just called. My wife had been released and had to travel with Michou directly to Nesslau.

In this way life's events surprise us: we wait and wait and suddenly developments redirect our lives. As my wife left Brissago, she did not count on never returning and not seeing her friends again. She too had laughed when the camp director requested all the ladies give their exact vacation addresses, so they could be reached at any time: somebody might be released.

And now the pain for her became reality, and she did not concur. She wanted to travel with me and not alone into this remote area. I had not yet been released. The synchronization attempt by OSAR was not totally successful. All her luggage was in Brissago. She had nothing with her. After all, how much do you need for three days?

How ironic: my goal was to have my wife return to Brissago for some time to put her things in order and wait for me. Also Michou wasn't totally well. On our first vacation day, he caught a cold and ran a temperature going out into the foggy, cold, damp fall weather. We wanted to wait until he was fully recovered. I called the Brissago internment home, but the strict camp director didn't want to know anything about my wife's return. She would let her stay in Geneva and await Michou's improvement if she wanted, but under no circumstances could she return to the home. Her camp comrades would pack her things and send them on to Nesslau. Travel expenses had to be conserved. Nothing could change this position. So my wife did decide to travel that Sunday to Nesslau. She left against her will, the fear of the unknown even outweighing the joy of taking Michou. And even that can happen. You yearn for freedom, and when it comes, you fear the unknown and regret for a moment leaving the well-ordered care of camp life.

Paul was moody and resentful. The release of my wife and Michel triggered mixed emotions. He resented being left behind in Geneva while his little brother accompanied his mama. "Michou doesn't even know his parents," he argued, "but I know them, and I want to be with them. It doesn't matter to Michou to stay behind in the home." At our good-byes he sobbed heavily. At the time he was in a children's hospital on account of his recurring rash. I only took him out for two days. I brought him back on the eve of our departure. Even chocolate would not console him. We went to the hospital, and I gave him a long kiss and quickly closed the door behind me. My eyes too were tearing. It hurt me to see him so inconsolable. I promised him: he would follow by Christmas.

On Sunday, the three of us left Geneva. I accompanied my wife until Olten and then traveled back to Mezzovico.

The last weeks in the camp…So it was true that I would leave my good and decent comrades with whom I shared so much joy and sorrow.

For five months, table 11 was our regular place in the dining barrack. The tall, serious, somewhat melancholy Pole from France sat at the window seat. He felt the entire bitterness of the Jewish destiny. Would he again see his loved ones? In Paris, as he was renewing his papers, he was sent to a camp—he and his brother. In that camp, hunger was rampant, such that people paid a thousand francs for bread and hundreds for a cigarette. Sometimes the gendarmes offered their hands to assist in smuggling, for handsome pay. Bread was stolen regularly. When the bread wagon came, a group covered a daredevil who with a quick hand grabbed the bread and let it disappear under his protective coat. Both German soldiers and French gendarmes guarded them. One day, while doing carpentry work in the guardroom, an opportunity arose. A window stood open. A quick decision: they jumped into the fields, spurred on by shots, and they succeeded. His brother was left behind and was deported. Every day he questioned his right to escape and to leave his brother in the lurch. And he thought he should have stayed with his brother and shared his fate: together free or together dead. No discussion or consolation helped. Dejection spoke from the black eyes of this most decent human being.

Next to him sat another heavily tested man. A refugee for the third time—this Pole had lived in Germany. First he went from Germany to Spain. Just as he succeeded to establish himself, the civil war broke out. He experienced the war bombings in Barcelona, which without defenses was left to the mercy of the enemy fliers. He experienced the terrible collapse of Catalonia and the terrible flight over ice and snow into France. Again came war years and again flight. I was not astounded that this person was so nervous; I was not astounded by the tick in his eyes; but I was astounded that, despite everything, this man was so lively, was able to bring himself to be funny and upbeat, and was always ready to tell another story. Great and wide was the anecdotal bag of a traveler. He always made us laugh, and even the serious Pole smiled, when he told us of his lengthy and involved adventures as "Galicianer" (from Galicia in Spain, not Galizia in Poland).

The young man to my left came from Italy. His family emigrated from Germany to Italy. In July 1940 he went to Croatia. When Yugoslavia collapsed, he was placed into a Croatian concentration camp and then went back to Italy. One day he received the order to report to a concentration camp—again flight, this time into Switzerland.

Which country in Europe did we not flee from? In which country were there not concentration camps with death staring you in the eyes? The Jew knew geography—a unique kind. It consisted of naming hundreds—thousands—of ghettos and camps all over Europe. Not all of them were marked on maps. But in them the Jew lived, knew them, experienced them. And threads were spun from one country to another and from one camp to another. They were not visible on maps, for soon they were cattle cars stuffed with people ordained to die, soon they were streets, trails, soon just directions over meadows, fields, snow-covered mountains that led from country to country and from camp to camp. A people in flight—that we were (and are). A people without a country—that we were. The world was ours because nothing was ours. Who could be happy when others cried; who could be free when others languished? I'm thinking about a comrade in Africa who did not want to go to Europe. "As long as people are in camps, I will stand by them," he wrote. "I belong to my comrades."

And I? Didn't I belong with these three comrades, with this group, my group from Prêles? What right did I have to be free and happy when they remained as the good gentlemen in camp? A melancholy drop mixed into the joy of my impending release. The war storm swept us together and now it was blowing us apart. Each carried their fate, small worlds in themselves circling the universe tugging at us, together for a time and then parted to follow their particular path through the course of time until death installs us in the last camp, into the earth from which we came, and bids us to our last rest.

Yes, parting was very difficult. Two days I postponed my departure, and should have gone to my wife and child. My colleagues waved for a long time. For a last time, I gazed at the barracks, the construction site, the comrades. And then the train abducted me. New landscapes. New developments and life.

* * *

On the way, I stopped for two days in Zurich. I needed to personally thank OSAR .

It was a broad building located in Lavater Street. On top, offices were crowded together, and below a stream of refugees mingled. A true Cerberus conducted and channeled the throng flowing through this building from early morning until late at night. And everyone carried their own lot, one that needed to be heard, understood, consoled, and eased. There were twenty-two thousand Jewish refugees in Switzerland, but only eighteen thousand Swiss Jews—more than one refugee for each resident Jew. Heavy was the burden, and not just materially, resting on the welfare organizations.

The refugees were not lacking in professions. They had established a notable rank in society. They were now—one earlier, the other later—locked out from society. But just as they were conscious of their declassification, so they remembered better times.

These memories were often very painful. Certainly, not all Jews were rich. Many knew the hardest struggles of survival. But all knew the meaning of material independence, dreamed about how wonderful the fulfillment of their wishes would be, without the need to beg, and without surrendering any rights. How many things seemed essential for the refugee but were rejected by the organizations because they couldn't approve everything?

Administering the needs required much tact and sensitivity. People who once were in a position to help others—for them it was now doubly painful to turn to others for every concern. Welfare is only real welfare when the recipient is spared every feeling of humiliation. The qualities of a welfare worker include empathy, sensitivity, and human understanding. It became difficult to preserve these qualities under the pressures of a heavy workload. And every petition had to be carefully reviewed. People cannot take advantage of the welfare organization's resources for egotistical purposes. These resources were limited. As a result of the currency transfer freeze, the amounts coming from abroad, England and America prevented a generous financing of welfare, so the contributions to the welfare funds were augmented by the Swiss people.

In this situation, the delicate task of the welfare worker is to do as much as possible, and do it in such a way that the recipient feels it happened willingly. The refugee must feel that these people are only driven to help them.

This spiritual caring of the refugee is the most noble and distinguished job of the relief organizations. The human destiny, squeezed into a paper file, here again takes on a structure and demands love and sympathy. Is there a more noble work than to help disenfranchised refugees again feel like whole and worthy human beings?

* * *

I had to wait a long time to be admitted. I had time to talk to the comrades. I saw so many I had met in Geneva, in Büren or Schönengrund. There and in the large dining hall—a restaurant that the welfare organization established in Lavater Street in which you could have a complete meal for eighty centimes—were the central meeting places for refugees passing through or vacationing in Zurich. There you went not just to eat inexpensively and adequately, but also mostly to see again the people you met and then lost sight of in the many Swiss refugee stages. There was the big news exchange for the latest from the camps, the central exchange of the previously mentioned bush telephone.

Finally I was admitted to the social worker concerned with the free places. I was warmly received. I sensed that inner sympathy that was so beneficial to the refugee, because we could then step away from the masses and become an individual. The social worker showed me my file. It was fat and heavy, with every letter I had directed to her since that first letter I had written in January 1943. It was still there—this letter—cleanly filed. The file began with this letter, and then came the many correspondences, inquiries, return inquiries, and so forth, and finally the crowning decision from the police department. An outsider could not comprehend the work each individual case entailed. It was not just about finding the free place. That was sometimes the easiest task. Then the technical work had to be done. The approval of the community had to be obtained, then the approval from the canton, the police department in Bern, the central directorate for labor camps in Zurich, and sometimes, when it concerned release from the reception camps, even the military authorities. And every case was different. There were time-limited dispensations and leaves of absence and total releases from work service. A whole staff of officials sifted through and worked on the many refugee files.

Yes, it was difficult to achieve my liberation. I think that consideration for my wife and child also played a role and, together with my illness, at least helped me obtain this vacation. And in three months I had to renew my request. Yet in the meantime, I was free.

In the afternoon, I was off to the office of Pastor Vogt[23], in Streuli Street, to the Evangelical Free Place Action to whom we owed our little house. Even there people were waiting, but not as many as in Lavater Street, and the reception was a little more personal. I was received with overly effusive friendliness, as if they were expecting me. Here I experienced for the first time the commitment of Evangelical cooperation, of those who did social work, not as regular work, not as regular cooperation, but as service to God and Bible fulfillment. The newly awoken and born-again word of God guided and led these people and engendered their words with a particular warmth and kindness. Later, the compelling strength radiating from the rooms of Streuli Street became clear to me. The need of the refugees, so I frequently sensed, evoked an internalizing and rebirth of Christian principles in the Swiss.

As a refugee, I perhaps have seen too much so that I may not judge everything correctly; yet I believe, it appears to me, that the debate over the problem of the refugees brought about a spiritual movement, a movement of renewal in the church, which in no way has been concluded. We see how much space is devoted to the refugee problem, and we must tell ourselves that for many Swiss the question of refugees and its solution has manifested itself into a problem that from the person on the refugee aside has become a problem of maintaining the worthiness of the Swiss people. It's nice to see that and be able to observe it. And after the war, the church, having come back to life as a spiritual movement renewing humanity through the renewal of God's word, aims to fulfill its mission.

* * *

---

23 Founder of the Evangelical Free Place Action. Independent Commission of Experts—Second World War, *Switzerland and Refugees in the Nazi Era*, page 68

Late in the evening of the next day, I arrived in Nesslau. Vicar Schaffert awaited me at the train station. Without him, I would never have found the way to the small house. My wife was not expecting me until the next day. She was totally surprised at my sudden appearance. And the joy was that much the greater.

Again together and again in a home.

24

THE HOUSE ON THE MOUNTAIN: NESSLAU

The next day, as I view the house, my heart fills with warmth. There it stands—the Swiss chalet about which I fantasized on my trip to Büren almost a year ago. And therein we can live all by ourselves.

"Our" little house is located in the Bühl, about a half hour to three quarters of an hour distant from the town, about two hundred meters above the valley. Over gentle, climbing green hillsides and forests, the view slides east to the seven Kurfürsten; and in the distance to the south, the Säntis, with its sharp jagged peaks, reaches for the sky. Bare cliffs tower vertically and reflecting snowfields, between supporting rock faces, surround its flanks. To the west, rounded forested hilltops stretch in quick succession along the horizon. The gaze penetrates into the no-too-far distance, where the peaks steer toward the heavens, on whose structure rests God's vault.

The peaceful and tranquil valley, with its petite, clean, well-cared for little houses with gabled peaks, lays nestled in this house of nature. The homes crowd along the perfectly straight street, like a herd surrounding its protective herdsman, between the two churches: on the left the Catholic and on the right the Evangelical. Emanating from the main street, proud paths climb the hillside and dead-end at individual residences.

Industry has barely made inroads. A weaving mill is situated in the middle of the town—an advanced outpost of technology. Otherwise, the inhabitants live off income from farming, dairy, cattle, and timber harvested from the rich forests. Now and then a little train hurries through the landscape. An autobus provides connections to the more outlying villages. Every breath inhales peace, security, and permanence. Somewhere the war rages on, the hustle and bustle of the big cities exists; here everything is unhurried, tranquil, and good-natured. The fortune of nature lives here in the green valley, by these good people who stand solidly on their home soil, their faces weather-beaten, with secure inherited gestures fulfilling their customary daily work.

In the evening when I'm walking home from the village, I often rest and breathe deeply. That feels good—peace. Magically transformed, the peaks glow against the horizon, awash in a delicate red in the last rays of sunshine. My gaze seeks the roof of our little house, the chimney's rising smoke telling me that the stove has been lit and the evening meal awaits me. I'm searching for the light from the small petroleum lamp that is both compass and trail marker. How cozy is it—the light in the broad landscape bidding welcome from home to home.

Our home is the typical Swiss peasant chalet, with the kitchen next to the woodbins, to which are attached the stalls[24] for dairy cows. A left turn from the threshold leads into a homey living room. Here stands the magnificent piece: the huge, green, tile oven. The ovens of the Toggenburg are unique. They have a rather large girth and are built into the wall between the living room and the kitchen, from where the firewood is fed. A bundle of branches and twigs, about twenty-five centimeters in diameter and tied with a wire, and some logs are all that is needed to defeat the freezing winter storms and spread comfortable warmth in the living room with its low ceiling. With a long wooden spade, the burning wood is pushed to the rear into the living room, and when it is completely burned, the air vent is closed. The oven stays warm the whole day, and even in the morning is still tepid. It's a real

---

24 The attached stable was only used in the winter to house the dairy herd while the main stable was cleaned.

perpetually burning oven constructed with the best principles of furnace science.

The description may be long, but the oven is worth lauding with proper praise. Imposingly, it stands on well-rounded, sturdy wooden legs—a bulwark against the harsh winter. Life centers on it during these long winter evenings. Nowhere else have I seen such ovens. I must think back to our pitiful oven in Büren, around which fifty to sixty frozen people shuffled.

A small workroom adjoins the living room, from which narrow stairs lead through a trapdoor to the bedrooms and the attic. Everywhere are narrow stairs and trapdoors—in the foyer, leading to the attic; in the kitchen, to the cellar—which separate and connect the rooms and make the house into a closed unit. Our young one has baptized our home, "The Trap Door House." But we will stick with its original name *Schneckenbühl.*[25] We find it so fitting for a refugee house, within which we retire and quietly dwell.

After the crowding in the camps, this home seems so absolutely spacious. How many families can even claim a house for themselves? And in the camp, what belonged to us alone? The narrow locker of the central directorate kept our possessions in the dormitory barrack, in which forty men slept, made noise, snored, and argued. When and where could you be alone?

Our little house has one shortage—but I will not describe it as a shortcoming. We have no electrical light. It astonishes how quickly you get used to kerosene lamps and how cozy and homey their light shines on the table. It reminds me of my childhood, when we also only had kerosene lighting. We have enough progress. Better to have sufficient kerosene than to have the electricity turned off because the meter indicates that the quota has been exceeded; better two cooking pans on the small woodstove than the beautiful gas range we had in France, whose flame so sadly flickered; and certainly better the logs in the woodbin than the central heating in Lyon, on which we sometimes had to stand just to warm our feet.

* * *

---

25 "Snail house"

My wife is busy the whole day. Here it counts: to maintain the residence, to cook, to do laundry, to take care of the little ones and do all the important, numerous little things that comprise the life and work of a housewife.

But she loves doing it. Her face shows satisfaction and peace of mind. She doesn't regret the eight-hour days and the sewing repair room in Brissago. She gets up earlier, but there is not a signal that forces her to rise. She doesn't have to tremble that she might not hear the bell and find the dining hall locked. Neither is she afraid of a room inspection, in which the camp director moves the beds to find a forgotten trace of dust. The steady danger of a reprimand no longer hovers over her like the sword of Damocles.

In June 1943, I was in Brissago shortly before we were forbidden, through our presence, to disturb the quiet of the women. Understandable curiosity drove me to enter the internment home, although that was then forbidden. It was a wonderful modern hotel, a masterpiece of the Swiss tourist industry. The war scared away the flood of tourists, and it then only knew the flood of refugees—all these women, in this hotel, wearing their uniform aprons. I had the impression of being in some kind of penalty guesthouse. These were no "young girls in uniforms," but women of every age. By the way, I wasn't in there for long, as my frightened wife immediately led me away. One day my wife was visiting our camp along with other residents of her home. We had planned a bright afternoon to give the ladies a chance to see our camp. At a quarter past eight, the ladies were supposed to leave. At eight o'clock my wife became all excited. "Shouldn't we be going to the train?" Okay. We went to the train: not a soul on the platform. "Surely they will count the women prior to departure, and I won't be there!" she said. Always present was the fear to do something wrong, to miss the roll call, to be reprimanded. That tugged on the nerves and made the women fearful and insecure.

To be reduced to schoolgirls at thirty, forty, or fifty years of age, always subject to supervision—that is a bitter lot. This lot no longer burdens my wife. For that she is thankful.

Here she works for herself and her loved ones. She has the satisfaction to see how little Michel, under her diligent care, develops into a handsome and lively boy. He certainly had excellent care in his

Maternelle. The sisters are attached to their charges and do everything for the well-being of the children so that the thought that other children are being protected and raised by their parents doesn't enter into their little heads. And yet, here, how so totally differently Michou blossoms. It shows that for such a small being there is no substitute for motherly love. The loving eyes of a mother are like the life-giving sun; the air of the parental home is like the warm air of a greenhouse that stimulates and promotes development and growth. We can't be accused of blind adoration thinking this way. Didn't we separate from Paul without much ado? But Michou is still a small baby, who can hardly babble. He is doing well in the fresh mountain air. Gone is the cough from Geneva. Michou has red cheeks and has developed a little pouch. He romps around, climbs on the stairs, and his childlike, bright voice fills the whole house with life.

* * *

When my wife set foot into the house, she found flowers on the table. With much love, the entire community of Nesslau contributed to the furnishing and hominess of our little house: one contributed a wardrobe closet; another, a bed; a third, a bed for the children; and a fourth, a sled for the children to use in the winter. All contributed clothing, linen, tablecloths, towels, aprons, children's clothes, and warm sweaters—everything but everything a household needs.

In the kitchen cupboard and on the cellar shelves were stocked: rice, sugar, noodles, cooking fat, jams, potatoes, and fruit. Everyone was proud to do something for the refugees. What work the vicarage had to carefully provide for the life of a family.

And as we were then taken care of, so it has remained. We are guests of the community, and it constantly thinks about us. Again and again, people want to bring us pleasure and surprise us. It's nice to be a guest. I needn't be ashamed to receive gifts. Haven't I always worked to earn the bread for my loved ones? Now we are refugees: I can't, I am not permitted to earn our bread. I must live from other people. But I don't beg. We don't go into houses to ask for donations. I don't feel degraded when people come to us and give us something to provide some pleasure. It's not my fault I became a refugee. The war will be over, and I'll be able to work again and be proud to once again earn our own bread. And I will endeavor to be good to my fellow humans and do my duty to humanity and spread kindness. Sometimes there are moments when it hurts to receive and not be able to reciprocate with much. Sometimes old pride and arrogance rear up against the test God has put on us, to learn the lesson that no one can exist without others.

As I came to Nesslau, I feared the inhabitants would not understand that I lived without working. The people here work hard. The soil surrenders nothing easily. It only gives to those who sweat and toil in its presence. Early morning lights announce that they have risen and are at work. The cows must be taken care of. And here we are: we eat, but we don't work. We live from the efforts and toils of others, who every month make their contribution to the vicarage. How can peasants, who have nothing handed to them, understand that?

Certainly I work. No one can live without working. The person who has grown accustomed to doing nothing is to be regretted. That person loses the best life offers, the ability to emote and find pleasure. How tasty is the rest after the strains of the day; how well we feel in the warmth the stove offers after a cold, snowy, wintry day outside. But when we have lost every measure of comparison, rest becomes boring, and warmth just makes us sleepy; food passes through the mouth without our thinking of God. Nature itself gives man the need, implants the impulse to be active, to work. I'm working too. Yet I work in comfort and on what I like. I write. I hope I am creating something good and worthwhile. If it's good and worthwhile, the time is not wasted. But if the people know that I am working, do they recognize this work as such? I don't know, and I don't know if I have the right to write while others are earning my bread. I want to—I wish to be rich and pay back everything with interest. Often we think how cozy and comfortable we are here in Nesslau—too nice maybe—and that one day this too will come to an end. I'm not talking about the end of the war. One day, when we think we are totally secure in the quiet of this little house, a whirlwind will eject us from here.

I'm certain that I am hardly capable to perform manual labor. In the spring of 1942, I took on a garden to plant potatoes for the winter.

Four weeks later I was hospitalized. What with the poor nourishment and stress of those days, it might have been inevitable, but I'm certain the unaccustomed work hastened the crisis. In the labor camp, I barely toiled four weeks at the construction site when the crisis that has afflicted me periodically, struck. And now with God's help, I have not been ill for three years. Except for some symptoms in December, I have been spared. Relaxation is good for me, and perhaps I'll succeed in remaining totally healthy for a long time. I'll need my complete health for the peace—this eagerly awaited time that will be filled with work. May we be guided by God's will. The people around us may think that we need recuperation, and may they grant us that in these months—that should be the last months of the war. For them, how peculiarly strange and terrible our fate appears. They sometimes do some really nice things for us, as one does to ward off an impending disaster, to beseech fate.

I once stopped off at one of the peasants to buy potatoes. Our stock was depleted. As I was ready to pay, the woman refused any payment. Her husband gave her strict orders to do so. Awkwardly, in Swiss dialect that I hardly understood, she explained she could not take any money since they had been blessed to remain in their own place.

Sometimes I think that our position seems even more difficult to them than it does to us. We have become accustomed to our fate. It makes no sense to moan, as we can't change anything about it. Our bases for comparison are not the same. People ask us if we still have a residence someplace. If after the war we expect to find our possessions again. We don't know. And if after the war we will be able to call it our own. The people don't understand how we can talk peacefully and with composure about these things. For us, the greatest value is that we are, after all, at least the immediate family, still together and alive. What are apartments, houses, furniture, and stuff when we have stood in danger of paying with our lives? Yet for the people here, freedom, peace, family, and home are such familiar and trusted concepts, such natural things, that they find it hard to find the right measuring standards. Perhaps it is our assignment here, through our presence, to warn these people of the questionable worth and impermanence of earthly goods.

* * *

The relationship between the refugees and the Swiss, from purely a personal observation, is such a delicate and sensitive problem, often distorted and poisoned by politics. As if it weren't already so totally difficult and entangled, the contrast between the Swiss and the Jewish refugees, particularly the Eastern Jews, is huge and far-reaching.

Few people are so bound together through their soil. Often nature, in constricting splendor, pushes to the city. She dominates the landscape, and nobody can escape its influence. Everywhere, the Swiss breathes the free air of the mountains, sees mighty peaks, or lives on the broad shores of lakes. To brave the mountain world, to not be tossed by its storms, the harsh and rough Swiss environment has penetrated the Swiss character and even found expression in its speech.

Such a land, whose climate and living conditions promotes strong people and full individualism, by its nature has predisposed the creation of a flourishing democracy. It's no coincidence, for example, even in the neighboring Tirol, that the peasant has never fallen into serfdom, that only free men have always inhabited Scandinavia. The environment, as the original factor for the human development and character development, promotes here the unity of the whole person, a person that is free.

Place next to this person, deeply rooted in this land, permeated with rights to freedom, for whom the will to fight for freedom and independence is self-evident, the lissome refugee, the Jew, pushed around in all countries of Europe. The Jew could never in over two thousand years fight for life on par with the Swiss. Rigid perseverance would have eradicated such a one long ago. The Jew is thankful for the ability to get out of harm's way and to flee for survival.

And even when modern developments of city life have not been without influence on the structure and further education of the Swiss, so the original trends weakened but were never abandoned. The Swiss is an inner and outer closed person. There is no contrast between an inner urge for freedom and an outer way of life. How different from the Jew, particularly from the Eastern Jew. In the course of several hundred years of seclusion and suppression, the Jew needed to succeed in differentiating between inner strife and permitted living structure. A certain scorn for the environment compensates for monotony, sometimes becoming bitterly aware of its shortage.

Two types, in which such a totally different development has led to such totally different character traits, can only understand each other and come nearer to each other with great difficulty. These differences show their effects particularly in the camps. Many such seemingly sad camp incidences are traceable back to these original contrasts, coming to a common understanding and resolution is not easy.

That aside, and speaking in generalities, the Swiss overtly tends to judge the refugee from a one-sided view, a view that so strongly influences that it sometimes makes it impossible to come to terms with the total personality of the refugee. The Swiss looks at the refugee mostly through the eyes of pity, personally having little contact with them, knowing them mostly through descriptions in the newspapers. The clergy persuasively and forcefully, again and again, keep the plight of the refugees before their eyes and appeal to their humanity, their pity, their compassion, their conscience, and their duty to help. The refugee is to the Swiss sometimes exclusively a person who has suffered a great deal.

An anecdote that refugees told me in the spring of 1943 characterizes the relationship between the Swiss and the refugee: A Swiss and a refugee approach each other. The Swiss greets, "*Gruetzi, gruetzi.* You're a refugee?" "Yes," responds the refugee. "You must have suffered a lot," says the Swiss. And again the refugee responds, "Yes." In a single syllable, the conversation ends, and each continues on their way—because they have nothing in common. In this anecdote at least the circumstances are interesting, in that many refugees actually imagine that the relationship between the refugees and the Swiss takes this form. They think that the Swiss see them only as objects of pity and not as fully valued people. I know it's not so, but in the limitations and shackles of camp life, many comrades think in this way. I will put it this way: the refugee, with the sadness of those experiences, appears to the Swiss to be in a cocoon; the terrible state seems so un-embraceable, that the Swiss is often embarrassed to raise more banal themes of life, just as in a house of mourning you silently extend your hand to the mourner and go on. But you can consider it as you will. The reality is that this suffering extends the rampart of isolation between the refugee and the Swiss.

But one can't live forever in a house of mourning. Neither can the refugee live forever in the world of thought of its fate. Since the beginning of the influx of refugees into Switzerland, the concept of the refugee problem has evolved considerably. Only when we argue about a problem do we become aware of its complexities. Surely, at the beginning of the organization, which really could only develop over a longer period of time, the refugee gained the impression that the Swiss took a very one-sided position toward us. And these first impressions, as so many other experiences from that initial time of our stay in Switzerland, are still influential and hinder a better mutual understanding.

The mutual misunderstandings and mistakes are of such infinite shame. They hinder so many refugees to dignify OSAR in all its greatness. I have already spoken of how OSAR appears to me as a spiritual current, a spiritual movement that in response will and can sustain beyond the person of the refugee. And that is the beauty in a democracy—even when everything earthly has its shortcomings—the struggle about questions of daily living through the participation of people and groups, advocating their ideas, can disassociate from the disputes of honest objections and lead to even more meaningful pure mental arguments that are so fruitful for the spiritual life of a community because they hinder paralysis and give life to new ideas.

Between the starting point of the movement and discussion of the refugee question stand tradition, compassion, and knowledge of religious duty. A good deed is done for the refugee because a religious commandment and humanitarian duty is fulfilled. The refugee is an impersonal object on whom kindheartedness may be practiced. Human relationships don't exist yet. Certainly, human relationships can develop even between strangers. And isn't it an enormous expectation for people to act according to the commandments of the Bible. If all people fulfilled God's commandments, there would not be any refugees.

You can't blame the refugees when their treatment as plain objects of compassion leaves them unsatisfied. For we would like so very much not to be refugees, but people like all others. It's a matter of coming closer together, because when you do so and know each other better, then the heart and the person speak, not just compassion and conscience. Particularly, we in Nesslau have the opportunity to see that it's possible and natural. But unfortunately—unfortunately—such opportunities are much too rare.

And so it happens, that also the refugee doesn't properly emphasize a connection with the outer world. In the small world of the internees, one finds the best rapport with those in the same situation for needed support and understanding. The same strict fate that contributes to the separation between the refugee and the Swiss, forms the bridge on which refugees can approach each other.

Fate, mentality, and statutory barriers separate the refugees and the Swiss, who in their great numbers remain in a limited relationship, particularly between the refugees and the Swiss authorities. And on these relationships rests a heavy burden of guilt that can be traced back to the experiences in the reception camps.

In light of the aforementioned, can we comprehend the enormous significance of the relief organizations? They are the authoritative mediators between refugees and officialdom. They are its representatives and lawyers. Above that, for the refugee they are the true representatives of the Swiss people who have the distinguished task incumbent upon them to establish contact between the refugees and the Swiss.

We have seen how difficult this task is. And sometimes I think the time has not yet arrived for a real understanding between the two. Perhaps a time will come after the war, when the Swiss and refugees will see each other in a new light and speak with each other. Then the Swiss will see them as a free people. And then will come a moment when they will both understand each other better. For in reality, only a free person can be an equal friend to a free person.

* * *

In the middle of December, I went for my medical examination in Zurich. The insurance doctor of the central directorate examined me. I described my condition honestly, saying that I still had some issues, but nothing to really complain about.

And then I waited for the results. I couldn't tell anything from the doctor's demeanor or his facial expressions. Finally, I received the report from OSAR. The doctor determined that my ulcer was healing, and I was entitled to a transfer to a home with dietary supervision. OSAR added that the regulations regarding discharge from the camps had tightened and not to count on a release under these circumstances. Perhaps a request for a vacation extension could be successful, less on account of my health, but more in regards to my wife and Michel, for whom I have been a worthwhile help with errands and shopping.

What have the refugees done now to be treated more strictly? Were the internees in free places guilty of transgressions in connection with their freedom of movement? The privately interned individual cannot leave the confines of his community. For leave beyond these limits, one needs special permission. Not that you wouldn't be given permission, but you feel awful having to check in at the police station for every little outing and give a reason that may be of a personal nature or just a matter of wishing to breathe the air of a different community and from time to time visit a larger city. The refugees are for the most part city people and don't fare well with certain displacements. Certainly it came to those kinds of failures. It's human nature.

It may also simply be the case that, as a matter of principle, they didn't want to place non-working refugees into the areas of working people, to avoid criticism from the inhabitants of the countryside. I have spoken myself of this danger. The reasons must have been persuasive to give rise to such an intense reconsideration, which even outweigh the internment costs of a camp or home. We didn't count any more with our continued release, at best an extension of our vacation.

Imagine then the happy surprise, as in the middle of January I received a letter from the police department authorizing my total release from the labor camp. We counted so little on it that I had already made plans for my return trip. And now for the time being, I was free, and we could live together. My file was to be returned to the central directorate. My number was eradicated, and I again became human. Certainly still many limitations governed; but what grace to live for oneself alone and for your dependents. Few Jews today have been granted the privilege, and few refugees enjoy this advantage.

* * *

On the return trip from Zurich last December, I picked up our Paul from St. Gallen. The Children's Relief Organization on account of our living in the canton of St. Gallen, transferred him to the to the children's home Speicher, near the city of St. Gallen. We very much regretted that it was not possible to have him stay in Geneva for a longer time and in particular to continue school there, but there were many refugee children in Geneva awaiting placement so that his continued stay in Les Murailles became impossible.

So here again was the rascal with his red cheeks and face like milk from which his blue eyes looked into the foreign world with great curiosity. Here, he again looked forward with great joy to his papa, mama, and little brother. The mouthpiece went on as if propelled on wheels, for he had to recount his trip to St. Gallen and then to Speicher. In his rucksack he brought toys for his brother. And he traveled alone from Speicher to St. Gallen and made conversation with the conductor, who wanted to talk to him in Schwytzerdütsch and so on and so on.

I told him that the Schneckenbühl was on a mountain. All the while he was searching for our little house. We loaded his things on a little hand wagon, and he helped push it vigorously. "No, that's not the Schneckenbühl yet." But now we were only about a hundred steps from the little house, and the boy was burning with curiosity. "Now you can run up there." Right away he stormed away and held to Mama's neck, who embraced him joyfully. Then quickly he went to the neighbors, where little Michou happened to be. And although Michou did not know his brother, he jubilantly approached him, and with their arms tightly around each other, they two rolled on the ground. Now the family was united. We were together again in a home for the first time in thirteen months.

* * *

Yes, we are all together and happy about it. For refugees, nothing is a given, and everything is granted by God's grace. When we sit at the table and I see the children eating our good but simple fare with hearty appetites, when Michel heartily bites into an apple, when Paul savors his cheese, then my heart opens. When the children play with each other on the floor, sometimes affectionately and friendly, sometimes even in anger and annoying each other, then we are joyous and happy. And sometimes we get angry from this rabble-rousing that never gives us rest, but it quickly dissipates when Michou trustingly cuddles up to us and bends his head to be stroked. He has self-awareness and can be difficult and contrary, our little Prince from the Orient, as we call him because of his dark complexion and radiant black eyes. When Paul and Michel stretch out and cheerfully blabber away in the small bathtub next to the warm oven, then my wife beams from her whole face. It is so wonderful to observe children in their development when they are healthy and thrive. That is the highest and purest fortune for parents. How few people, how few refugees and Jews can do that today. To observe these affectionate, sweet, innocent little bodies and to be close to them—how few are granted that today.

* * *

Christmas has come and everything that this festival expresses, love and humanity, goodness, passion, and caring—how richly we share in it. Never have we received so many presents; never have so many people thought of us. Packages come by post; gifts at the vicarage are brought to the house with best wishes. One morning a little package hung on the door from an anonymous donor. It isn't just the gifts as such that gives us such pleasure, but the warm, kind, and sympathetic way in which they are given. We need so much, for sparse is the wardrobe of a refugee. And there have been so many baked goods and things to nosh. We suffer from a guilty conscience. It is all well and good; we like it, and they taste so good. But we think about the many refugees in the camps who do not have ties to the Swiss, who are not guests as we are, who are not so generously and richly showered with gifts. Why are we so differentiated from the others? Fate is not always just.

With embarrassment we regard the many gifts for which we can only be thankful with words and our hearts.

Good people are here. They are happy to do good for others; they feel they have been spared and feel the grace of their destiny. And how different can it be in a community so carefully guided by its shepherds? We don't always communicate well, for Schwytzerdütsch will always be difficult for me to understand, but you don't need to say much to understand each other. On the contrary, sometimes too many words serve only to whitewash mutual misunderstanding.

Since New Year's, Paul attends the school down in the village. Just short of eight years of age, he plods valiantly and undeterred to the school, an hour each way every day. He has missed school on only one day, when the snow blocked every trail. He is tough and well developed for his age. He likes the country. He would like to stay here forever. Children quickly get used to new environments. They know nothing of destiny, citizenship, borders, and passports. He loves the cows and calves; he is crazy about sledding. He looks forward to the spring and working in his own garden.

Now there is almost too much snow for sledding. In the fall, we were told that the snow sometimes reaches up to the windows. At that time, we laughed in disbelief. At first the winter was relatively mild. Then, one day in February, it started to snow, and it snowed, and it snowed without interruption for two whole weeks. What use is it to keep shoveling a walk? The next morning, hardly a trace of your work remains. And yet you have to do it, do it again, and again, to get out of the little house, to go to the village. And all the peasants shovel untiringly. The path at our neighbor's is like a promenade, so wide, clean, and regular. And I have to shovel out the path to our house; I would be ashamed to have someone do it for me. It has to be nice so that our little one has some room to run around and my wife and Paul not make fun of the little narrow path. This work tires me out at times, but I'm happy to be able to do this minimum alone. And so it is in life that we need to shovel our pathways, to start every day anew; undaunted and untiringly one must map out one's directions even when evil has submerged the path. And then one day you will be rewarded for your staying power: the sun shines, and the effort is not for naught.

No, the snow doesn't scare us, for we came here to enjoy peace and quiet; we seek no constant socializing. It doesn't bother us when days go by without us leaving our little snail house. Three times a week, I go to the vicarage, where I may help out a little. These outings, shopping, and visits with our neighbor, who has so taken Michou into her heart, limit our interactions. Now and then people come to us, but we rarely return these visits, because these people are very busy and we do not want to be a bother. We like staying at home with the children. We are never bored. My wife is always busy, and I am always totally occupied with my work.

On Sundays we usually go for a long walk, depending on snow conditions. It's so nice to climb up the mountainside, just up to the skiers' huts. Nature here is so pristine and almost magical. The firs wear a white winter coat of laden snow. When a wind gust wakens them abruptly, they shake unwillingly, and their white burden descends to the ground. The sun shines. The ice crystals glisten and sparkle, the light gleams and dazzles, until we must avert our eyes, as we were not created to live in so much light.

In the evening we sit around our trusted petroleum table lamp and chat. We talk about the past, the future, about our loved ones so far away. Our thoughts always return to them. We wish and hope to find them all again. We get letters, but not from everyone. The grandparents, my parents, yearn to see their grandchildren. They are already old. The time is getting long to see the children. They only know Michou from pictures. They dream about their grandchildren, as grandparents are wont to do in their old days, whose life approaches its end and see only in their children and grandchildren the fulfillment of their existence. They would also like to do something for us and send us something. They fear we may be lacking in something, despite all the letters to the contrary. But there is a war, a war that doesn't want to end. It is forbidden to send remittances even to refugees. That's what the strict law demands. And the parents of my wife! Will we see them again, these good and kind old people, who stayed in Vienna because never in their life did they travel without passports or visas until the authorities declared them "with unknown regulation" and deported[26] them? No luck is absolute, and always we must pay tribute to our hard fate.

---

26 Martha's parents, Marie and Ludwig Kraus, were deported from Vienna to Theresienstadt in July 1942 and then to Maly Trostinec, just outside Minsk, in September. From "Totenbuch Theresienstadt."

Where will we go after the end of the war? What will the world be like that will be shaped for us? Will we go to Austria, the old homeland, or to France, the new? Or perhaps even to Palestine, to finally get into a country where we can feel at home, in which a Jew may do everything, pursue any vocation, without noticing or thinking that in reality one is still a Jew and not a hereditary Austrian, German, or French? We yearn for peace, a homeland, to be at home, engage in a profession. Riches don't entice us, as they can't buy happiness. But we also want to finally see quiet, peaceful times, we, the generation that between two wars has seen unemployment and poverty and suffered the entire tragedy of our epoch. We yearn for times in which things will be a little better for us, in which a vocation secures the support of the family, in which the housemother doesn't have to turn over every penny ten times before she dares to spend it. Will the new world bring us these times? Or will it demand in exchange the disavowal of personal freedom and independence?

But our thoughts don't always soar to such heights. The mind is not always engaged in such splendid discussions. Often, too often perhaps, we are caught by totally earthy and small wishes. Then I have to solemnly promise that once, before we leave Switzerland, we will all gather in one of the finest patisseries and eat, eat as long as we want without regard to money. During this war we have developed nosh envy. Oh, before, none of this mattered. But now, five years of war have covered the land. We are emaciated like the entirety of humanity and are plagued by all kinds of desires.

I remember the last war in Vienna, the whole misery of the inflationary period, which for the poor prolonged the war's poverty for many years. I was fifteen years old when I brought home a particularly good report card, and a rich uncle invited me out for ice cream as a reward. With concern I asked, "It's true, I can eat as much as I want?" "Of course it's true" was the encouraging answer. I devoured eight hazelnut ice creams under the astonished eyes of the waiter. At home I had to still my hunger with cabbage soup and dried vegetables.

Now it's not like that. We eat well, and often we think that later we should fare no worse than here in the Schneckenbühl. And still, we dream of cake and chocolate. We also dream of having a homey, beautifully furnished house or apartment of our own, of terraces with music and merriment, of theater and cinema and more. And so dream millions of people in this war and wait and wait.

* * *

The new world: the postwar period. At the end of January, I was invited by our dear social worker in St. Gallen, who is always thinking of us, to participate in a discussion with a few people dedicated to social aid and planning in the postwar period. It was a conference of the League of Swiss Women for Work Relief, which already is actively concerned and working for the postwar period. This meeting was a revelation to me. While the cannons are still firing, innocent victims are claimed, and every day poverty and misery climb higher and higher, and here are people thinking and working for the needy. I say innocent victims, for it concerns foremost the care and upbringing of children, who through this war have particularly suffered so much. We read quite a bit in the newspapers about UNNRA, AMGOT, and God knows what else, but here acronyms are becoming living realities. The woman that spoke to us is really preparing for the future. The people that were assembled here, hardly more than a dozen, they are to be educated in the implementation of social welfare. It's wonderful to work on the future; it is certainly the best assignment that the postwar period can give us. Unfortunately, I can't travel to St. Gallen every week, but I wish these people, who through goodness and cooperation seek the way to a new time, that their dreams can soon become reality. I regret not attending this course, though I doubt my capabilities to lead a children's home. But aren't there other jobs in such an organization? I'm still searching my way and waiting. But this evening has remained actively in my mind—a veritable promise for the future.

* * *

And so I have arrived at the end. Our lives will continue, yet our future is uncertain. But at this point, I am happy to be able to finish. People love happy endings. They seek and wish it. Yet when a story has a happy end, they are tempted to think of it as kitsch, because life doesn't guarantee a good ending. But, mercifully, it sometimes grants a fortunate end. I am more than happy that I could see that my illness, this harsh test, opened the possibility for us to be together and for me to be free. I could discover for myself that nothing in life has to be bad. And then I am happy that I could end this story of a refugee with such a positive outcome. I am happy because I am thankful to be allowed in Switzerland and to have rescued myself with my family.

And yet we experienced such harsh times; even here in Switzerland, we experienced such misery. But slowly, slowly things improved for us. This rise that we experienced is also the rise in the evolution of the welfare for refugees. Surely, I know that thousands of people still live in camps, and thousands of divided families still suffer. But we are moving forward. Goodwill is at work. Whoever was granted the experience of devoted people working on their behalf and to secure their welfare, they will also feel less keenly the tough times in Switzerland. They will only feel the start of a development, moving steadily forward toward a better future, to a time that, God willing, will no longer know refugees. And if people should knock on our door, seeking entry and rescue, so they, as we were, shall no longer be refugees, but humans—our brothers and sisters.

25

BACK TO ONESELF

I have concluded my report in which I captured our way through Switzerland. And despite the many portrayals, I have the sense that I have not made all the key points, as if the essence of the book is missing. The essence cannot be found in the events, which flow through time, sometimes with great fury and sometimes with even temperament. The essence is expressed by what of ourselves I put into the events, how they are imbued and the impressions they make, as far as we are willing to accept them with our full soul.

As I sat down at my desk, it became so infinitely difficult to write this report. I spoke about that at the outset. But now I see that it is even more difficult than I had anticipated. Imagine you are sitting in a confessional and confessing all of your sins. And here you speak to only one man, who absorbs everything you say and seals your fate like the grave the body. But what I have recorded here should be read and known not by one but by many, many people. You recede into your most inner self and always find new layers surrounding the core. Each page is like a hard forced confession. You sit before an examining magistrate and tell all. You lay bare your most inner self, your thoughts, and give the world praise, and with every word you think, "Now I stand completely revealed; everyone sees my ugliness and my nakedness." It's easy to say, no one is without blemish. Surely, but when others don't know that? I have at least tried to make myself no better than I am. When I overstepped restrictions—think about that from our morality, out of the morality of the disinherited—I could not even recognize certain restrictions unless at the same time I denied my own right to live. I say this in connection with my sins in the reception camps, those that I have confessed and those that through my reluctance I have left buried and not included in my writing.

These words are both a complaint and intercession on my behalf.

But it's not just that alone. Again and again, my conscience bothers me. I am a guest here in Switzerland, a thankful guest. How could I not be thankful in this peaceful sanctuary, the Schneckenbühl? Do you think I don't know how the others are doing, not just the unfortunate souls in the storm-battered areas of our tortured part of the earth, but also the refugees here in Switzerland that despite rescue still suffer? They must suffer because they are not free and aren't recognized as belonging together. I think of the possibility that unconsciously, somehow, somewhere, I offended our hosts, who wish to treat us well, so I want to express my gratitude. This conflict may not be resolvable, and in the eyes of truly good people, I may well be forgiven.

The goal that is at stake here is worth the struggle. And it is not just what my experiences have taught me, that individual freedom is paramount, not just that it has been proven to me anew—as if I needed this knowledge—that our social structure is in disarray and in need of revolutionary restructuring.

We would be wretched creatures if we didn't recognize the lasting consequences of our experiences and clearly articulate our feelings. And of the observation: I have written sometimes against my will because I wanted to be as honest as possible from the start and to remain apolitical to the end. I had to write, nevertheless, if I wanted to do justice to the developments, which for us started on November 17, 1942, when with petrified hearts we locked the door to our residence and set out onto the street.

What can a refugee think when someone tells you—during your flight, at the border, in the reception camp, at an interrogation, or in a conversation—that you are banished from society, a second-order person. Wouldn't you yearn for the coming of a world in which second-order persons won't exist, in which everyone travels in one class only, even if it's not first class, but even just third class for all. Refugees must remain socialists, not because they own nothing, but because they have been affected more deeply than just in their pocketbook.

We would earn our lot, should we decide to return to our diverse countries after the war, to resume our lives at the point where we once left them. Then we had no interest in life, as we were just mere objects. After the last world war, Karl Kraus maintained that a bullet entered humankind in one ear and exited from the other. And yet it seems to me that this time it will be impossible that our experiences will be extinguished and we will become humans as before.

Sometimes I stand at the window and stare into the dark night. The earth is sleeping, wrapped deeply in a white snow cover and awaiting the life-giving sunshine, which will remove this blanket and grant freedom for a new life. So we sleep and wait. But exactly as the earth does not remain dormant but collects fresh strength and suddenly through its built-up energy transforms its fertility into the ever new wonder of spring, so we collect new strength for some perhaps not all too distant day. At the window, the lights of Nesslau twinkle back—and so waves the promise of an auspicious day of liberation.

Recently we were in the midst of a snowstorm. Thick flakes fell the entire day. The sky was covered in gray as if several snow loads were suspended there. We climbed high through the snow; the trail had been blown over; our heavy boots sank in deeply, and the wind whipped white crystals into our faces. Suddenly our little house stood in front of us. Its warmth surrounded us with secure protection. In the evening, I stepped out. The wind subsided after scattering the snow clouds. The star-spangled heavens vaulted over us, and the moon shone bright over the unblemished, fresh snow. The forces of nature parted and left space for a deep peace. So, too, the war will one day part, and peace will enter into our hearts.

* * *

You see, I ended at this point just short of two weeks ago, and today is Easter Sunday. And spring is coming. It comes with the blowing of the Föhn that nightly sinks the snow into the earth. It comes with the sun making its appearance hot and firm over the countryside. In our neighbor's garden, the first snowbells emerge; with us it's the chives that are the first to answer. It's the first time we have experienced the metamorphosis into spring in this way. Every day we are amazed at the impetuous urging with which nature wants to catch up when the harsh winter has forced its surrender. And what will be, when peace comes and all inhibitions are swept away, when all the dams have burst, and when one's long-asphyxiated life is broken free with powerful force? What will happen then, and how will peace affect us?

We don't know and can't predict it, because we don't determine our destiny. Other powers control us, and they determine the future of the peoples of Europe.

Can you still remember? Do you still think about the many long years when the big frenzy over Germany developed? When empty, power-drunk rogues spit on, tortured, and martyred the nearest one, what was the reverberation of the world? Did anyone think or feel that whoever wounds and insults God's creation also disregards the creator? One didn't want to see the injustice or give it credence. The Jews were so annoying, so uncomfortable...the Jews with their atrocity fairytales... the Socialists, the Communists. The world wanted quiet. The quiet of the satiated should not be disturbed. One took comfort from the daily scorn, the daily degradations of these people, as these were not insults at all because the insulted were of such low standing. So we deceived ourselves and remained silent, until the lies and the silence turned against the world, until the search for peace joined with the fear of the criminals and sought to buy their goodwill through shameful accommodation and selling out. Thus humankind degraded itself and extinguished its own dignity. Currency devaluation threatens. Long newspaper columns are filled with complaints and wailing. Yet, in cold blood, we let the moral devaluation of humanity go on, for we know only money and live in fear of passing ownership, until one day everything falls apart and the fires of war grip the world.

And today what has become of humanity?

Is it then any wonder, when instead of upright self-conscious people, shy indolent people come forth, incapable of any internal reaction, like a robot waiting for external redemption. They think what a government commands them to think. They hear and read what is being spoken and printed for them. They eat from the menu that has been prepared for them. Deep in the heart, still some wishes lie buried, more unconscious than conscious, for they are no longer their own person, they have lost the power of self-determination and are owned by an arrogant state. So it is today in many countries, in some more than in others. Yet in which country today is the individual free, in which country do you find what was once called "the fundamental rights of man"? Humankind has sacrificed its freedom for less than a dish of lentils. Sunk into materialism, people in their criminal striving for power have sacrificed dear spiritual goods. The striving for power has deceived, the dream of world domination is finished, and only an unending misery, boundless wailing, admonishes us not to forget that humanity is just a pathetic creation.

We were so proud of our progress and of our culture. Who would dare be proud today? The progress today is the hundred thousand—the millions—housed in barracks, shelters, and holes in the ground, in places where straw sack adjoins straw sack in two or three layers on top each other. They were happy if they received straw sacks and not bare straw. Happy when the promiscuity in the sleep places references only men and does not include women and children. Happy to be in peaceful barracks and not awaiting death in some fear-filled cellar or in wretched hiding, in which worrisome people continue to schlep through a shameful existence. Who wouldn't yearn to return to cave dwellings, to huddle in furs, peacefully housed with their clan, spared from field kitchens, mess buckets, roll call, and signal whistles? How sad and indicative of our shame that today we must hide the light, the message of life, because tomorrow, were it visible, it may become a death threat message. The person who in the last few years could peacefully spend time within four walls, who wasn't in any camp, didn't participate in the war, and wasn't subservient to anyone—can this person ever grasp the grace that has been granted him? You had to experience it, to know, to measure what it means to switch off one's person, to swallow one's thoughts and to remain silent, to remain silent when you wanted to speak—no, wanted to scream—to be stepped on without resistance, without batting an eyelash. This desire to run headfirst into a wall, feeling powerless to counter the orders, the regulations, and evil will: leads inexorably to defeat after inner revolt and finally boundless apathy and tiredness. The degradation of people to objects in the hands of servants and the loss of the most primitive dignity of humanity cannot be obliterated or forgotten.

Living by the whistle, constantly listening to the next order—so live millions of people, beings who were once free. On orders, they rub the sleep out of their overtired eyes and step up: to work, to eat, see the doctor who determines the fitness of the human animals for slaughter. They step up in single file, in double rows, in three or four columns, to march and to fight. On orders, they speak; on orders, they are silent, they throw themselves on the ground and crawl over the earth through wire entanglements. On orders, they kill fellow humans because they wear a different uniform, speak a different language, have a different nose or skin color. On orders, they are free: to laugh, to make love, and to create new life. It is always necessary to continue giving life, to always have new beings ready to listen to orders.

* * *

For the past years, every day and every night, I see in front of me my comrades and fellows in destiny. Will they still have the strength and courage to fight for a better world? For we want peace. We are tired; we have wandered through the dark street of life and are searching for the rays that will destroy the dark and bring light. What has the world done with us? We want to settle up with the guilty; we want equality, a new social order guaranteeing peace, and bread for all.

Where are our brothers and sisters? What will they do tomorrow, and where will they be? Alas, you don't learn, year after year, without punishment that annihilation is an end in itself. The daring soldier, whose rows of medals proudly attest to his bravery, can tomorrow change into a disturbing, useless ruffian, and the courageous, coolly intrepid freedom fighter may turn into an antisocial anarchist. So, the sequence of sacrifices is not terminated. After the war dead, we will bury the peace dead. And who will make thinking humans of the robots? It's easy to put on blinders; only slowly does the eye accustom itself to all the light.

Will we have the strength to fight? Will we raise the strength to become people with conscience, whose passions will not be misused by misguided egos?

Will we build a new world, or have the forces of war so sucked the marrow from our bones that we, like zombies, will drag around life's burden until death calls?

I will not and cannot believe it. I will not and cannot hope for it.

Did we only have the strength to fight in the war, but not to earn true peace?

For now it will come, the fight worthy of our participation, the fight for freedom and equality: only now, when our bonds are loosened and deadly discipline frees us from our shackles. Let's not lose the opportunity. For woe to our children—and us—if we do.

Together we will create a better world. It is our duty.

And you, reader—who I may call "friend"—if you know our lot, will you help us?

Camillo Adler

Schoenengrund. Unknown date.

Camillo Adler

Schönengrund. February 23, 1943.

Woman's Home, Brissago, Tecino. Martha Adler in rear row, left.

Woman of Brissago. Martha Adler in center.

Woman of Brissago visiting Mezzovico. Martha Adler hidden behind Camillo Adler (with glasses).

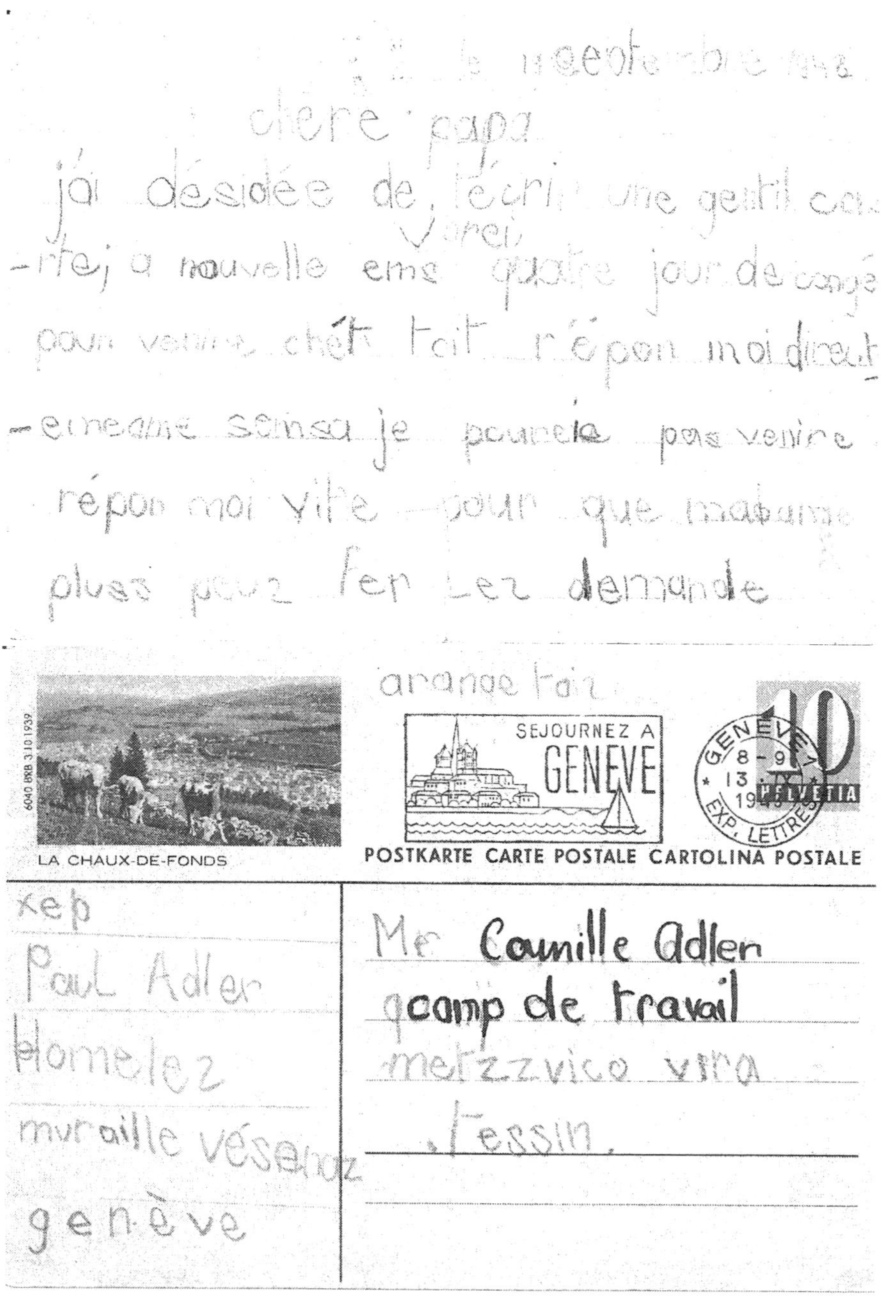

le 11 septembre 194

clere papa

j'ai désidée de t'écri une gentil ca
-rtej a nouvelle ems quatre jour de canyé
pour venir chét toit répon moi direct
-ement sinsa je pourcia pas venir
répon moi vite pour que mabume
plues peuz fer lez demande

arange toi

SEJOURNEZ A GENEVE

LA CHAUX-DE-FONDS

POSTKARTE CARTE POSTALE CARTOLINA POSTALE

xep

Paul Adler

Homelez

muraille vésenaz

genève

Mr Camille Adler
qcamp de travail
metzzvico vira
Tessin

One of many postcards from Paul from the children's home.
Home les Murailles, Geneva.

The house on the mountain, the Schneckenbühl.
Left: late winter, 1944. Right: June 1944.

Erklärung

des unterzeichneten Flüchtlings: A d l e r   Martha, geb. 25. Oktober 1901,

staatenlos.

Ich bestätige, dass mir der Aufenthalt in der Gemeinde: N e s s l a u

bei: Fam. Scherrer, Richelschwand, Nesslau

unter den folgenden Bedingungen gestattet worden ist:

Ich verpflichte mich:

1. Mich periodisch bei m Polizeiposten Nesslau zu melden und

zwar jeweils einmal wöchentlich

2. Das Gebiet der Gemeinde Ness-lau nicht zu verlassen.

3. Meine Unterkunft nicht ohne behördliche Bewilligung zu wechseln.

4. Mich in der Zeit zwischen 2200 und 0700 in meiner Unterkunft aufzuhalten.

5. Keine Bars, Dancings und Spielsäle zu besuchen und folgende Lokale nicht zu betreten:

6. Jede politische Tätigkeit und jedes Verhalten, das geeignet ist, die Neutralitätspolitik des Bundesrates zu stören, zu unterlassen.

7. Keine politischen Versammlungen zu besuchen.

8. In keiner Weise öffentlich aufzutreten z. B. durch Vorträge, Publikationen in der Presse, Herausgabe von Druckwerken usw.

9. Nicht in Gruppen von mehr als 5 Personen auszugehen.

10. In keiner Weise erwerbstätig zu sein und auch nicht ohne Entgelt für Dritte zu arbeiten. Es ist mir nur die Mithilfe im Haushalt oder Landwirtschaftsbetrieb meines Gastgebers gestattet.

11. Die kriegswirtschaftlichen Bestimmungen, namentlich die Vorschriften über die Rationierung (Verbot des Schwarzhandels) genau zu respektieren.

12. Den vom Armeekommando erlassenen Weisungen über das Verhalten der Zivilbevölkerung bei Kriegs-mobilmachung und Ueberfall genau nachzukommen.

13. Jederzeit den Behörden über meine finanzielle Lage vollständige und wahrheitsgetreue Angaben zu machen und ihnen von Aenderungen sofort unaufgefordert Kenntnis zu geben. Ich bestätige, dass ich den Behörden über meine jetzigen finanziellen Verhältnisse erschöpfend Auskunft gegeben habe. Ich ermächtige alle natürlichen und juristischen Personen, namentlich Banken, Treuhandstellen, Rechtsanwälte usw., die mit mir in finanziellen Beziehungen standen oder stehen, den Behörden über meine Vermö-gensverhältnisse Aufschluss zu geben.

14. Alles zu tun, um die Schweiz sobald als möglich verlassen zu können und habe zur Kenntnis genommen, dass mir eine Festsetzung in der Schweiz unter keinen Umständen gestattet wird.

15. Mich jederzeit und überall eines diskreten und korrekten Verhaltens zu befleissen, das der Stellung eines Flüchtlings, der das Gastrecht der Schweiz geniesst, Rechnung trägt.

16.

Ich erkläre, mich genau an die vorstehenden Bedingungen halten zu wollen, und nehme zur Kenntnis, dass Abweichungen nur nach vorheriger schriftlicher Zustimmung der kantonalen Fremdenpolizei gestattet sind. Sonderbewilligungen werden von der Fremdenpolizei nur in wirklich begründeten Ausnahmefällen erteilt.

Widerhandlungen gegen diese Vorschriften werden bestraft und ziehen sofortige Versetzung in ein Inter-niertenlager oder -Heim, in schweren Fällen Ausschaffung nach sich. Die Bestimmungen des allgemeinen Strafrechts bleiben vorbehalten.

Ein Doppel dieser Erklärung wurde mir ausgehändigt.

Unterschrift: *Martha Adler*

Nesslau , den 6. Oktober 1943.

Geht an: Die Eidg. Polizeiabteilung
die Kantonale Fremdenpolizei
die Gemeindebehörde
den Internierten

II. 42 - 6000 - 92 - 71635

Agreement to the conditions of residency in the community of Nesslau.

PART III

OBSERVATIONS AND REFLECTIONS

Original Manuscript dated April 1944

26

REFUGEES AS SOCIAL AND ECONOMIC MANIFESTATION

Internments, the limitations on the freedom of movement, have always existed. The original use of internment was applied to citizens whose government, for one reason or another, found them undesirable, dangerous citizens who threatened authority and were capable to depose it, and to keep them distant from the other citizens and to prevent their contamination with dangerous ideas. Governments have always exercised this practice against those who did not agree with and support them.

How many thousands of people did czarist Russia send to Siberia to endure forced exile? They were subject to several, limiting police regulations and classified according to special legal status. From the earliest times, opponents of the regimes of Russia, Italy, and Germany were placed in internment and forced labor camps as enemies of the state. In accordance with the principles of sovereignty, interference by foreign powers into the internal affairs of a recognized government is not permitted. If we were to succeed in establishing a supranational, international organization, whose decisions were respected and carried out, with mandatory membership of all nations, then an interference that benefits political victims of persecutions would be entirely conceivable. But, in such an ideal political order, would there exist those in need of protection? For the time being, we are still far away from that goal.

People whose lives were threatened, who were viewed as undesirable citizens in their homeland, have always attempted to leave the affected country and find another, in which, foremost, their life would be safe and in which they hoped to establish another life in accordance with their principles. The diversity of governments, the expanse of a world hardly explored, guaranteed the possibility of flight and a search for asylum.

There have always been refugees. Every great social clash—the Spanish Civil War and the current world war are examples—brings with it the denial of the right to life, so to speak, for a minority. So it was in the time of the Reformation, with its spiritual objective that was similar in many respects to that of our epoch, forming the background of an ideological struggle. The striving for knowledge that once spread over the world strengthened the bonds in the search for an improvement of earthly order. The struggle over the Bible paralleled the struggle of the peasants against parasitic nobility. Exactly as today, the struggle for the spiritual target of humankind goes hand in hand with the struggle of the working class against an oppressive system.

In the struggle to create a single regional religion, whole areas were then depopulated. En masse people had to leave their ancestral homeland if their prince didn't embrace the same principles of faith. They were made refugees in search of a new homeland. The princes, often as a method to ease the domination of a homogenous mass, considered unity in religion not just an honor to God, but a prerequisite to the art of governing.

Even today, there are again questions of social declarations of faith, which this time gave rise to the masses of refugees. Never have people submitted to a common denominator. And where there is a government that demands total subordination and seeks to totally seize the people, there must be those who prefer the loss of their homeland and its character to the alternative.

The aspiration for unification, for an integration of the citizen has become greater than before. In earlier times, a prince satisfied himself

340

to have his subjects embrace a belief—his belief; government violence today far exceeds these demands. Nonetheless, faith was a universal concept and appeared as a very strong unifying bond so that other differences became secondary. Today religion has lost its power as the final objective. Instead of the search for God, people pray to machines; the banal has replaced spiritual aspirations, and the question of a new ethic has not been solved.

The search for the principles capable of unifying a broad circle of people gave rise to the idea of a national, united state. In the name of this new god, race and ethnic origin were the motives to expel people from their land. If faith and affiliations were nonetheless subjective concepts dependent on the individual, so in race and ethnicity, objective facts were elevated to trial subjects and criterion and the measure of a human's worth. In this category belonged: the Armenian refugees—that is, those Armenians that could rescue themselves from massacre; the Greeks, who on the basis of a treaty between Turkey and Greece had to give up their homeland in Asia Minor where they had lived for thousands of years prior to the Turks arrival; and the Jews, since the power grab in Germany by the National Socialists,.

When you see how much sacrifice, how much suffering and tears, the worship of false idols as unified faith—as if it were possible to force into line millions of people on what affects their innermost emotions—the primacy of a people brought upon humankind or a race and when you observe the unending suffering in which the majority of humankind lives, you must really ask yourself when a true socialist and just community, not a national but a human community, will be established and raised as the exclusive goal of humankind's struggle. Preached by evangelists, wished for by the poor, written into the program missions of numerous organizations, people talk at cross-purposes instead of working together.

Next to the refugees, in a narrower sense the refugees without a homeland, stand the actual war refugees, who had to temporarily give up their home because it was destroyed, because their homeland was occupied by a foreign power and they sought to evade an economic action against their own homeland by the exploits of this power.

* * *

The persecution of the Jews, possibly an outcome of the idea of a homogenous people's state, is in its way, in which the Nationalists brought it to maturity, just a part of the social argument that fills today's world with struggle. It's a matter of whether a worldview, ethics, and morality founded on the Bible and the New Testament, derived from Jewish thought, will continue to serve Western culture with its spiritual guidance, or whether a hedonistic philosophy, an amoral nihilism, will fill Europe.

The Jew as person was just the demagogic façade of a thoroughly materialistic and political plan. In the end, Jews are people like any other. You cannot deny that many Jews would have joined the National Socialist order had they not written the struggle against Jews into its objectives. Even a Jew must admit that. Yet for the National Socialists, the struggle against Jews was a demagogic propaganda method for the purpose of winning power and assertion through the exploitation of people's lowest instincts. Yet how foolish to assume, even if National Socialism had succeeded in annihilating all the Jews, that the spirit that identifies Jews and can only fill all Jews with pride, can be made to disappear from the earth. Should they survive as an ethical society, the world must surrender to the only possible moral basis that is not just a part of the Jewish spirit but belongs to the thought of all high-minded people of all cultures. The same ethical norms, which the Western world inherited from the Old and New Testament, are found in classic Chinese philosophy. It is characteristic of the Jewish lot, that Jews, respectively the Hebrews, in a moment of extreme danger and need appear for the first time as a community of people. The threat of extinction, which in Egypt brought into question their existence, has for them always been a question of fate.

At the time of Moses, the land of Goshen was nothing else but a forced labor camp. Even the deepest attacks into the family did not deter the Egyptians, as the decision to kill Jewish boys proves. Again and again in history, these typical individualists had to bear the forced concentration and destruction of the family. I don't want to overstep the framework of this essay but only to quickly note that at the time of the Roman-Judaic wars, the Romans deported thousands of Jewish youth capable of heavy manual labor into civil work projects in the Isthmus of Corinth and mining works in the mountains of Sicily. The aged were killed, youth abducted into forced labor, if not used for the pleasure of the Romans in circuses where they met their end, and Jewish girls sold into slavery. Today it's fortification construction on the Atlantic coast and the laboring in the coalmines of Upper Silesia as far as they were not annihilated for the greater glory of National Socialism. And in the Middle Ages, weren't Jews and their children abducted to forcefully baptize them to assure their salvation? Didn't Jews then prefer to kill their own children rather than deliver them into the hands of the enemy? And again, there were Jewish girls in bordellos, not for Romans but for German soldiers in Poland. The same suffering, the same sorrow filled Jewish families, then as now. *Arena of the occurrences*, *name changes*, *concentration*, and *deportation* were then unknown expressions, but the effects were the same.

The Romans' determination to eradicate the Jews rested not on the obsession of conquest, just as today the conquest for greater living space has nothing to do with the annihilation of the Jews. The Pax Romana, the Roman peace, didn't have in mind the eradication of subjugated people. Had the Jews recognized Roman sovereignty, they could have calmly continued to live in Palestine. But their spiritual concepts, as opposed to all the other people of the Mediterranean, made it impossible to recognize Roman rule. The hedonistic, materialistic worldview of the Romans and the ethical thought of the Jews could not coexist, and this led to pogroms and eradication measures against the Jews, whose extent has only been achieved by the Germans in this war.

And yet, despite this terrible butchery, the Jews have outlived the Roman Empire, and their spirit has become a part of Rome's inheritance. Under analogous circumstances today, may it be a consolation. We don't have any other choice.

* * *

Although the lot of the refugees has always been a sad one, in earlier times it was easier to bear than today. The world stood open. There were so many countries in Europe and elsewhere, where it was possible to

343

find a new homeland. Even the absorption of White Russians, whose numbers exceeded at least a million, brought no insurmountable difficulties in France, where live several hundred thousand, or likewise in the United States (where also live the greater part of the Armenian refugees). Admittedly, their wanderings benefited from the fact that they fell during a period of postwar reconstruction and replacement of destroyed goods.

In an economy in which excess production from labor is slight and the satisfaction of needs are performed at a low level, the influx of a fresh labor force is equally welcome as in a country in the midst of development. After the abolition of the Edict of Nantes, which had given assurance to the French Huguenots the freedom to practice their religion, they easily found refuge in Germany, Switzerland, and England. They brought new industry and inspiring thought into the economies of their adopted countries. For example, they founded the textile industry in Manchester. In the fourteenth century, the German Jews, amid the horrible persecutions they were subjected to, could find new homesteads in Poland. In this totally undeveloped land, they took over the important functions of artisans and trade, and became important contributors to the economy. For this reason, pursued nationalities, faiths, and freedom fighters could in the nineteenth century easily immigrate to America, which then took in several million people. In the years prior to the First World War, up to two million people crossed the world's oceans. Today the acceptance and placement of a few million fewer people appears to be a worldwide problem, the solution of which constantly assembles new conferences and commissions that fail to achieve a satisfactory outcome.

Market saturation in developing countries was reached even faster than the productivity, which had climbed into the immeasurable without succeeding in reaching a harmonious balance between social structure and the distribution of goods on one hand and the production capacity and the manufacture of goods on the other. As a result of the apparent overflow of goods, humans appeared only valuable as consumers, but only insofar as they could consume as much as they were given space for production and offered income. This aspect of human existence was neglected. While at one time states protected themselves more from the influx of foreigners, reserving the labor capacity for the native work force, at the same time they expounded a great propaganda to attract rich foreign tourists into the country. Rich refugees could hope to find asylum in that they could spend their money brought in from elsewhere, but the poor—the greatest portion of the refugees of the Second World War—tapped to no avail on the portals of this hardened world. What nonsense.

We recognize today that self-sufficiency is an absurdity. In planning for the postwar period, we assume that the exchange of goods is absolutely necessary in order to lift the world standard of living. But doesn't exchange of goods enable the exchange of production factors? Don't we achieve the same result, if we exchange finished goods in order to raise our own inventory, or if we as people, who are also production factors, allow ourselves the risk of experiencing an increase in the production capability? For how far will the standard of living of a country be raised through trade? Which prerequisite shall we assume? Surely every worker is capable of producing a great quantity of goods, greater than oneself or one's region can use. A piece of the production for consumption in manufacturing center is in excess. If we can succeed in exchanging excess goods in one center of production for different kinds of excess goods from another, so we can raise the total inventory of goods that can be consumed, while otherwise unused goods will deteriorate. This kind of thinking destroys international trade, and it is correct.

Yet how illogical is the world, how materialistic and low its way of thinking. We want to guarantee the entry of goods, for they create nothing for people. As necessary and proper as it may be, trade will never alone guarantee the balance of the future order if it is not connected with a reorganization of our societal order. And a new order can only be created when not just goods but also humans, according to their scaled worth, are granted the right to a proper ranking in society. Today, every state wants to have as many citizens as possible; every state moans about the reduced birthrate and the danger this may create for society. It has always been pointed out how critical growth is to the existence of society. Many industries depend on the production of children's needs, and many people's livelihoods support children, workers, business people, teachers, educators, publishers, and so forth, and depend on other people to have children and to raise them. The child is valuable not just as a human being in itself, but through the jobs it offers other people. We can estimate the investment to raise children and how many people find work and exist on this investment. In the child brought into the world, don't we see a being that should be made happy, aside from the consumption of milk bottles and diapers? As long as we haven't liberated ourselves from this truth of human mercantile observations, so we will not succeed in reconciling economic and social order—even were a miraculous gold mine to make us all millionaires and finally, finally makes us only consumers with no longer the need to produce.

Right after the war, we will again see promotion for foreign travel. Visit the natural beauties of our country; visit the last surviving museum, the last cathedral spared by bombs; visit the ruins of the once famous abbey and the cemeteries; observe the ten thousand crosses that have arisen here. Come all, ye that labor and are heavy laden, laden with money and currency, so we can welcome you with a deep bow and earn money from you. Come here, consumers with money from all lands. Everything is available to you: clothing, shoes, food, and luxury. But work—no, that we don't give away, that we need ourselves. Alas, how many would be happy not having to work because they are old and sick, if they could work less and could share more in the goods of life, but can't because although they have work, they don't have enough money.

The states will count their victims—one, two, three, five million and more dead in this world war. Make children, fill in the holes, and continue life. But you outside, you stateless, do not enter, for we need the room for our citizens. We have our own unemployed. If you have money, you can buy our goods; be nice and stay outside and don't bother our reconstruction and redevelopment.

Does the world really believe an order will come to exist that will finally prize human value? I don't want to say how it was seen after the last world war; that war was waged for humankind, for freedom, and so on—for why tell yourself lies? A new world will be constructed, whether a better one remains to be seen. It appears to be the direction of today's development of the postwar world. God protect us from this new world. Soon even I will believe in the Third World War that has been so promisingly painted on walls everywhere. I am reminded of the French proverb: "A force de parler du diable..."

Poor refugees, poor stateless, poor people.

346

The world order that is to restore humanity's rights has not yet been born.

And refugees? These will again come into existence if we continue in this manner. You, so diligently going about your work, sleeping and eating in a secure home, you can become a stateless refugee at the next confrontation being prepared by well-meaning people.

The refugee question is a question of humankind foremost. If these observations are to have any value, they must stir the human con-science and guide moral principles. In the instant people value people as humans, as fully valued humans with the dignity to live anywhere on this God-given earth, the refugee question will disappear of its own accord. However, as long as there is a refugee question, it is a reminder, a portent for a world that has not yet found its way.

27

FROM "THE LEGAL RIGHTS OF A REFUGEE"

W e have seen how the refugee question, aside from sympathy and antipathy, has been decidedly influenced through the structural changes of the economy. Added to this were the worsening political conditions in the years prior to the Second World War. The refugee question became a sheer irresolvable problem. New ways were sought and pursued.

In 1938, with the collapse of the Spanish Republic, a half million people were forced to cross the Pyrenees. The end came so suddenly that the people in all haste had to cross the nearest border just to escape with their bare lives. A leftist government in France appeared to guarantee the offer of more friendly treatment.

The dispersal of such a large mass of refugees into the country appeared for the time being impossible. The suffering French economy, with its constant currency devaluation, couldn't reestablish stability. In any case, the absorption of such masses could at best be done in stages, necessitating the screening of individuals. For political reasons, dispersal seemed undesirable. On the contrary, many reasons spoke for containment and guarding of these people. France chose the way appropriate for undesirable people whom one doesn't want to subject to an even worse fate by sending them back over the border.

Despite all the sympathy of the greater French population for the unfortunate fighters, the Spanish and Spanish fighters were interned in camps. One can hardly comprehend the size of these camps. Argelle alone sheltered eighty thousand people. Gurs was also a barracks city that could easily compete with the mid-sized cities of the provinces. As an omen of the bombing war, these settlements gave us a foretaste of what the human settlements after this war might look like in places where once thriving cities stood. The organizing strength of the French authorities were not competent to handle the influx, the more so since the refugees arrived within a few short weeks and the time for preparing for their acceptance was exceedingly scarce.

For years, masses of people lived in these camps. Excluding Mexico, no other country bothered about the Spanish refugees besides France, which sheltered them. Today there are very few Spaniards in French camps. In the face of the prospects to spend an inordinate amount of time in the worst of circumstances, many preferred to return to Franco's Spain and face the risk of harsh punishment. Thousands joined the French Foreign Legion with the false hope that through the investment of their lives they could garner a better future. After the 1940 armistice, they were interned again, and not until 1943, five years later, did they regain their freedom.

In Holland as well, German Jews, refugees, were placed into camps. I'm not speaking of retraining camps for refugees, as operated in Belgium and England. For these camps existed for the sole purpose to give refugees the opportunity to prepare for other professions. Such a camp is not an end in itself, as in the case of internment.

The internment of refugees and civilians searching for rescue is consequently certainly not a novelty. In the line of our little promising development, it corresponds on the one hand to abolishing the freedom of movement and work and on the other to the always greater limiting of individual human rights and individuality.

Nonetheless, it appears interesting to look closely at the paradox portrayed, that it was a middle-class society that introduced these means, a society that, as opposed to collectivistic order in another country, wrote individual freedom on its flag.

Or do the refugees appear of such low value that the reduced limits of their legal rights in the eyes of the rest of the citizens don't arouse notice? It would be something like ancient Athens, which some praise as a marvelous democracy, whereas in reality, the democracy existed only for an upper tier, and the lower classes, the half-citizens, servants, and slaves carried on their lives with little connection to democracy.

Here I must write openly what I think, and I don't believe that even this ill will can be interpreted as a reproach addressed to the Swiss. Switzerland is a small country surrounded by states of differing attitudes toward Switzerland. When we consider what other countries with a wealth of possibilities have done, or rather have not done—for example, the United States that in 1941 at a time of greatest need drastically revamped its immigration policy such that thousands of Jews had to suddenly abandon every hope of emigrating, many of whom were deported to their death a year later—then it can certainly not occur to me to argue with Switzerland, which in the middle of a hostile world did what it could.

From the previous, it is clear that Switzerland, having decided in 1942 to accept refugees, also followed the route of internment camps. It's not my task here to discuss in detail the decisive motives for the Swiss government's decision to implement internment camps. That only the Swiss who can avail themselves of the relative background advisory material can do. My task is only to clarify the human side of the refugee problem. I must emphasize, however, because the reaction of refugees is of measurable significance, that the refugees know they have the Swiss people to thank most of all for their acceptance and rescue. The Swiss people then engaged in the kindest ways in the matter of the refugees and expressed its will in spoken and written word. All refugees know what they owe the Swiss people and are thankful.

As refugees, we must always pay attention to Switzerland's exposed position at the time and acknowledge that despite that it fulfilled one of its most beautiful traditions in accepting a large number of refugees and saving them from certain death; we must also not forget that this political and economic situation, not just in the question of refugee absorption but also the sheltering of and caring for the refugees, played an outstanding role.

Even if we can understand and grasp it all, it naturally can't change the fact that certain regulations hit hard, exactly as several regulations imposed on the Swiss as a result of the war—military service, rationing, the limitations on certain freedoms and rights—appeared hard on the citizens, though they understood their necessity. When we explain the situation of the refugees and consider their reactions, it has nothing to do with gratitude.

* * *

What is the legal status of a refugee?

It is clear the acceptance of a refugee is uniquely and solely determined by the accepting state.

Through the reality of flight, the refugees position themselves outside their prior communities. They can therefore no longer assume the protection of their countries of origin. On the contrary, their countries of origin—more accurately, the dominant authorities there—have become the enemy. That was so massively the case with the refugees from Germany and Austria that they didn't even have the chance to leave their communities there. The prevailing party from their state community, more often prior to flight, forcibly evicted them. Since there is no international authority above the national state, to which the refugees could turn, the ejection from their community turns them, so to speak, into abandoned property. They must totally place themselves into the sovereign hands of the state that took them in. In the sense of Rousseau, for the refugees there is no social contract, for the refugees the state appears as an autonomous concept. The guest country alone determines any refugee entitlement as a result of absorption. As long as it carries the burden and responsibility for the refugees, the guest country can exclusively evaluate their potential and suitability for absorption.

What is a right? If there were to exist anywhere just a single person, that person would have no rights. The concept of rights arose from the standardization of the inter-communal relationships of people. The refugees, having left or having been evicted from their communities,

352

have also lost the rights from these communities. They can only regain rights in so far as another community gives them. As long as this is not the case—that is, as long as the refugees cannot participate in the life of the communities that have sheltered them and can in no way get closer to those communities—they have no rights. In other words, the guest country totally determines the extent of a refugee's legal rights.

The right of asylum is not a refugee right. It is the right of a sovereign, independent state to absorb and shelter people. These are abandoned people—in the sense that another community has not found any reason, nor has been permitted or refuses, to claim them. The refugees are delivered to the community to which they belong when it elevates itself to accepting a stake in them. Political events and criminal intentions deny the refugees' communities of origin no stake in them. Toward them, an international right for asylum is needed. A brutal criminal doesn't enjoy the protection of the right of asylum because the crimes have given the human community the right and even the duty to punish. To exercise the right and duty to punish, entitles the injured community, which need not be the community of origin, to demand the criminal person's extradition. Extradition treaties specifically govern the procedures for dealing with base criminals.

The exercise of asylum right protects freedom of thought and conscience. With the absorption of Jews, certainly nonpolitical refugees, it's not about the protection of conscience. But exactly as it appears inhuman that people should suffer because of their views, so it is morally inadmissible to let people suffer because of their race and ancestry. Yes, even more so. Thoughts and ideas belong solely to each person. One must represent and vouch for one's own thoughts and ideas. They are one's personal, mental possession. But one's ancestry? Ancestry and race are for each person a fact of birth that can't change.

To make one responsible for that, to martyr and eradicate for that, is blasphemy. We are all God's creation. We take into consideration the right to exterminate harmful animals. They can't help that nature created them as harmful animals—that is, harmful to humans. We eliminate and pursue them because we have presumptuously claimed judgment and decision over them. To pursue and exterminate people on account of their race is to equate them the same as wild animals. Whoever isn't emotionally sensitive to race persecution as a mockery of all human moral laws doesn't deserve to be viewed as human, as a creation of God. The analogous use of the right of asylum, originating with persecuted Jews, is a most primitive duty of humankind.

Where do we stand with guest rights and hospitality? A so-called guest right is nowhere established. In ancient times travel was undertaken with great risk because robbers, wild animals, and natural catastrophes were great threats. The traveler might lose the way, die from hunger and thirst; it was a situation in extreme need of compassion. Travelers were dependent in large measure on the kindness of people, evincing the highest moral commandment. All religions of antiquity incorporated rules to practice hospitality. The moral duty to show hospitality was so binding, its practice so natural, that the traveler with an implicit understanding could assume the hospitality of strangers as a guest right.

It is peculiar, and I want to point it out as a revenge of fate, that a state such as National Socialist Germany was left to set aside hospitality and raise it from a moral to a legal obligation, the contempt of which resulted in death. In this war in Germany, a married couple that refused shelter and food was condemned to death. The disregard of the very first of the ethical commandments must be revenged, and a society that thinks it can dismiss them is condemned. Fate has methods to bring back those insubordinates to the way of morality with force if necessary. Where are the times that human life in Germany appeared so cheap that the state could recommend the eradication of incurable cripples? Today in the face of the continuing bloodshed that the German people endure, to preserve their population they are even obliged to fall back on mutilated cripples. A big German institute seeks women who are willing to live together with these cripples to produce children. The school that teaches even nihilistic respect for life is gruesome. Though, the National Socialists' contempt for humanity even here can't be denied. Through propaganda, from the heroic consciousness of the moment, poor women are moved to make sacrifices, an oppressive burden that will be mortgaged over their entire life. And does anyone think about the children, about the spiritual burden of these innocent beings growing up in such an abnormal home?

* * *

The internment of civilians takes its legal form from the internment of military personnel. The difference is enormous, however, because the interned soldier enjoys the protection of its homeland. His internment is allowed and governed by international agreements. As we can see, this cannot be the case with the refugee, as the refugee doesn't have a homeland. On the other hand, similar to the soldier, the civilian internee loses certain legal rights. The soldier has given up a part of his legal status the moment he, along with the civilian advance, denies the civilian person's rights. The soldier, in exchange for his loss of rights, has the knowledge that he can protect his family and country. His sacrifice is compensated by the significance of his mission. But what mission, what special assignment, had and have the civilians, men and women who, because of their ancestry and the "people" they belong to, had to flee? Nonpolitical refugees— whether Jews, Alsatians, or Italians—aren't aware of a particular mission, and they find it difficult to accept their situation.

For on the ladder of social worth, the refugee stands on the lowest rung. First are the citizens with their many rights and duties, then the foreign citizens whose treatment is regulated by mutual agreements and who can leave the guest country at any time to return to their country of origin. They enjoy the protection of their consulates and their representatives, who can always intercede on their behalf. Last are the refugees, who enjoy no national or international protection and who have no authority to turn to when feeling injured or wronged. The refugees live only by the grace of those that have taken them in and who sometimes let them feel this grace; and the reality of their loss of rights finds its parallel, its proper supplement in their defenselessness.

* * *

The limitations that Switzerland has put on the refugees stem from the fact that they, as abandoned property, have no authority over their own person. They have been legally incapacitated to handle their affairs, of limited fitness to manage on their own behalf. This loss of authority, the limiting of their legal rights, finds expression in the following points.

Foremost, the freedom of movement. Internees are people whose stay has been authorized by the state. They may leave their residence only with special permission. They are tied to their assigned residence. The need for the freedom of movement is so ancient that to get special permission for every step is oppressive. Freedom of movement was once seen as an original right, and today we are slowly losing these original rights. And when even the free citizen is tied to a country and doesn't enter other countries to settle there, it's not amazing that the refugee's bond is even tighter.

Further, the question of labor. The employment of internees is a very complex problem. We will analyze this in the next section in great detail.

Further, in regards to wealth ownership. Internees are obligated to declare their wealth and any jewelry they have brought with them and to deposit them into the national bank. Only with permission from the authorities and only within limited bounds can they exercise control over their wealth.

Since Switzerland, by taking in refugees has saddled itself with a great burden and responsibility, it is only natural that in cases where wealth exists, they have reserved for themselves a vote in the disposition of this wealth. The right of administration that Switzerland has secured for itself should also advance a certain equality under the refugees.

Finally, in regards to the expression of political opinion. Refugees are prohibited from every activity of a spoken or written nature. The limitation of the expression of political opinion stems from the duty of a neutral state to strictly observe its neutrality. You cannot engage in politics in a foreign country. Politics belongs to its citizens.

These are the main limitations of refugees as far as they are established in law. For most refugees further limitations, which arise from the organizational solution of the refugee problem, are added to these. These limitations to which the refugee is particularly sensitive are in regards to the situation of his family rights.

When spouses, as a result of their separation, can no longer share in a common household, the matrimonial community, the foundation of marriage and society, crumbles.

In the concept of marriage, established intentions, such as the obligation of the spouses to help and support each other, cannot be realized. Married life in the camps of sheltered, separated refugees is limited every six weeks to three days. It forces into hibernation almost all aspects that define the essence of marriage.

After the war, what will be the structure of family life? Not considering material circumstances, which I won't analyze here, based on human judgment, the outlook is good.

Of course, internment has by necessity its dark side. But besides the particular problems of adolescents, which by the way are less of a problem of family life than a general problem of puberty during special circumstances, certainly no damage has occurred that threatens the destruction of the family.

The attitude of the refugees toward family is more positive than ever. From their unity, the message is singularly clear: they sense the planning and rationalizing of family and emotional life as a straightjacket. They are definitely against the collective organization of the family. Furthermore, for them it is an idea that is dominated by individual independence. I don't want to talk of the men, if they have learned to appreciate more the women's role as homemaker, a role absent from life in the camps but one that defines a home. But the women too, who perform the largest share of work in a home, think only to the moment they are again in their own homes. Work assignments in an internment home give some women more leisure than they have in their own homes. Women who in freedom take care of a household with many family members don't have the luxury to end their workday at six in the evening or to dedicate Sundays for rest. And yet no woman would trade those advantages for her own home and family life. You needed to observe them, the great efforts they made toward their loved ones during their vacations, with what love and care they served their children a favorite food, prepared sandwiches, and regarded their clothes. In other words, they mothered. The motherly instinct of a woman demands their dedication. The allure of free time in the collective community does not compensate for all that.

The reaction of the refugees to an organizational solution, which encompasses all aspects of living, shows us the limits to which a collective community can go. The emotional life of the individual sets the limit. Every regulation will here be sensed as a disturbing and an unjustified attack.

The success of the collective effort that has resulted in such an increase of human production in goods has seen our general judgment over the value of individualism made unhappy and falsified. Individualism appears today only then and in so far as it is valuable as a member of a community. That is the logical conclusion of a development, which from the worship of mass production, has succeeded in the formation of human masses.

We speak of the danger of uniformity. It has come. But, I don't believe that it will last forever. As exemplified by the refugees, the over-stating of a regulation, which is all too powerful, shows how the natural reaction leads to a total rejection of collectivization. We must slow or mitigate the creation of uniformity, to which we are witness, lest it give rise to anarchistic instincts.

When I view the world of the refugees in these camps, I must think of the book by Aldous Huxley, *Brave New World*, the world of tomorrow in which everything is planned. Although this world assumes that also the humanity that inhabits it is planned. A plan that develops humans through genetic manipulation is decisively prepared. By happenstance a normal human being comes into this world, but can't accept this creation, as the emotional world is not suppressed and not biologically regulated. Humanity's spirit can never be put into shackles. Every person strives for a defined life. The most peaceful humans are capable of becoming revolutionaries when their emotional life is attacked, when they are dictated to—when they can love, how they can love, and when their influence on their children is to be withdrawn.

What use is the well-intentioned planning of the refugee organizations when so often the spiritual sector is left unsatisfied? When you ask, why is it that so many refugees don't appreciate or don't know how to respect what is being done for them? I would answer that too much is being done, that their independence has been taken away, and they are treated as children. It's obvious that families are severely impacted by the strict regulations, and often regulations that push too far and leave very little room for an independent existence. "For myself alone" may well be the motto of many who experienced this war "with everyone together."

Further, to the parental authority over the children, nowhere is it articulated that parental authority and the parents' supervision and education rights over the children has been abrogated. These rights have been put aside as long as the parents are interned in camps or homes.

The moment the family becomes separated, the parents, who through internment have lost authority over their own person, are no longer in a position to exercise the same over their own children. Someone must therefore take the place of the parents, in other words make decisions for them with respect to the education and supervision of the children. Of the refugee organizations, the one to provide the decision-making authority over the children is the Children's Relief Organization. The parents retain, at most, rights to object and complain, which they can, should the situation arise, voice to the Children's Relief Organization. They must, however, abide by its decisions. There is no appeal.

A broad, sensitive limitation for which there is no provision in the law for refugees, but which stems from the realities, is the limitation, one could say, of the loss of matrimonial fitness. According to Swiss marriage laws, the bride and groom must produce a certificate of matrimonial fitness. In it, the home community of the bride and groom confirm that the wedding is not contrary to any legal barriers. Analogous rules apply to foreigners. I'm not speaking here of marriages of refugees with Swiss. These are special cases. I'm only speaking of marriages among refugees. Refugees, as all foreigners, are asked for such a certificate of matrimonial fitness. In normal times, it is certainly possible to obtain such a certificate through the home community or through consular representatives. Today, it is not possible for the internees to obtain such a certificate. With the observance of such regulations, it becomes impossible for the interned to consummate a marriage.

The Swiss authorities well understand the burden of these restrictions on the internees. There are people who have known and loved each other for a long period of time, for whom a legalization of their relationship signifies a first step in the establishment of a family and a home, in other words to the normalization of their lives. Refugees are not social subversives. They are civil people and also in these things with civil attitudes. An unblessed joining of two people is for most refugees just a relationship and not a marriage. That is for them even more the situation since the marriage of refugees is reduced by the short and occasional togetherness without the other content of a marriage. A passionate connection signifies for the refugee, for the time being, more or less just a sexual relationship. The blessing of their relationship seems doubly valuable because in their eyes as in those of the environment—even if it is just the environment of the refugees—that relationship has been raised from one with purely sexual meaning to a higher level.

The well-meaning attitude of the Swiss authorities can be seen from the semiofficial recognition of so-called Jewish marriages. The Jewish marriages are marriages that, particularly in France, were finalized by Jewish refugees. In France, these people no longer had the possibility to consummate their marriage before the registry, be it because they lived with false papers or under false names or in hiding, the registry would have been the way to deportation. For the most part, shortly before their flight, similar to soldiers' weddings, they had a rabbi consummate and bless their relationship in order to make the test of fate that flight signifies easier to bear in the awareness of their togetherness. And these refugees, naturally, have the burning desire to totally legalize their relationship.

It is thus not just the law but also the realities of heavy limitations that are foisted on the refugee. It seems that the limitations of the realities weigh more heavily on the individual than government regulations because they touch the personal sphere.

* * *

In light of current conditions, internment in camps appears as a requirement of the state-led economic and social conforming form of collective hospitality. It is reminiscent of protection and security, which is likewise connected with the limitation of freedom.

The reduction of the legal rights of the internee is time limited, as the duration of the internment depends on the war's end. It extends further, as we have seen, only to certain spheres of legal rights. But it is tightly connected to the question of regaining a new homeland for all the stateless.

The legal rights of an individual are the total of rights that an individual possesses and mirrors the rights embraced by the community to which the individual belongs. The freer the community, the more and expansive are the rights that the individual person can exercise.

Naturally the responsibilities that the person must voluntarily fulfill are also greater because doing so will continue to guarantee the free existence of the community, the individual and the individual's rights.

The refugee, standing on the lowest rung of the social order, cannot participate in these rights and responsibilities. But the social cleft that necessarily separates him from those on the highest step of the social ladder is that much greater, and the refugee is so much more sensitive the freer the community is in which such a one is just a refugee.

It wasn't always so. In the previous world war, and even earlier, refugees enjoyed a certain freedom and much broader legal rights than today. The embrace of the collectivism of our lives brings with it a narrowing of the entitled rights. It is self-evident that the intervention by the state crystallizes more and more into an independent concept, impacting in the broadest sense the situation of the defenseless refugee without rights. Here, in the life of the refugee, the development under which we all suffer is its most precise expression. To the concept of the total state and the total war belongs the concept of the total refugee who must not only forfeit material possession but also legal rights. Of these realities, little can be changed. The only source of light that can ease the existence of the refugee is humane treatment.

28

LABOR AND LABOR SERVICE

T he employment of internees poses a very complex problem. Its solution is determined by the number of refugees relative to the guest country's population through its professional stratification and through its economic possibilities.

A yearlong internment without regular work wears one down and is capable of rendering such a one unfit for work, just like a worker can become unfit for work through prolonged unemployment. Each capability we don't use atrophies, like an organ that can't function slowly dies.

The right to life implies the right to work. As far as the act of nature makes sense and has purpose, every creature through its creation inherits entitlement to life. You may argue whether work is a blessing or a curse for humankind. The Bible says, "By the sweat of thy brow shall you earn your bread." In the end, work is both. The harmonious structure of labor according to ability and strength is, for one's need for activity and satisfaction in that capability, certainly a blessing. It fulfills us. Where this harmony is disturbed, labor becomes an oppressive burden. Labor can only be viewed as a blessing as far as it is free, not for the slave or those in bondage.

Nevertheless, to live one must be able to work. It is immoral to live from the labors of others. This assertion naturally changes nothing of the reality that in this regard human conscience is very elastic. But it doesn't change the moral principles of labor either. Just in the last years, in which the curse of unemployment afflicted millions of people, the right to life gave way to the concept of the right to work. Society has the obligation to give work to its citizens in order that they may live. In eras of deadly unemployment, the ability to work was seen as a favor—nay, a blessing. Work decreed an individual a useful member of society, for which the unemployed is a burden. The reality that the worker is useful to society gives those legal rights a firm basis in society and is visible in the dignity of the free worker.

It is self-evident, and I am the last one to misjudge, that also our guest country, Switzerland, such a small country, could not escape the structural changes that have occurred in the world. What I write is never directed against our guest country. It's a matter of portraying the situation of humanity and in particular the refugees in general terms: the situation of the refugees in particular, in part because their treatment has been so clearly expressed, to where we are headed, not just in Switzerland but the world in general. When at first we get used to finding it possible to observe a group of people granted their own lifestyle, should even the case occur—and that is not excluded in the long run—then let us not forget that what we are accustomed to can become second nature, that such a group of people could really be content with their lot, how close lie the attempts in the course of the generous planning that the postwar world has in store for us to expand the stereotyping of people into other groups. It must be clearly articulated what the reaction of such regulated people to these control measures is and what they sense as confining. The reflection of a thoroughly organized and guarded world, the world of the refugees, must be held up before the eyes of humanity as a deterring example.

I don't deny that there are conditions made necessary by war, but where they lead in the age of the total war, what devastating effects they bring upon humanity, must be recognized should the world muster the will to avoid a return to such conditions. Only so can we recognize the limits that the state can impose on its citizens without using them for its own purposes.

364

* * *

But let us return to our theme. In the discussion of accepting refugees, the question of their employment and their care stood in the foreground. In accordance with the dominant principle of protecting domestic labor, one could not in general think of giving them labor permits. The labor service for Swiss was introduced by necessity despite that mobilization reduced the sources of labor. This gave rise to the principle that no refugee could perform work that could be carried out by a Swiss. This was no innovation that Switzerland aimed at the refugees. Exactly the same regulations existed in England before the war for those seeking refuge there.

The strict enforcement of these regulations is evident from the fact that even intellectual work and artistic creation—the freest activities par excellence—were closed to the refugee. No painter could paint, no singer could sing, no artist could perform, and no writer could write. Of course, they could, but they were prevented from making public the fruits of their labor. The refugee practices intellectual self-sufficiency. In regard to the refugee, no country can live in intellectual isolation, and books and works by foreign artists penetrate Switzerland, and foreign plays and movies exist as well as recordings of foreign musicians—in short, everything except those of the refugee. But we refugees are so fortunate to have rescued our lives that I dare not criticize. I have no right to do so and am simply stating the facts.

In the foreground of the discussion, next to the question of employment, stood naturally the question of providing for the refugees. These two factors resulted in the labor service. To this belongs the purpose of easing the supply situation with the individual employment in agriculture. For this, specialists and those in occupations with shortages may be granted work permits. In certain occupational shortages, such as furriers and goldsmiths, several labor permits have been granted. There are also working specialists whose numbers I cannot quote. Their numbers are very limited as the abovementioned principle is rigorously enforced. Only farming actually accommodated a relatively goodly number of refugees. Their number is quite considerable when you reflect on how few refugees were trained and where also the language of individuals can be a great hindrance, for the farmer wants not only people who can work but also those with whom he can talk. The farmer gains nothing by employing refugees who, relative to regulations, are just as expensive as hiring Swiss. The farmer will therefore only reach into the refugee labor force as a last resort. The labor service rested as a means to provide massive care for work capable refugees. By its various aspects, it is also one of the most interesting themes for a detailed discussion of the refugee question.

The labor service serves the purpose to make the internees, even if in a limited aspect, useful to the country and to provide work after their own interests. The usefulness that the labor camp brings to the country should be lasting. The work camps are assigned land improvement, the execution of which, on commercial principles, would be unprofitable. Only because people, whose labor force would otherwise be lost, can carry out this work, and only because certain improvements could not be profitably carried out with Swiss workers, one arrived at including this work in the plan of the agricultural supply organization and transferring it to the internees.

Beyond that, the labor service should help the internees overcome the sad experiences that drove them to flight. Regular work should divert them from the worries brought about by the loss of homeland and dear kin. It should serve the refugees' spiritual healing. Further, it also gives the workers in service the awareness of usefulness. They should feel they are fulfilling a place in society and through their activity leading to a permanent gain of arable land; as such they should convey at least in part their gratitude to the guest country. Lastly, work gives back to the refugee a certain dignity, the dignity of earning one's own bread by one's own hands and not by the handouts of others.

What is the attitude of the refugees toward the work service? For the refugees, the transfer to a labor camp signifies a marked improvement of their situation. Based on the previous, it is sufficient to say, the labor service, contrary to the reception camp, comes as a great relief. The refugees recognize that and greet the transfer to a labor camp with joy. But the refugees recognize it as an emergency measure. They think, too, that the labor service is in fact not a democratic creation and look upon it as a necessary evil, compared to the reception camp, the lesser of two evils, and they know and realize that Switzerland can't offer them anything better. The transfer to a labor camp inevitably leads to the tearing apart of the family, and fathers, and married men in general, find it difficult that in order to care for their families they must be separated from them. This separation from their families justly shows them the extent to which they are in fact pariahs, a mixture of individuals belonging to an organization with little regard to their lives.

The Swiss themselves find the separation of families a reality contradicting their own social concepts. Now, where they can, they make every effort to bring an end to this troubling condition for the greatest number of refugees. Just recently, I received a letter from a comrade in which he relates that a very large number of men had been placed into homes in which they could be with their wives. Yet you will never eliminate an evil condition in its entirety that has been founded in the essence of the organization, an organization that in our society, and the only one possible to gain, naturally reflects the lack of order. The way to the loss of identity in the refugee organization expresses itself rather clearly as our order evidently proves so much more the lower we climb down the social ladder.

The social discomfort that the worker in the labor service seized must be released—a discomfort from which certainly also Swiss workers in the labor service are not exempted. There comes also the slimmest satisfaction with work that is foreign to them, which in most cases shows not the slightest connection to their usual employment or can be seen as preparation or retraining for a job after the war. It is clear that the effect of worker education can only take place—at least only fully take place—when the employee is satisfied with the job. And in so far as this is not the case, the aims of the organizers of the labor service cannot always be achieved.

As the work only achieves its educational effect when the worker is satisfied, and since this is hardly the case in the labor camp, how the free time is filled and the work of an individual becomes so much more important for the establishment of a harmonious balance. The structure of free time—yes, even its extent—depends a great deal on the camp leader, and it is not easy to recruit personnel, psychologists who comprehend the hard-tested mentality of individuals no longer in their youth.

One cannot, therefore, expect too much from the work camps. As it is, it is certainly carried out by the best will of the organizers. Everyone knows the ills of such creations but can't change much about the given realities.

* * *

How is the worker recruited to the labor service?

All refugees in the reception camps are given physical examinations, and those proven fit, depending on existing possibilities, are sent to labor camps. The refugee's principle obligation is to pass into the labor service. The consent of the refugee does not come into question.

This condition appears essential to me, because here, the right to work, which is not denied the refugee fit to work, diverts to the duty to work and the consent of the worker in the labor service appears superfluous.

The question, whether a working relationship comes about through a two-sided consent agreement, meaning a contract, or whether through an open legal record through an authority's one-sided consent, is of great significance.

Up to now, in the modern age, one was always partial to the standpoint of work freedom. That wasn't always the case and is not self-evident. In ancient times and even into the modern age, people worked as slaves or in bondage. They didn't have freedom of work. They didn't possess the dignity that work bestows on the free person. Their working relationships were bound; that is, they came about without being asked or giving their consent. In the modern age, in free states, bound working relationships apply only to prisoners of war and those convicted to prison. The motives that led to their integration into a work process correspond to the motives of the labor service.

It's interesting to me, in this connection, to refer to the obligation of *pre-station* that the stateless in France had during times of war or emergency. Every stateless who found asylum in France was obligated to pre-station in so far as he was fit to serve. The pre-station consisted in carrying out important military work, such as fortification labor, or to supplement labor in war factories. The *prestateures*, who wore military uniforms, contributed to the war service as soldiers without weapons.

We are dealing here, without a doubt, also with a bound labor relationship. Yet pre-station is to a great degree similar to that of the soldier's position. When labor service, a type of pre-station as such, can summon the obligation of the stateless to render service in return for the guarantee of asylum right, so this idea carries much more strongly in the military pre-station than in the civilian labor service.

* * *

The elimination of the bound labor relationship in modern times, the liberation of the worker, doesn't just trace back to the moral and religious idea of respect for people, but in particular to the material element, namely the recognition that personal interests are the most important drivers of people. A personal interest in work, which induces people to the highest display of their strengths, can only then be availed when the free worker voluntarily does the work. The full legal rights of the worker, as security of a complete employment, and the respect for human dignity form the foundations of the modern right to work.

While in the bound labor relationship one-sidedness in the development of an informed opinion is sufficient, the labor agreement of the free worker comes about through the voluntary assumptions and laying down in common the conditions of employment with the consent of the employee and the employer. The freedom of the worker is manifest in the two-sided consent.

At the time the worker was given freedom, manufacturing methods had advanced very little. It depended on the skill and enthusiasm of each individual to achieve the highest possible performance, and toward this purpose society gave the worker freedom.

As manufacturing methods became more refined, the performance and output was no longer dependent upon the will of the worker, and with the application of newer manufacturing techniques, interest in the freedom of the worker waned. Production no longer depended on the person, but on the speed of the production line, from which an establishment achieves a degree of efficiency. Productivity had become so great that personal contribution to the means of production was without significance. As viewed by society, it had the effect of enabling the means, from the production side, to limit individual rights.

Every economic system deals the worker the degree of freedom necessary to fulfill its production quotas. This is self-evident in a society driven by egotistical motives.

And so, in the moment when overproduction called for regimentation and planning, our society fell victim to these attempts, trusting in the belief that the limitation of individual rights is a condition of regimentation and planning. As the freedom of the individual was advanced not from moral considerations but from selfish motives, lay defeated the moment that selfish motives no longer mattered, more so in the limitation of individual rights made possible by production techniques, which offered a way out from the dead end to which technology brought society.

Production is the result of the functional production methods on one side and the human production powers on the other, acting in combination. As the societal equilibrium was disturbed by apparent overproduction, two methods were available to restore the equilibrium: collectivizing the methods of production or the collectivizing of individuals. Our society rejected collectivizing the methods of production, and the result was a collectivizing—that is, the stereotyping—of the individual. This loss of individuality did not advance equally worldwide, and its purest embodiment is fascism.

A society, for whom the freedom of the individual is not just a goal but a necessary foundation for societal order and development, would never consider that people are superfluous and could be pushed aside. As a result of the esteem that such an order would bring to humanity, the stateless, refugees, unemployed, and undesirables would not exist. A person would be at home by people everywhere.

Alternately, an egotistical society as ours, in its strife to mask the obvious defects in its order, forcefully arrives at solutions, which signify a collectivization of the individual and the loss of individualism. To maintain production, they must again and again build up a mass of people that become superfluous, unemployed. These unemployed must be brought to disappear so that at least superficially equilibrium is maintained. The methods to sweep up the unemployed entail the disregard of people unique to such a society and peak in uniting them in groups to fulfill particular assignments through which they are segregated from the work process.

And so these developments bestowed upon us fascism, weapons buildup, and war. At the time in which German rearmament did not embrace its entire people, Germany introduced the labor service. The labor service was the solution to a society that gave up on the freedom of the individual, in which its uniformity might make it easier to direct and lead.

Society declared itself ready to guarantee the workers sparse bread under the condition that they declare themselves ready to give up their freedom, which for them was expressed by the fact that their work relationship rested on a free contract.

The distortion of the understandings from which we all suffered made it possible that the duty or the right to work led to the coercion to do, more or less, useless work and the consent of people to employment deemed superfluous.

As already said, the limitation of individual rights leads inescapably to the glorification of the meaning of state and distances us from the social contract of a free democratic state. Society seeks its way out by defining the state for its own purpose with full authoritative power over its citizens.

It may appear that I have overstepped the framework of this essay dealing with refugees, but it only appears so as the refugees, as seen and treated by our society, are useless people that can't be integrated. That refugees could become such an overwhelming problem is a conditioned reality of our economic order. They are superfluous people exactly as others have become unemployed through different means, a product of our time.

Is it evident then, that in time of war, a small country like Switzerland deems refugees as a problem, and to solve it intervenes with measures that were unwelcome even by the Swiss themselves and clearly a painfully embarrassing stopgap. We need only look at what happened to refugees before the war, at the time the world was big and no war discipline dominated that pardoned what is happening today.

Several types of refugees came to France. Since 1933 came the German emigrants. They received no work permits but could build an existence in commerce and as traveling salesmen. The Spaniards arrived in 1938. They were interned. Later, several thousand Austrians arrived. They were not interned but left free and given a very generous assistance, but prohibited from any employment.

I speak from experience. In Lyon in 1938, I belonged for a time to the Austrian Refugee Committee and know what we did—that is, what we didn't do, as we could not do more. Those Austrians, totally without means, received eight francs per day, too little to live and too much to die. For the most part, they whiled away their time in coffee houses playing cards, and after the armistice, if they were not "cared for" in camps, they engaged in the black market. Naturally not in the great black market reserved for the French but in accordance with their small existence, they dealt in small quantities of groceries, several yards of cloth, and again and again a triumphant propaganda would show how a Jew had been caught and charged with selling five yards of unauthorized material at an exorbitant price. I remember a particularly crass case, truly a wretched case, where a black market dealer had been convicted of attempting to sell carbon paper and pencils at high prices and without a salesman's license.

No, it needs to be said. Our society has until now found two ways to deal with this evil cancer portrayed by superfluous people. Either the negative, which meant certain deterioration of the people because nothing was done for them or their concentration in a framework in which they melted into society and lost their individuality. It must be emphasized and articulated. If our society does not change radically, then after this war there will again be many stateless, refugees, and unemployed. One speaks of reconstruction, and so much reconstruction will take place in countries whose destruction is so total that it is no longer a matter of reconstruction but one of new construction. And most importantly, how will we reconstruct? I lift my head and look around me. What do I see? On one side, UNNRA beckons; and on the other, authoritarian collectivization.

I fear the authoritarian collectivization, which apart from the collectivization of the means of production also seems to me a collectivization of the individual. Equally, I fear UNNRA, the aids action that combines philanthropy with business, a combination that portends nothing good. And nowhere do I really see the emergence of a new order that combines equality with true freedom.

Illegal

Illegal

Kleines Wörtchen, "Illegal"
Wie oft hab ich Dich Gehört,
Seit den lang vergang'nen Tag,
Da ein Führer hat ein Volk betört.

So viel Menschen mussten damals
Plötzlich über Grenzen geh'n
Und ich fand des fast banal:
"Ja, sie waren illegal."

Ich, ich lebte mit Papieren,
Durfte vor der Welt mich zeigen
Und es war mir fast egal,
Dass so viele illegal.

Eines Tages hat die braune
Flut sich bis zu uns ergossen,
Was noch gestern war legal,
Heute ist es illegal.

Und mit Weib und kind und
Rucksack
Auf die oft gehörte Weise
Bin ich über eine Grenze;
Illegal war uns're Reise.

Seit her bin ich illegal,
Ich und alle meine Lieben
Und legal ist nur die Liebe
Zueinander uns verblieben.

A small word is "illegal"
I have often heard it said
since that day now long ago
when a Führer cast a spell on
those he led.

So many people then were forced
at once to cross o'er borders.
And I found it most banal:
"Yes, they were illegal."

I, I lived with valid papers.
Could show the world my face,
and I almost didn't care
that so many were illegal.

Then one day the brown torrent
gushed
and caught us in the rising flood
What yesterday was legal
Today, it's now illegal.

With backpacks, wife and children
in the oft prescribed order.
Our journey was illegal
we too trespassed o'er a border

Since then, we remain illegal,
I and all the ones I love.
Only our love is legal
As in each other we entrust

Und ich hab' viel Zeit zum
Denken,
Die Gedanken die sind frei,
Und es ist mir ganz egal
Wenn mein Denken illegal.

Und ich denke , dass gar vieles
Auf der Welt wär' illegal,
Viele Werte möchten schwanken
Vor dem höchsten Tribunal.

Not und Armut, Hunger elend,
Unterdrückung, jede Qual,
Sind for uns'rem höchsten Richter
Ganz gewiss sehr illegal.

Und so will ich Gott geloben,
Werd' ich wieder mal legal,
Will ich helfen, dass die Welt sich
änd're
Und dass nur dass Schlechte
illegal.

And I have much time to think
Free are my reflections,
And I don't care
When what I'm thinking is illegal

And I think that so much
In the world is illegal
Many principles would totter
in the highest court of justice.

Need, hardship, hunger, suffering
oppression, every torture
before our highest judge
are surely most illegal

And I pledge to God
when I'll be once more legal,
to do my part to change the world
so that only evil is illegal.

Original Poem by **Camillo Adler**   Translation by **M.A.**

AFTERWORD

After the war ended, my father received his work permit and found employment in Zurich with the Swiss Labor Assistance (SLA) organization, a Swiss NGO dedicated to achieving a socially, politically, and economically just society. At that time, this organization assisted in building orphanages in Italy and Austria, and through its arm Collie Suisse distributed aid packages. The family moved to Zurich, but with our status as Displaced Persons, the Swiss authorities obligated us to make every effort to leave the country as soon as possible. We received visas to Australia and America, and despite also simultaneously receiving the Swiss residency permit, we immigrated to the United States in August of 1951. We settled in a one-bedroom tenement apartment in the Bronx, and my father found employment as an accountant with Pan American World Airways, affording us inexpensive flights to vacation in Europe and visit our relations in England and France. I was fortunate to make several summer visits to my aunts and uncles and travel to many countries, as well as ski in the Alps. In New York, my parents rekindled friendships with many other DPs from Austria and Switzerland. In 1954, my father accepted a one-year assignment as Pan Am stationmaster of Robert's Field in Monrovia, Liberia. On his return he was able to advance at least two grades, with a substantial increase in pay, and we moved to Flushing, Queens, to a two-bedroom apartment. At that time he passed an aptitude test to become a programmer, and Pan Am sent him to IBM school. Today, of course, he would have been called a software developer. My father had started from zero in three countries and mastered the language in each. Even as a child, his family moved back and forth between Poland and Vienna. He was the first in his family to attend university and receive a doctor of law degree.

My mother eventually worked as a German secretary for various employers, including an agent for German-speaking performing artists and a mail order house for German goods. She was proud to earn her own source of income for clothes and regular visits to the beauty parlor and eventually qualifying to collect her own Social Security.

My brother and I attended public schools in New York. Without fail, my mother always attended parent-teacher meetings. Paul and I were both fortunate to attend City Colleges, which at that time had no tuition fees for New York residents. Paul graduated from Queen's College and became a certified public accountant. He worked for several firms and eventually settled in San Francisco. I received an electrical engineering (EE) degree from the City College of New York and later a master's degree in EE from Northeastern University and worked for many years for Raytheon Company in Massachusetts.

In June 1969, my mother died from a rare form of cancer (retroperitoneal sarcoma). My mother's death devastated my father and was the only event in his life with which he could never come to terms. They had, after all, endured so much together and had finally begun to enjoy life. His health gradually worsened. His ulcers returned, and he was hospitalized on several occasions. He suffered a heart attack, stroke, and Parkinson's disease, and dementia set in. I saw him for the last time in the San Francisco Jewish Home for the Aged on March 17, 1985. He died that evening. He was a real hero—idealistic perhaps, but decisive—and through his actions saved at least four people's lives and after the war helped others through the bureaucratic maze of resettlement and restitution claims from Germany and Austria.

I am now retired and live in Lexington, Massachusetts, and also share a house in Franconia, New Hampshire, where I have skied for many years. Not surprisingly, I was introduced to this sport in Switzerland. I also stay busy volunteering in middle schools in the science classroom, working with the teachers and students, and taking courses with the Brandeis Osher Lifelong Learning Institute.

M. A. July 26, 2012

26434198R00216

Made in the USA
Charleston, SC
06 February 2014